DATE DUE

DEC 4 '01			

DEMCO 38-296

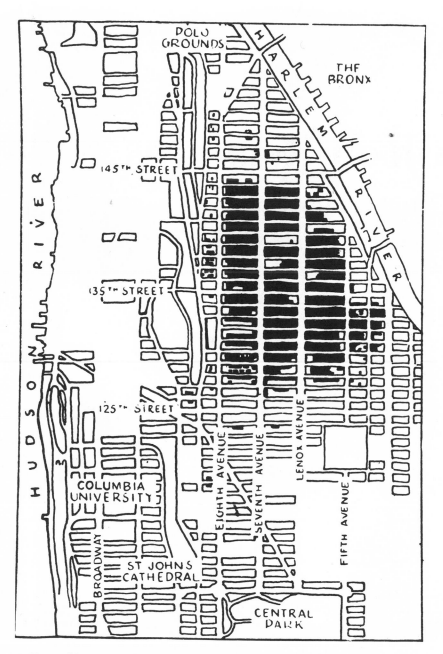

Uptown Manhattan and Harlem African and Caribbean American population, 1924.
Source: Urban League Survey

Blood Relations

BLACKS IN THE DIASPORA

Darlene Clark Hine, John McCluskey, Jr., and David Barry Gaspar

General Editors

K

Blood Relations

Caribbean Immigrants and
the Harlem Community, 1900–1930

IRMA WATKINS-OWENS

Indiana University Press
Bloomington & Indianapolis

the Photographs and Prints
in Black Culture,
nox and Tilden Foundations:
pear in chapter openings);
St. Thomas, Charlotte Amelia Street Scene (detail from
SC-CN-95-0406), p. 11; St. Philips Church (detail from
SC-CN-80-0162), p. 56; "Dispossess" (Morgan and Marvin Smith,
photographers; detail from SC-CN-81-0176), p. 92; Advance
Division of the U.N.I.A. (detail from SC-CN-95-0766), p. 112;
outside the Lafayette Theater (detail from SC-CN-84-0181), p. 149;
West 134th Street (detail from SC-CN-93-0296), p. 165.

© 1996 by Irma Watkins-Owens

The paper used in this publication meets the minimum
requirements of American National Standard for Information
Sciences—Permanence of Paper for Printed
Library Materials, ANSI Z39.48-1984.

∞ ™

Manufactured in the United States of America

Library of Congress Cataloging-in-Publication Data

Watkins-Owens, Irma.
    Blood relations : Caribbean immigrants and the Harlem community,
  1900–1930 / Irma Watkins-Owens.
      p. cm. — (Blacks in the diaspora)
    Includes bibliographical references (p.) and index.
    ISBN 0-253-33024-6 (cl : alk. paper). — ISBN 0-253-21048-8
  (pa : alk. paper)
      1. Caribbean Americans—New York (N.Y.)—Social conditions.
  2. Afro-Americans—New York (N.Y.)—Relations with Caribbean
  Americans.   3. Harlem (New York, N.Y.)—Social conditions.
  4. New York (N.Y.)—Social conditions.   I. Title.   II. Series.
  F128.9.C27W38   1996
  305.8'009747'1—dc20   95-37260

1   2   3   4   5   01   00   99   98   97   96

For Idell Epps Watkins and J. D. Watkins

Contents

Acknowledgments

THIS BOOK HAS had a long life cycle. It began with my interest in Harlem while an undergraduate at Tougaloo College. Early research was aided by fellowships from the Rackham Graduate School of the University of Michigan and a Ford Foundation Fellowship. Summer Faculty Research fellowships from the African American Institute of the State University of New York and Fordham University helped support crucial new research and revisions of the manuscript. I am grateful for the technical assistance of Linda Martin who typed the first draft, Kathy Primus, Jane Likimani, and Monica Pons who typed subsequent drafts.

Several scholars have provided active support and feedback over the years. My husband and friend, Leslie H. Owens, provided intellectual feedback, editorial and word processing assistance, and help in countless other ways. Joyce Moore Turner and Burghardt Turner, Robert A. Hill, Mack Jones and Thomas Holt read my work and have given constructive feedback over the years.

Darlene Clark Hine, a general editor of the series in which this book appears, graciously read the manuscript at a particularly busy time in her schedule and gave advice that led to its publication. I will always be grateful for her support. I also wish to thank my IU Press editors Joan Catapano, LuAnne Holladay, Terry Cagle, and Stephanie G'Schwind for the friendly professionalism and guidance.

In the formulation of ideas and for the reconstruction of the fabric of Harlem community life, I have relied heavily upon oral interviews and unrecorded conversations with first and second generation Caribbean immigrants and others. All formal interviews are acknowledged in the bibliography, but a note of gratitude is due those who helped shape my thoughts. In addition, several interviews led to other important research. Harlem resident Dr. Muriel Petioni, who arrived at Ellis Island from Trinidad at age five, provided valuable information about her parents' generation and her own, and the 131st block where she grew up; she enthusiastically conveyed a feeling for the life of the period. Dorothy Burnham, whose parents arrived from Barbados at the turn of this century and whose family today maintains close ties with their St. Michael home, helped me to understand the importance of family and friendship over the migration network. I was able to reconstruct this network through interviews and meetings she arranged for me in Barbados. There, centenarian and return-emigrant Violet Murrell, a cousin of Dorothy Burnham, graciously talked with me about her experiences as an immigrant in New York. Ismay Smith, my informal host in Barbados, provided invaluable assistance in setting up other important interviews. Although the topic is not explored at length in this study, in New York Emma Carroll, a southern migrant now in her eighties, helped me understand the similarities between female southern and Caribbean migrants.

I am also grateful to other second and third generation descendants who graciously responded to my request to quote from family papers or use photographs. Special thanks to Dean Warren Schomburg, William Pickens, III, Grace Watson, Dorothy Burnham, and Monica Smith for permissions granted.

Acknowledgment is due to the staffs of the libraries which facilitated use of their collections. My deep appreciation goes to the staff of the Schomburg Center for Research in Black Culture where much of the research was conducted. Special thanks is due Ernest Kaiser and most recently curators Diana Lachatanere and Mary Yearwood and archivists Andre Elizee and Anthony Toussaint for guiding me through the collections. Thanks is also due librarian Barry Moreno of the Ellis Island Research Library of the National Park Service for help with prints, oral history, and other research information. The staffs of the Schlesinger Library, Radcliffe College, Columbia University Oral History Office, Beinecke Rare Book and Manuscript Library at Yale, West India Research Library in Jamaica, National Archives and Library of Congress all aided me in my research.

I also wish to acknowledge the support of individuals who shared my vision about the importance of this project. My Fordham colleagues Mark Naison, Clara Rodriguez, and Peter Schneider gave me their moral support and much appreciated advice at a crucial stage. I am especially grateful to Fawzia Mustafa and Susan Berger for sisterhood and Gustavo Umpierre for collegiality and friendship.

My most heartfelt appreciation is reserved for my family. My children's healthy impatience was an important incentive to bring the project to its conclusion. My son, Shomari, especially reminded me of the importance of recreation or "fun," as he put it, during the most intense stages of the writing. He provided a refreshing and much needed perspective. My daughter, Imani, while suggesting that I change professions advised that if I *must* keep my present one, I should select much shorter projects in the future. I appreciate her youthful insight. While providing the most engaging scholarly exchanges my husband, Les, performed double-duty in our household, adjusted to my peculiar work habits, and encouraged me to keep the faith. A special thanks is owed to my elderly parents who were deprived of much longer annual visits while I completed this study. Their patience and understanding provided important emotional support when they needed my own. In addition, it was they who sparked my interest in the "telling of history" through their own stories of our African American family's survival of slavery and reconstruction. Though the subject of this book seems far removed from these stories, the merging of people's experience with the actual telling of it has been a goal, however successful, of this project. For their unwavering support and the many things they taught me, I dedicate this book.

Blood Relations

Introduction
Intraracial Ethnicity in Harlem, 1900–1930

BETWEEN 1900 and 1930 some 40,000 immigrants of African descent, most of them from the British-held colonies of the Caribbean, settled in Harlem as it was emerging as a black community in New York City. This settlement converged with that of African American migrants from the states of the southeastern seaboard and elsewhere. The result was the creation of a new ethnic community, unique in the American experience. Few contemporary observers in or outside of Harlem failed to notice its diversity or express an opinion about it. It was a "seething melting pot of conflicting nationalities and languages," a "homegrown ethnic amalgam," a "diversified and complex population." A 1930s WPA guide to New York City noted, "Negroes blended into their New York environment habits and qualities carried from the southern states, Africa, and the West Indies."[1] Yet more recent investigations rarely emphasize Harlem's diverse origins, or explore the intraracial ethnic dimension as an important dynamic in African American community life. In part this oversight might be due to the attention most Harlem scholars have given to the community's importance as a center of cultural production during the 1920s. Most historical studies have simply continued this focus.[2]

The present work is not a general history of Harlem, and it differs from previous studies in that black ethnic heterogeneity in an emerging community is the central theme.[3] A number of topics which exemplify this theme are the subjects of the ten chapters that follow. The controversies and conflicts evident in the interaction between black immigrants and native black Americans are explored, but these are placed in the larger context of a community's coming of age between 1900 and 1930. Thus ethnic relations are not viewed in terms of conflict alone, but as an integral dynamic in Harlem's formation. Finally, ethnic relations are examined within the context of gender as well as the concepts of race and class.

At the scene of their encounter in America, migrating southern and Caribbean[4] blacks found themselves in the midst of a changing New York African American community after 1900. In this year blacks began moving from scattered and crowded downtown Manhattan communities into previously all-white sections of central Harlem. Due to over-building in the 1890s African American real estate agents such as Philip Payton were able to induce a few white landlords to accept black tenants. He leased and then rented several houses on 134th Street to black tenants and with his wife, Maggie, purchased and moved into 13 West 131st Street in 1903.

When the IRT Lenox Avenue subway line was completed in 1904, central Harlem became more accessible. In addition the race riots of 1900 and 1905 convinced many that "there is no safety for any Negro in this part of the city at any time." Families and single adults deserted old tenements on crowded West 53rd Street and the San Juan Hill section (West 63rd to 66th Streets, later Columbus Hill), doubled up to pay the rents, and poured into Harlem. Others were displaced by the construction of Pennsylvania Station on the site of their old homes around 34th and 35th Streets and sought better housing in Harlem. White tenants and landlords bitterly resisted this "invasion" at first. But spurred on by ambitious real estate agents like Payton, the migration from downtown took on the character of a crusade. By 1910, African American ministers joined real estate entrepreneurs in spearheading an "On to Harlem" movement.[5]

In 1915 African American Harlem was centered in the 130s. The blocks between 5th and 7th Avenues reflected the diversity of the community. In addition to many migrants from the southeastern seaboard states, residents living in the area came from Jamaica, Barbados, Montserrat, Antigua, Bermuda, the Bahamas, the Virgin Islands, Martinique, Haiti, Guadeloupe, Puerto Rico, Cuba, Panama, Suriname, West Africa, etc.[6] The majority were single and young, lodging with kin or someone from their homeland or southern town. Families, native and immigrant—over 80 percent—were two parent.

Harlem became a desirable community, attracting a new black elite from all over the country and abroad. Intellectual activist W. E. B. Du Bois came there from Atlanta in 1910 as editor of the new NAACP's monthly journal, *The Crisis*. Florida native James Weldon Johnson, later the NAACP's executive director, returned to New York from the diplomatic service and settled in Harlem in 1914. Jamaican poet Claude McKay dropped out of Kansas State College in the same year to move to New York and later lived near the "hub" on 131st Street. In 1916 millionaire hair-care industry pioneer Madame C. J. Walker moved from Indianapolis to Harlem, and Marcus Garvey also arrived that year. Amy Ashwood, who had been a cofounder of the Universal Negro Improvement Association (UNIA) in Jamaica, joined Garvey in 1918.[7] But the vast majority of Harlem's new residents were working-class single women and men from the South and the Caribbean seeking opportunities, if not their fortunes, in the great metropolis. Together they formed the new urban generation.

Native-born African American leaders hoped the masses as well as the poets and business people would help establish a "representative Negro" in a model twentieth-century community. This community was to be patterned after the race's social-class aspirations ("uplift"), engage in organized demands for social equality, and move toward an economic foothold in a capitalist society. As men and women of color, African American leaders expected black immigrants to conform to the native-born black majority's interests and work toward the race's directed goals. In 1920 W. E. B. Du Bois wrote in the *Crisis* of the possible impact Caribbean immigrants might have upon black Americans:

It is this mass of peasants, uplifted by war and migration that is today beginning to assert itself at home and abroad and their new cry of "Africa for the Africans" strikes with a startling surprise upon America's darker millions. The movement is as yet inchoate and indefinite, but it is tremendously human, piteously sincere and built in the souls of hardworking, thrifty independent people who while long deprived of higher training nevertheless have among them very few illiterates or criminals. It is not beyond possibility that this new Ethiopia of the Isles may yet stretch out hands of helpfulness to the 12 million black men of America.[8]

Here Du Bois appears to have seen the new Caribbean immigrants as cultural heroes from whom the masses of native blacks could learn lessons of thrift, hard work, and independence—true qualities of a representative Negro.[9] Within the context of a social-advancement program institutionalized with the formation of the NAACP and the Urban League a decade before, and with the emergence of the post–Booker T. Washington New Negro, newcomers already "uplifted" by the optimism and expectations of the postwar era could bring special talents to the formation of an African American urban community. Educated Caribbean immigrants interacted on many levels within the Harlem community. Their presence was conspicuous in the Harlem Renaissance, in radical politics, and in the ranks of a fledgling professional class. Contemporaries also took special note of their addition to the tiny African American business class.[10] But who were these newcomers whom Du Bois described as "this mass of peasants"? Caribbean immigrants were not all peasants coming directly from rural districts. Only 14 percent entering between 1901 and 1935 were classified as agricultural workers according to the *Reports of the Commissioner of Immigration.* A majority had spent some time in small towns or cities before immigrating to the United States. An undetermined number of male and female immigrants were secondary migrants who had traveled to Panama, Central America, or other Caribbean islands in search of work before coming to America. A small but visible educated elite—a Caribbean "Talented Tenth"—were among the immigrants. Other middle-class immigrants possessed a sound grammar school education and often a skilled trade. Thirty-one percent reported occupations in industry and 10 percent in commerce. About 40 percent of those arriving reported occupations as laborers and servants.

Until 1924, Caribbean immigrants entered the United States virtually unrestricted, although previous congressional legislation mirrored Americans' growing intolerance of immigration, foreigners in general, and "undesirable" racial strains in particular. This legislation singled out Asians, particularly Japanese, for exclusion altogether by 1924. The 1924 Act sealed this ban and instituted quotas based on national origin. This law also placed Caribbean colonies under quotas set aside for their mother countries. As subjects of European nations, fewer African Caribbean people qualified for visas after 1924. The bulk of the immigration which helped to shape Harlem's intraracial ethnic character took place before that year. When compared to the millions of Europeans who entered New York through Ellis Island between 1890 and 1920, their actual numbers appear insignificant, but their historical importance lies with their social and cultural impact. The heaviest years of black immigrants' entry were between 1911 and 1924. The vast majority of these immigrants—82 percent—came from the English-speaking Caribbean and will be the main focus of this study.[11]

The ethnic character of New York's black communities evolved with the immigration of increasing numbers of foreign-born black people between 1900 and 1930. Within the city's total African American population of 60,000 in 1900, 5,000 were foreign-born. By 1930 the total African American population was nearly 328,000. Of this number 224,000, including 40,000 foreign-born, resided in Manhattan. The vast majority of these latter individuals lived in Harlem, which possessed the highest concentration of Caribbean-born immigrants in the United States. Miami ranked second, and Boston third.[12]

Caribbean immigrants generally settled in already existing or evolving African American communities. Exclusionary racial and housing practices enforced this pattern. "Unlike others of the foreign born," wrote Jamaican journalist, entrepreneur, and activist W. A. Domingo in 1925, "black immigrants find it impossible to segregate themselves into colonies; too dark of complexion to pose as Cubans or some other Negroid but alien tongued foreigners, they are inevitably swallowed up in black Harlem."[13]

For the immigrants this situation resulted in an inevitable reshaping of identities and raised a number of questions for newcomer and native alike. How would white American society perceive foreign blacks? Would black foreigners become allies with black Americans in the great American race struggle? And how would native blacks and their leaders react to a new expanding ethnic and nonracial dimension to community life? Contemporaries raised these questions though recent historical investigations have rarely explored them.[14]

Initially the presence of significant numbers of dark-skinned immigrants from diverse cultures, speaking a number of European languages or possessing a variety of English accents, disrupted old interpretations of race for white Americans as well as for native-born blacks. One of the earliest observations African Americans made was about the foreign newcomers' reception in places of accommodation or in the workplace. Booker T. Washington reported the following incident in his 1901 autobiography, *Up from Slavery*:

> I happened to find myself in a town in which so much excitement and indignation were being expressed that it seemed likely for a time that there would be a lynching. The occasion of the trouble was that a dark-skinned man had stopped at the local hotel. Investigation, however, developed the fact that this individual was a citizen of Morocco, and that while traveling in this country he spoke the English language. As soon as it was learned that he was not an American Negro, all signs of indignation disappeared. The man who was the innocent cause of the excitement, though, found it prudent after that not to speak English.[15]

Immigrants' own accounts about white Americans' selective treatment of them are even more revealing. While working on the Pennsylvania Railroad during World War I, Jamaican Claude McKay found himself with free time to spare in Pittsburgh. In his effort to find a little relaxation at a local African American cafe, he unfortunately got caught with other innocent black men in a police dragnet to catch "draft dodgers, slackers and vagrants." As he was without his registration card, police arrested McKay and threw him in jail overnight. The next morning officials marched him into court along with "a motley gang of men, bums, vagrants, pimps and honest fellows," all caught in the same net. The judge handed out five- and ten-day sentences like "souvenirs." When his turn came, McKay explained that he worked for the railroad and had left his draft registration card in New York.

> To my surprise, as soon as I had finished, the judge asked me if I were born in Jamaica. I said, "Yes, Sir" and he commented: "Nice place. I was there a couple of seasons ago." . . . Turning to my case, again, the judge declared that I was doing indispensable work on the railroad and he reprimanded the black detective who had pressed the charge and said the police should be more discriminate in making arrests and endeavor to ascertain the facts about their victims. My case was dismissed.[16]

After this experience McKay resolved "to cultivate more my native accent." Even black American citizens could sometimes avoid being removed to Jim Crow accommodations if mistaken for foreign-born. In 1903 a Florida train conductor asked James Weldon Johnson and a dark-skinned Cuban friend to move to a Jim Crow car, but when he heard them speaking Spanish "his attitude changed; he punched our tickets and gave them back, and treated us just as he did the other passengers in the car."[17]

Ira De A. Reid (*The Negro Immigrant*, 1939) reported an observation about a Caribbean black who "does not suffer much from the American race prejudice. On the job he speaks French or Spanish. The white boss lets him by." The *Negro World*, the newspaper of the influential Garvey movement of the 1920s, editorialized in "The Value of Knowing the Spanish Language" that the Spanish-speaking black enjoyed exceptional freedom and opportunity in travel and accommodations and in employment as bookkeepers, stenographers, and typists. Many were reported to have occupied positions as managers in large importing houses. The writer of the article urged American-born blacks to learn the Spanish language in order to find jobs. But the paper had on other occasions recognized this selective discrimination as "the strange ways of U.S. prejudice." A 1926 article reported that a Kansas City Pullman passenger agent refused a berth to UNIA international organizer Madame Maymie De Mena, a Nicaraguan of African descent, until she produced her passport.[18]

The interplay of race with foreign background both in the context of the Harlem community and the larger white American society is important to an investigation of the dynamics in an intraracial ethnic setting. Do these examples of selected treatment illustrate more about the functioning of racial caste in America than the actual experiences black immigrants had with discrimination? How would the vast majority of black immigrants fare in the opportunity structure? What new perspectives on the idea of race can we gain by examining the experiences of foreign-born blacks? In the chapters that follow, these questions and others raised by contemporaries about conflict and ethnic attitudes, cooperation, and community interaction are explored in the larger context of Harlem's development as a community.

The backgrounds of Caribbean immigrants just prior to their first massive modern migration into the United States since slavery had a significant impact on the manner in which these newcomers interacted with the emerging Harlem community. The historic waves of migration within the Caribbean and neighboring Central America preceded and continued to affect black immigrant populations in Harlem. Social and cultural patterns institutionalized in the region distinguished immigrant communities from those of southern African Americans. Yet it was no coincidence that Caribbean immigrants and southern migrant blacks arrived in New York at the same time. Both seemingly disparate movements were in part labor displacements influenced by the growth patterns and needs of industry in both regions and the expansion of transportation networks making northern cities more accessible.

Both southern and Caribbean migratory impulses were aided by "myriad kinship and community networks" that directed individual and family groups toward employers and housing.[19] Extended family members and down-South or Caribbean neighbors often lived in the same building or on the same block. These socio-familial networks formed the basis of community life in Harlem.[20]

The fabric of community life, including the ethnic dimension, can be understood by an exploration of kin networks and lodging as well as the varieties of institutions created by the Caribbean and southern migrants. The "On to Harlem" movement forms the backdrop for an important contribution of this study: an examination of the Philip Payton block, located on 131st Street between Lenox and Seventh Avenues. A study of this representative block, based on an analysis of the New York State manuscript censuses of 1905, 1915, and 1925 allows empirical observations about the evolution of the block from predominantly white middle-class to predominantly first-generation New York African American, and African Caribbean working class. Occupational and lodging patterns provide a sample of the heterogeneous social setting against which previous assumptions about ethnic relations can be evaluated.[21]

Indeed community development in Harlem—which is exemplified by the formation of social networks in voluntary associations, political movements, churches, and other organizations—was often the result of cooperation between Caribbean immigrants and native blacks. But it is misleading to define this cooperation too narrowly, for it sometimes emerged even when areas of group friction were not fully ameliorated.

Historian Darlene Clark Hine and others have suggested central roles migrating women played in northern institution building, especially of churches and mutual-aid organizations in the midwest.[22] Similar patterns within voluntary organizations are evident in Harlem. In contrast to the midwestern cities, New York and other northeastern cities such as Philadelphia attracted greater numbers of young women than men. W. E. B. Du Bois and others took note of this early in the century. "The first noticeable fact is the excess of women. . . . [H]ere more than in Philadelphia the demand of negro housemaids is more unbalanced by a corresponding demand for negro men." Their numbers obviously had social significance for an emerging urban community. In Du Bois's estimation "this disproportion acts disastrously . . . on the women and the men."[23] But a female vanguard took important steps toward developing the emerging community, and this was true of Caribbean immigrant as well as southern migrant women. Although the Caribbean immigration during this period is generally regarded as male-led, this point needs re-evaluation in the context of family and chain migration. There is significant evidence that women were very important in creating migration streams from regions as well as from families, although male migrants may have outnumbered women in the 1900–1930 period.[24] Yet women rarely gained visibility in leadership roles of major organizations or churches. In many ways gender operated as a much more exclusive category than ethnic background.

In Harlem's formative period and in African American communities elsewhere in America, a class structure, though changing, was clearly observable. Class hierarchies were evident in the reactions of New York's older aristocracy to new arrivals. As early as the 1880s native New Yorkers formed societies to solidify members' social positions and perceived advantages against the intrusions of talented newcomers. In response to these limitations, migrating southerners of the "better class of Negroes" formed their own associations specifically excluding native New Yorkers. Caribbean immigrants formed similar groups, which promoted adjustment to New York and advancement in the class structure.

Old New Yorkers continued for awhile to dominate the social life of the black elite. But a new elite formed—well-educated professionals, politicians, journalists, and business people. Immigrants and southern blacks seized opportunities in the new expanding communities in the San Juan Hill and Tenderloin sections of Manhattan and later in Harlem. By 1900 most of the clergy, business people, physicians, politicians, and artists had been born in the South or the Caribbean. Mary White Ovington noted in 1911 that the "old New York families, sometimes bearing Dutch and English names, have diminished in size and importance. . . . And into the city has come a continual stream of Southerners and more recently West Indians, some among them educated, ambitious men and women, full of the energy and determination of the immigrant who means to attain prominence in his new home."[25] In certain situations social class was just as important a defining feature of social relations as ethnicity.

Churches as much as any community institution reflected the class and sometimes ethnic background of their members as well as the interests of the growing population. New denominations emerged, and old churches expanded and bought or built uptown by 1920. Although some Caribbean immigrants joined native-born

churches, another manifestation of the community's ethnic character was the formation of new, predominantly Caribbean-composed congregations. The Caribbean migration also added entirely new denominations, such as the Moravian, Wesleyan, and
Unitarian, to Harlem's ample list of congregations.

While the origins of often ethnically distinct institutions such as churches,
benevolent societies, and fraternal orders in Harlem exemplify the community's cultural and social diversity, other aspects of Harlem's development help illustrate some
of the defining characteristics of race and ethnic relations.

Harlem politics, both traditional and nontraditional, evolved in the context of a
disfranchised and segregated African American community. Unlike other urban
settings, such as those in Chicago for instance, Manhattan African Americans made
little advance in electoral politics before 1930. Sharp competition for political position characterized an environment where power was based on a system of individual
patronage—rewards and favors—doled out by the white establishment. Harlem's
struggle for autonomy and direct representation took place within this context, and relations between the key political players—Caribbean and native-born, usually male
professionals—were often strained if not bitter. The interests of Harlem's mass-based
community—a legion of female domestics, service workers, and newly arrived southern and Caribbean immigrants—went unaddressed.

In this atmosphere another kind of politics emerged, which both bypassed the
political establishment and challenged the concept of an imagined "representative
Negro." A heavily Caribbean-born male and female cadre of street speakers, dismissed by some critics as "West Indian rabble rousers," nevertheless helped to
undermine the prestige of traditional leaders. Although old-line politicians, especially black Democrats, had used the street corner to recruit voters, they had never
used the open-air forums to agitate for the kind of change that would have obviously
jeopardized their own positions. Street corner forums between 1917 and 1930, symbolized by the stepladder platform, forced a more public expression of community
concerns by leaders, both immigrant and native, who might not have been previously
inclined.[26] Moreover, community issues of every description were contested and
sometimes literally fought for at street corner forums.

The stepladder forums also spawned important national and international social
movements. One of Harlem's famous street orators, Marcus Garvey began the largest mass-based movement before the civil rights era on the corner of 135th Street
and Lenox Avenue. Garvey's career has been extensively studied elsewhere. Here
a focus on this Jamaican-born leader's nativity and the controversies surrounding
it helps identify how ethnicity and competition for political space intersected in
an emerging community. Garvey's most controversial Harlem period is also examined in the context of the U.S. government's pursuit of the UNIA leader on the
basis of his status as an "alien." The Garvey case helps illustrate and highlight the importance of discrimination some blacks faced on the basis of national origin and not
race alone.

Yet even Marcus Garvey's most virulent native-born critics pointed to the UNIA's business enterprises as among the most important contributions to Harlem. Economic problems of the developing black community and African American hopes of advancing in the business world were topics widely discussed on street corners and elsewhere. If critics characterized Caribbean-born street speakers as "rabble-rousing foreign agitators," some Caribbean entrepreneurs were singled out as good examples for all African Americans. The thinking behind this rather selective role modeling was bolstered by a widely held faith in a capitalist age, as well as racial solidarity tied to an economic base. Indeed outsiders, often white ethnic entrepreneurs, dominated black Harlem's commercial fields. "The saloons were run by the Irish, the restaurants by the Greeks, the ice and fruit stands by the Italians, the grocery and haberdashery stores by the Jews," noted Claude McKay. "The only Negro businesses, excepting barber shops, were the churches and the cabarets."[27] In one context black immigrant involvement in business could be regarded by contemporaries as a stimulating community influence as well as proof of the race's capabilities in a field where blacks had faced historic exclusion. But in another context the examination of immigrant/native entrepreneurship offers an opportunity to examine in historical perspective controversial assertions about the immigrants' edge or "superiority" in business.

Historical circumstances also provide the framework for understanding immigrant entrepreneurs' participation in the informal and underground economy of the Harlem community before 1930. The few legitimate black-owned businesses—real estate firms, grocery stores, specialty shops, and so on—often stood beside and sometimes joined forces with the community's leading underground enterprise, the illegal lottery system known as "numbers" or "policy." Caribbean immigrant men and women were among Harlem's most successful numbers bankers, who, as the community's wealthiest entrepreneurs, often supported legitimate projects.

A final chapter of this study is devoted to Caribbean immigrants' involvement in cultural production of the period, especially their contributions to the expansion of the African American press, often the first outlet for aspiring black writers. By so doing, their writings become identified as an essential part of the present discussion providing a view from inside the black immigrant experience. Immigrant and native writers of fiction also responded to diversity in the Harlem community, and their work often adds vital understanding of the less public dimensions within multiethnic interactions.

It is clear from these topics that there is more to be explained about intraracial ethnicity than the theme of conflict. The encounter African American natives had with African Caribbean immigrants cannot be reduced to a black nativism which "spilled over to taint Harlemites' reactions to West Indians" and to create a "battleground" of intraracial antagonism, as Harlem scholar Gilbert Osofsky put it.[28] To be sure conflict was an enduring theme in immigrant-native interactions, but their relations were more complex than has been previously acknowledged. An important qualifying observation about conflict and cooperation made by John Higham in his valuable *Strangers in the Land* may be important to keep in mind here:

> I passed over the whole record of inter-group cooperation except where it bore directly on the story of conflict. Cooperation is also an impressive part of American experience; a study of bitterness and strife inevitably catches the people it deals with at one extreme of their temperamental range.[29]

Cooperation and interaction on many different planes may have been the more common theme of immigrant-native contact in Harlem. But an examination of the impact the entry of immigrants had in the native black experience helps us to understand more about the nature of American community life itself. New definitions were forced upon historic conceptions of race which previously defined the boundaries of black communities. Harlem's formation and development in New York City and America cannot be truly understood without sensitive probing of the intraracial ethnic dimension.

2

Panama Silver Meets Jim Crow

BETWEEN 1904 and 1917 Aletha Dowridge, a young woman from St. Michael Parish, Barbados, carefully saved the letters written to her from family and friends in New York and Barbados. There are letters from her mother and father; from Fred Challenor, whom she married in 1907; and from her close female friends and relatives. In September in 1904 she received a letter from her father, J. F. Dowridge: "I know that you are far from home. Trust in God will help you with your hard work." The younger Dowridge was living in Brooklyn and working as a household servant. The two dollars she sent home earlier had elicited "boasting over my daughter greenback to every body that inquired after you." Her mother, Harriet Dowridge, was undoubtedly proud as well, but she also offered the words of encouragement countless black mothers must have repeated to wage-earning daughters:

> Lea you doant know how it greaves me when I think of you a young girl have to knowck[knock] about the worl to work for yourself so hard. However my child you must be contented as you are not the onley one. For if I could dow better it coulent[couldn't] happen so but I must go back and say if you learn to work for yourself you cant suffer when mama is taken from you. So you must chair[cheer] up my bonney girl and god will help you thrue all. I trust that I shall live to see [my] american daughtor and eate one of her pies. I am now working for some money to make preparation for your return to your darling home.[1]

Migration in search of work, both within the setting of the Caribbean and to points beyond its geographic boundaries, has long been a way of life for the people of the region.[2] The strong personal ties maintained along the migration network, such as those evident in the Dowridge-Challenor correspondence, and the institutions created helped to sustain the distinctiveness of Caribbean cultures wherever people settled. The focus in this chapter is on the immediate historical background and the conditions under which migrations took place within the Caribbean. The process of migration, the social and cultural networks established, and American attitudes about black immigration are also important to our understanding of later ethnic encounters in Harlem and elsewhere.

Caribbean migration has been categorized in several phases. Movements between 1835 and 1885 were mainly interterritorial (between islands) in nature and directed away from plantations upon which African Caribbean people were enslaved until 1834. The islands Trinidad and Tobago and the nation British Guiana, on the northern coast of South America, were among the first destinations as planters from these areas actively recruited laborers and offered slightly higher wages than elsewhere. Severe economic conditions on other islands, for example in Barbados, encouraged this interterritorial movement. Whenever possible this first generation of newly freed slaves took possession of small, unoccupied plots of land. Migration was sometimes motivated by attempts to acquire small acreage on other islands.[3]

Despite the expansion of a local peasant economy, plantations employed the majority of the available workforce. Low wages and unemployment remained a problem. Colonial Jamaican government's estimates of unemployed individuals frequently outnumbered any other category.[4] Most of the cultivatable land had long ago been taken over by plantations. In truth, the colonial system was designed for freed slaves and their descendants to become laborers, not landowners. Lack of land reform after slavery was a source of considerable discontent among black Caribbeans well into the twentieth century. In 1865 the Jamaican Morant Bay Rebellion occurred when an angry group of peasants demanding land reform marched on the colonial administrators in St. Thomas parish while the parish council was in session. They set fire to the courthouse, killing several landholders and ignoring Queen Victoria, who earlier advised to them to work "steadily and continuously when their labor is wanted, and for as long as it is wanted . . . and thereby render the plantations productive."[5]

Even if a family acquired land, emigration of one or more family members was often still necessary. Between 1835 and 1846, 19,000 people emigrated from eastern islands of the Caribbean to Trinidad and British Guiana. In later years, between 1850 and 1921, a total of 50,000 people migrated from Barbados to British Guiana and to Trinidad and Tobago.[6] Smaller populations of blacks went elsewhere. For instance, 7,000 Dominicans (from Dominica) left for the gold fields of Venezuela. There were also movements from Barbados to Suriname and to St. Croix. These migratory patterns continued into the twentieth century.

The interterritorial migrations took place at the same time that thousands of Asian indentured laborers were imported. To ensure a stable supply of cheap labor for the sugar estates, colonial governments began importing Asian workers as early as the 1830s. Between 1838 and 1917 Jamaica, Trinidad, British Guiana, St. Lucia, St. Vincent, Martinique, Grenada, Suriname, and Guadeloupe imported nearly 500,000 Asians—mostly Indian but some Chinese—to work the estates.[7] The result was the evolution of culturally heterogeneous societies in the Caribbean with their own complex set of social dynamics. An interesting aspect of this development was the later migration of Caribbean Asians to Harlem and their interactions with native-born blacks as well as their former African Caribbean neighbors.[8]

From the 1880s through the 1920s, another phase of the inter-Caribbean movement was characterized by emigration directed to increasingly labor-hungry foreign lands on the borders of the Caribbean Sea. This included migration to the Panama

Canal project; to Cuban and Dominican Republic sugar estates; to banana plantations and railroads in Costa Rica and other Central American countries; dry dock work in Bermuda; and finally to the United States, where immigrants pursued jobs in a variety of occupations. Between 1900 and 1920 some 1,200 Bahamians went to Miami in search of jobs during the building boom there. New York, especially after the war and the completion of the Canal in 1914, in part attracted immigrants in its role as a major seaport on the transportation routes of the United Fruit Company.

Economic necessity was the principal but not the only reason for the inter-Caribbean movements. The better-educated classes—less than 2 percent of most islands' populations—those trained in the skilled trades or those with political or other ambitions, found it difficult to realize their goals in colonial societies, where they were excluded from significant social, political, and economic participation.[9]

The internal social structure also thwarted ambitions. The rigidity of color and class stratification varied from society to society, but David Lowenthal describes a widespread social pyramid organized along color lines that provides a reliable framework. According to these perceptions a small, white, colonial elite controlled access to power and rewards; a slightly larger group, mostly persons of mixed-blood ancestry, held many of the better jobs and its own exclusive social status; and the dark-skinned masses occupied the lowest economic and social level.[10] There were, of course, variations on this somewhat oversimplified description.

Class status and economic mobility were essential ingredients in achieving recognition in this environment. Education, a skilled trade, or acquisition of property might afford darker-skinned persons with a certain status if not acceptance into the most elite and influential circles. Acquiring property, also rooted in the peasant tradition of freeholding, became a major goal of immigrants wherever they settled.

Their gender severely retarded women's status in Caribbean society and made color and class barriers even more difficult to escape for them than men. Improving one's status and realizing ambitions was sometimes an important motivation for emigration.[11] But a labor system which fostered emigration was fashioned primarily for single, working-age males. Families nevertheless struggled to invent ways to benefit from wage labor away from home.

In the years between 1904 and 1914, after the American government took over the Panama Canal project, migration to Panama was a vital part of the movement of Caribbean people, which predated their immigration to the United States. Some twenty-five to thirty thousand—a majority of them contract laborers from Barbados—is a conservative estimate of the numbers of African Caribbean laborers on the Canal Zone during these years. The following description by historian David McCullough provides a more compelling picture of the importance of black labor in the Zone:

> Official visitors, congressmen on so-called tours of inspection, writers gathering material for books, could not help but be amazed, even astounded, at the degree to which the entire system, not simply the construction, depended on black labor. There were not only thousands of West Indians down amid the

turmoil of the Culebra Cut or at the lock sites but black waiters in every hotel, black stevedores, teamsters, porters, hospital orderlies, cooks, laundresses, nursemaids, janitors, delivery boys, coachmen, icemen, garbage men, yardmen, mail clerks, police, plumbers, house painters, grave diggers. A black man walking along spraying oil on still water, a metal tank on his back, was one of the most familiar of all sights in the Canal Zone. Whenever a mosquito was seen in a white household, the Sanitary Department was notified and immediately a black man came with chloroform and a glass vial to catch the insect and take it back to a laboratory for analysis.[12]

In spite of the point made here, the African Caribbean people remained invisible then and now in the historical literature. But the encounter of black immigrants from this region with the social and historical experience of blacks in the States really began in Panama. An unknown but substantial number of Caribbean immigrants came to New York directly from Panama or financed their own or family members' transportation to America with "Panama money."[13]

While emigration might have provided the Caribbean laborer with a better opportunity for earning a living, the quality of one's life did not necessarily improve in accordance with one's skills or expectations. Caribbean immigrants employed on the Panama Canal project had their first experience with American-style Jim Crow. Every aspect of life on the Zone was segregated. The color line was as clearly drawn "as anywhere in the Deep South." In all official documents, the post office, and other public places, white and black, or "gold" or "silver," designations were in place. Black employees, regardless of their actual skill, were designated "unskilled" and paid in Panamanian silver balboas, while white American skilled workers were paid in gold. "Silver roll" employees were paid at the rate of ten cents an hour, ten hours a day, six days a week.[14] During the decade of canal construction, thousands of black men died or sustained permanent physical injury through premature or delayed explosions of dynamite, asphyxiation in pits, falls from high places, train wrecks, landslides, and cascading rocks in the canal cut.[15] Harlem Renaissance writer Eric Walrond, a native of then British Guiana, appropriately entitled his collection of short stories about the Panamanian experience *Tropic Death*. Conditions in Panama City and Colon, where many black folk were required to live in three-story wooden tenements, contrasted sharply with government-sponsored white housing for white American employees living in the Zone:

> One passes through large sections of both cities where Belzian [*sic*], Jamaican, Haitian and other Negroes congregate in colonies according to nationality, any number of families occupying a single room, places with no more than one or two toilets for the whole building, without running water, without electricity or gas . . . where disease stalks and black bodies grow limp and juicy with the preventable scourge of elephantiasis.[16]

No housing was provided for silver employees and their families. (The lowest-paid married gold employee was housed rent free in a four-room apartment, with a broad-screen porch and a bath.)[17] The protagonist in Walrond's short story "Tropic Death," a young boy recently arrived in Colon with his mother to join his father, lived in one of the above tenements:

> Down in them seethed hosts of French and English blacks. Low and wide, up around them rose the faces and flanks of tenements. . . . Circling these one room cabins there was a strip of pavement, half of which was shared by the drains and gutters.[18]

Despite the ruthlessly exploited conditions which created these images, Caribbean immigrants in Panama and elsewhere developed their own traditions and created important social institutions as new permanent communities emerged. Churches functioned not only to guide immigrants in their spiritual lives, but to help provide a feeling of community in a new environment. They were especially supported by migrating women. "By way of the Sixth Street Mission, his mother rooted religion into his soul," wrote Walrond. "Every night he was marched off to meeting." There, he'd meet the "dredge-digging, Zone-building, Lord-loving peasants of the West Indies on sore knees of atonement . . ."[19] Benevolent associations organized for mutual aid also encouraged saving money and buying real estate. Rotating credit associations, known as "sou sou" or "partners," assisted small-wage earners and thus boosted an informal economy in the migrating communities.[20]

Women's increasing movement to Panama was important to the formation of permanent communities. At first, the absence of white and black women in the Canal Zone was striking. But to improve the stability of white communities, the American government encouraged the presence of white women and families on the Zone. The Isthmian Canal Commission (ICC), concerned more with providing servants than in stabilizing family life for black males, employed labor agents to recruit black women to work in various household jobs. In general, female migration out of the Caribbean steadily increased between 1900 and 1924. George Roberts notes that between 1911 and 1921, 44 percent of the population decline in Barbados was due to the emigration of women.[21] Most of this emigration was to Panama and then the United States. Women's migration from other islands was noted as well. A Martiniquean woman recalled, "[W]hen an American came and told us that we girls could all get good wages in Panama, and that he would take us for nothing, a lot of us wanted to go."[22] The first black women recruited as part of the workforce were Martiniquean and were officially listed as laundry women. Black women also worked as domestics and cooks in the commissary hotels operated by the Canal Commission. The commission's hotels were "dependent entirely on West Indian colored servants."[23] White Americans living on the Canal Zone preferred Caribbean women to native Panamanians as domestic workers. In the opinion of one paternalistic observer, the Caribbean women "were for the most part industrious and made very good household servants."[24]

Other women were apparently lured to Panama by bogus agents and forced into prostitution. According to an unsubstantiated *Independent* magazine article, some black women were being shipped into Panama at American government expense, solely for the purpose of prostitution. According to McCullough, to dispel the charges, "numbers of black women were asked to swear before a duly appointed [Isthmian Canal Commission] that they were leading a moral life and that they were in Panama of their own free choice."[25] The official colonial journal, the Jamaica *Gazette*, frequently published public warnings against this "evil." By 1910 emigration of women and children had reached proportions alarming to the planter-dominated colonial government. But the Jamaican journal *Our Own*, generally more sensitive to a lack of job opportunities at home, viewed this concern with suspicion. "Can it be true that Jamaican girls are being taken to Colon and other places for immoral purposes, or is it another attempt to impose restrictions on the movement of our laboring population?"[26] Black women clearly went to Panama to find steady, legitimate work at better pay than at home. But sexual exploitation of female household workers became an occupational hazard Caribbean women would share with their sisters in the States. Nor was the black American press ignorant of the conditions of female and male workers. The New York *Age* complained about the inconsistent manner in which the color line was drawn amidst the Zone's rigid segregation policies, where white males were on "most familiar terms with colored women."[27] At the peak of the construction, the Isthmus served as a kind of labor mart from which American government officials and private companies could choose laborers. By 1914 the United Fruit Company had a special agent on the Isthmus recruiting laborers released by the Commission. "Over 2,000 were sent to Honduras and thousands of others have gone to Costa Rica and Bogas del Toro" to work on various plantations.[28] In many instances workers had no choice but to accept United Fruit Company employment, although to serve its own needs the company provided transportation only between Panama and those points where labor was needed on its banana and sugar plantations, to Cuba or to its principal trading centers in the Caribbean and Latin America. In the end, the opportunity for economic advancement that many islanders had expected of Canal construction left scores little better off financially than they had been before. Unable even to pay fare home, some took the next available job, hoping to better their luck, to save more of meager wages elsewhere, or simply to move geographically closer to loved ones:

> The completion of the waterway Brought great Desolation on the W.I. employees. Some of us were Transfered [*sic*] to other places. Others were Sent Home to different Islands. The wage Scale during the Canal Construction was So Small that we could not put any Saving in the Bank. Hence the majority of us left Empty handed.[29]

Economic mobility in Panama and in all other migrant communities often depended on the skills, background, and experience of the immigrant. Laborers brought in on contract probably had the least opportunity to improve their condition, other than to obtain steady wages. The majority of these workers, according to Mc-Cullough's account, were illiterate. This description contrasts sharply with the later migration to the States, which was comprised almost solely of the representatives from the literate population. Those able to afford their own passage were individuals with education and other skills which they could use to better market their labor. A few of the latter found jobs as clerks in Canal Zone offices but were still paid in "silver," though on a somewhat higher scale than common laborers. Artisans could also advance to the degree that their labor did not compete with white American skilled workers. Caribbean immigrant Charles Zampty worked as a carpenter in the building trade on the Zone and recalled becoming politicized as a member of the black working class. Zampty was one of the organizers of the Colon Federal Union, and he recalled meeting Marcus Garvey in Colon during 1911 or 1912, when "he was publishing little pamphlets."[30] (Jamaicans like Garvey, a printer, who arrived on the Isthmus after 1904 were mostly skilled artisans not under contract.) Caribbean artisans often did the actual work for which their white American "bosses" were paid in gold wages. It was these men who were able to save "Panama money" or at least send substantial portions of their wages home to families.[31]

Other men and some women, particularly Jamaicans, traveled to Panama to set up businesses catering to migrant laborers. Jamaican Michael Ashwood, father of Amy Ashwood, one of the founding members of the UNIA in Jamaica, was a well-off baker who immigrated to Panama with his family and set up a food-catering service and restaurant in Panama City.[32] At the end of the construction project, Ashwood moved his business to Santa Marta, Colombia. Psychologist Kenneth Clark's father landed a token job as the black passenger agent with the United Fruit Company. He refused to leave this job, but his wife, a seamstress, and their two children migrated to Harlem in the 1920s.[33] For many common laborers, completion of the Canal in 1914 meant eviction from the Isthmus. Others left voluntarily to seek work opportunities elsewhere.

Cuba and a number of Central American countries became the destination of many workers immediately following the official opening of the Canal. In Cuba thousands of Caribbean people from the British-held islands were recruited to work sugar and banana estates managed or owned by the United Fruit Company.[34] After 1914 the United Fruit Company virtually controlled the Caribbean labor market and had an impact on the lives of workers and their families all over the geographic area.

With working conditions in the Caribbean and Central America deteriorating during the years of World War I (1914–1918), emigration began to focus on the United States, the dominant economic force in the Western Hemisphere. "Everybody is hopeful that someday he will get out north to the land of opportunity," noted one immigrant.[35] The attraction of jobs in America's industrialized war economy was only one factor inciting the flow. The economic link dating back to the slave trade between the United States and the Caribbean islands, particularly British-controlled colonies, was revitalized by the increase in island exports to the mainland by 1900. American investment in the natural resources of the Caribbean burgeoned and thus tightened economic linkages. The shipping industry, dominated by the United Fruit Company, made possible transportation to eastern-seaboard terminals such as Miami, New Orleans, New York, and Boston. And Caribbean immigrants in these port cities traveled back and forth to their homes, when they could afford to do so, and sent packages, gifts, and mail via commercial shipping lines. Ships carrying American tourists docked in Panama several times a week. Loved ones could hope to receive regular mail. "Why it is that you keep my letters so long to answer," wrote Amy Ashwood from Panama in June 1917 to Marcus Garvey in New York. Secretly engaged to Garvey since 1915, she continued, "I know there is a direct boat every week from New York." When accommodations could be booked for better-off African Caribbean immigrants, mail boats provided the most reliable service. "I will travel on the Royal Mail," Amy Ashwood informed Garvey. "I don't like the other boats."[36]

As might be expected the largest Caribbean communities developed at these coastal American trading centers. Most immigrants preferred not to debark at southern ports, because fewer jobs could be found there. Also the South's reputation for open racial violence and lynching was well-known in the Caribbean.[37] Still, the relatively large Jamaican and Bahamian immigrant populations of Florida cities such as Miami deserve further study in another context.

America, particularly New York, represented different kinds of opportunities for the Caribbean immigrant than did Panama, Cuba, or other parts of Latin America. The immigrant bound for the United States usually held high expectations that a wider range of life-improving possibilities would be available. "America," wrote Jamaican poet Claude McKay, "was the new land, the young land to which all people who had youth, and a youthful mind, turned. Surely there would be opportunity in this land even for a Negro."[38] America had a special pull for the youthful intellectuals like Wendell Malliet, who left his native Jamaica in 1917. "I set out for the so-called 'Land of Promise.' Owing to difficulties obtaining steamship accommodations from Kingston to New York," Malliet traveled to Cuba first. He remained there for a number of months before obtaining accommodations to New York City in late 1918.[39]

But travel to New York often required considerable planning and family cooperation. In an essay about Caribbean women immigrants, writer and novelist Paule Marshall recounts the experience of her mother's generation in the 1920s:

> Money was borrowed, a bit of family ground was sold, or a relative who had already made his or her way to the "States" and found work dutifully sent money home for the ticket. Then there was what was called "Panama Money," which in many instances paid the passage north. This was the name given to the remittances sent home by fathers and sons who had gone off to work building the Panama Canal between 1904 and 1914. My Mother for example, came to the "States" on money inherited from an older brother who had died working on the Isthmus. "Panama Money"—it was always spoken of with great reverence. . . .[40]

The cost of a ticket from the eastern Caribbean could be as high as sixty-five dollars, and family support was crucial. Like Marshall's mother, who arrived at age eighteen to settle with an aunt, most women were young. They were the daughters of estate workers, small land holders, and artisans. Marshall's grandfather was a cooper, a maker of barrels in which sugar was exported.[41] Aletha Dowridge's father worked as a carpenter.

Family support networks based in the Caribbean were important in providing emotional as well as financial support. Aletha Dowridge relied upon her mother's consoling letters: "My dare child I have been a young [unmarried] girl myself and I have had to toll [toil] about for my living and know the temptations that girls have to meet. . . ." At Christmas the elder Dowridge woman sent "everything that I think you would like and you must have a rail west india breakfast for xmas."[42]

But the expectations of relatives, especially those in the extended family, could be a strain on family relations. In the same letter the elder Dowridge wrote, "I am sorry that I roat [wrote] to tell you anything about ada coming over. However, you needin think anything about it. Poor girl she toal me she had written to beg you to help her in coming over and she beg me to help her by putting in a word for her in my letter."[43]

Although new immigrants drew upon the social networks previously established by older, nineteenth-century immigrant communities in San Juan Hill, sections of the Tenderloin in Manhattan, and Brooklyn, separations from families were often difficult for all concerned, and finding steady work was not easy. The Dowridge-Challenor family correspondence between Brooklyn and St. Michael, Barbados, documents the nature of family obligations and anxieties in the context of migration as well as the multiple levels at which friends and family interacted in a supportive network. Sometime after 1904, when the correspondence begins, J. F. Dowridge died. But before his death he expressed to his daughter "God I trust will let us see each other again before I die." He was also concerned that his son, Donald, who had immigrated to northern Brazil during the gold rush, "has never write me a line since he left home."[44] Harriet Dowridge, however, later indicated that their married son, Donald, owned a small business and had sent "a copel [couple] of pounds" for the support of the household. "He says his business is improving now and he hope to be able to send me something every month now that I am not working." Harriet Dowridge, who had worked as a baby nurse for white families as a younger woman, supplemented her income by selling homemade jellies, some of which she sent to New York for "aunt Lue [Louise]" to sell. Parents expected that grown children would keep in touch through a network of family and friends traveling between home and the States. Child fostering by grandparents and other relatives was an important support for working parents in New York. Harriet Dowridge helped to raise Aletha and Fred Challenor's first child, Elise, while they worked and raised younger children in New York. The inattention of those abroad, especially mothers, to close or dependent family could bring harsh sanctions from the community. One St. Michael mother who left her child behind to be raised by a relative drew criticism from Harriet Dowridge: "Fancy, lea his mother has never sent to ask one word about him from the time she leave him. Nor [has she ever] sent him a penny and we have herd that her husband is very good to her and that he is always beging her to send something for the boy. However she is very unkind even to her mother."[45] Based on the other letters in the collection, this woman was an exception.

The reader is struck by the frequency with which communications traveled the network of visiting relatives from the St. Michael area and New York. Some individuals may have traveled primarily to transport personal items to and from New York and Barbados. The Dowridge-Challenor family network frequently sent letters and packages back and forth between New York and St. Michael. "You must rite and tell me when Mrs. Francis is coming over," Harriet Dowridge wrote Aletha, just before her marriage to Fred Challenor in 1907. "I would like to send you a fue little things. . . ."[46] Island delicacies were especially appreciated by immigrants in New York. Very few stores in Brooklyn or Manhattan carried Caribbean food. Such thoughtfulness could perhaps help alleviate the hard life in the city.

Young women from the Caribbean often came to the city to assist older sisters, an aunt, or other female relative with household responsibilities or to help during pregnancy before themselves going out to work. "I would like to get May over here," wrote Wilhemina, a relative of Aletha Dowridge, during the early stages of a difficult pregnancy, "if it is only for a few weeks to do for me, then she can go out to work." She rejected the idea of her husband's female relatives "leaving work through me, as I would rather have my own family." Willie [Wilhemina] asked Aletha, who was working in the city, for a loan of $10 or $15 to help bring May over. "I have got her passage, but not the deposit."[47] May did arrive in New York and attended Wilhemina during her pregnancy. Unfortunately Willie did not survive the birth of her child. To Harriet Dowridge's relief, the child survived: "I am very glad to hair [hear] that Willey baby is dowing well and hope that God may help you to bring it safe for the old folks as it will be a great comfort to them."[48] Later Aletha Dowridge took the child home.

The loss of this young woman was mourned by her family and friends in Barbados, but the continued migration of young people from towns and villages all over the Caribbean raised concern from several quarters. The "Exodus" was the name locals gave to the movement. Many regarded the departures as a mixed blessing. The Barbados *Weekly Herald* editorialized that emigration was necessary, but its reaction was divided:

> We are sensitive in Barbados over this question of immigration. It is perhaps regrettable that with the West Indies and British Guiana full of undeveloped resources it should be necessary for nationals to seek employment elsewhere. But people must eat. . . . Who is to blame the ambitious, near destitute, who goes forth to find what he is not likely to find at home. We yield to no one in our understanding and appreciation of the excellencies of the British flag but we

cannot shut our eyes to the fact that in the present state of affairs emigration to America is indispensably necessary to the West Indies.[49]

The colonial government of Barbados had long directed a policy of government-supervised emigration to combat the "redundancy" of the working population. In 1897 officials set up the Victoria Emigration Society to commemorate Queen Victoria's Sixtieth Anniversary. The trustees and directors were given unusual power to assist financially the "emigration of poor women who are compelled to earn their living but are unable to do so in Barbados." According to George Roberts, most of the women assisted were white. But Aletha Dowridge's aunt Constance Payne was one of the few African Caribbean women to receive money—about eighteen shillings—for emigration. A resourceful woman, she eventually made her way to Brooklyn just after 1900 and, after working in white households for a while, rented a house at 246 Adams Street. The frame house, with three floors and a basement, served as a boarding house for relatives and friends from Barbados and provided an independent income for Constance Payne. Aunt Con, as she was affectionately known by her female relatives, succumbed to the flu epidemic of 1918, but she had initiated a chain migration which Barbadian officials undoubtedly could regard as an excellent return on their small investment. Three years before her death, the arrival of a niece, Violet Murrell, continued an important link in the chain migration from St. Michael. Letty, as she was known by relatives, arrived as a first-class passenger on the SS *Stephen* in May of 1915 at age twenty-two and went directly to Aunt Con's home on Adams Street. Assisting with the work of the boarding house at first, Letty soon went out to work on her own. Though she had been trained as a seamstress, she could not find work in this field, so she worked as a domestic in white households. After Aunt Con's death she shared the home of cousin Aletha Dowridge Challenor and family. Eventually she found a job in a Brooklyn garment factory as a presser and in time became one of the first black female members of the International Ladies Garment Workers Union. Though she remained single, this relatively secure job allowed her to purchase her own brownstone and to bring up her own nieces and host visits from St. Michael relatives over a 60-year period. She returned to St. Michael in 1972, where, at the age of 101, she hosted visits from Brooklyn relatives.[50] Aunt Let, as she was known by everyone, replaced Aunt Con as the central family figure linking the family in two cultures.

In 1920 the Jamaica *Daily Gleaner*, which often represented the views of the Jamaican elites, saw migration as beneficial to this class:

While it is perfectly true that Jamaica has lost a large number of her brightest and most industrious young people through emigration to America, it cannot be denied that such emigration has been on the whole a godsend to those who have gone and to those who have remained . . . we were never able in the past to afford a decent livelihood to all the young men and young women of our educated classes; in those days it was truly said that there were more "dogs than bones." If there had not been emigration to the United

States . . . the standard of living of quite a large and eminently respectable class of persons would have been sadly lowered, for these must have competed amongst themselves for such positions as were available. . . . [51]

But emigration was also an outlet for the working class. By 1920 the immigration of the more ambitious of this group was apparently of considerable concern to white planters. A letter to the editor of the *London Times* reflecting their point of view was reprinted in the *Daily Gleaner* in July:

A matter which deserves the attention of the British Government is the serious and rapidly growing exodus of the negro laborers from the West Indies to America and other countries where they either have been promised or expect higher wages and better conditions. This exodus will soon lead to an unprecedented labor crisis on our West India Colonies. From one small island alone 500 negroes have gone to America, 150 to Cuba and another batch of 150 will soon be leaving. The planters lot in the West Indies is not exactly a happy one.[52]

This writer also noted that "strikes, Socialism and Bolshevism are gaining the ascendancy," and considerable labor unrest was indeed evident among workers in the Caribbean. Authorities frequently blamed discontent on the agitation of Caribbean immigrants in New York. For instance, when rioting erupted among the black populace of British Honduras in July 1919, authorities blamed the eruption on the seditious content of the *Negro World*, the newspaper of Garvey's Universal Negro Improvement Association (UNIA).[53] The later provisions of the 1924 American immigration law restricting the entry of blacks from the European-held Caribbean countries could be seen as an endorsement of colonial administrative policies regulating population movements.

Antiguan immigrant H. R. Hodge saw the connection between labor unrest, social conditions, and emigration to the United States clearly. Meager wages had to be spent for food while planters controlled the best land and the people themselves did not have enough land to raise their own food. In the realm of education, he commented, schools formerly run by churches were now being taken over by the government and were being closed "one by one." As a consequence, "the majority of . . . [young men and women] are making efforts to get into San Domingo and Cuba and America and taking ships to nowhere trying to solve the problem."[54]

Yet efforts to get into America legally could be quite frustrating. "I am fretting out my heart," wrote the twenty-year-old Amy Ashwood to Marcus Garvey in June 1917. "I cannot get passage alone." Probably because of her age and sex, Ashwood was required to travel with an older female friend, whom she planned to tell authorities was a "cousin." Garvey, she wrote, would also have to pose as a married "uncle." "I can get my ticket . . . if I have a letter to show you are my uncle and that you will meet me in the States. . . ."[55] Each legal immigrant had first to satisfy the requirements of the United States Consul at the port of departure. And from the tone of government notices printed in the Jamaica *Gazette*, the procedure was not a simple one. Regulations were more complicated for women and children than for single male laborers:

> [I]n view of the stringency of the Regulations in regard to persons more especially women and children travelling to the Republic [USA] and in order to save disappointment and expense . . . persons desiring to proceed to the United States of America should before obtaining Passports first consult him [United States Consul] as to the probability of their being granted a visa to proceed thither and such persons are advised to consult the Consul accordingly.[56]

Each prospective immigrant also had to convince the consular authorities of "the necessity of their taking such a journey" before they were granted an American visa.[57] One Barbadian immigrant, in a 1932 letter to New York *Age* columnist Vere Johns, bitterly recalled the process: "Every possible means was adopted to discourage immigrants from the West Indies to America—when health officials looked for trachoma [a contagious viral disease of the conjunctiva of the eye] and hookworm they made girls appear before them in the nude—before they were fit to enter Uncle Sam's Domain." According to the writer, the American Consul, a white southerner who granted visas to the "Big City," charged ten dollars for what was termed an "examination."[58]

If inferior and costly transportation within the Caribbean had long been a major grievance of African Caribbean travelers, it was now a primary concern of prospective United States immigrants. There were few means of comfortable accommodation for blacks. The United Fruit Company steamers were the most regularly scheduled boats to the major American ports. It was also possible to get accommodations aboard private passenger steamers. This was the mode of travel of a striking group of twenty-three Guadeloupean women photographed at Ellis Island as they arrived in steerage class aboard the SS *Korona* on April 6, 1911. The women were traveling with a group of twenty other Guadeloupean women on their way to French Canadian cities where they had been contracted to work as domestic servants. Thirteen other female passengers from Barbados, St. Kitts, and St. Croix disembarked at New York, where they were to settle with family and friends. The African Caribbean passengers were given inferior, segregated quarters, usually as deck passengers subject to the whims of the weather, on these lines. "It is difficult for Negroes in the British Colonies in the West Indies and Africa to ensure passage to America in British Bottoms, for lack of accommodations," wrote African American journalist John E. Bruce ("Bruce Grit") in 1920. "Has this any significance to Negroes in America? Is the demand for more ships for the Black Star Line [owned by the Garvey movement] a reasonable and proper one?"[59] Bruce had a good point. The absence of decent transportation and humane treatment aboard inter-Caribbean and mainland-bound vessels was one reason Marcus Garvey's Black Star Line received so much support among immigrant workers in Cuba, Panama, Costa Rica, and Honduras as well as in the United States.

Once in New York, each immigrant had to be met by a relative or guardian who could demonstrate financial responsibility for the newcomer. Immigrants not satisfying this requirement were detained at Ellis Island and sometimes deported. An undetermined but sizable number of immigrants found it necessary to come as stowaways; by 1916 Caribbean stowaways were already a problem for American authorities. American Consul to Jamaica Ross Hazeltine wrote the State Department that there had been "quite a large number of persons" who had stowed away on both American and Norwegian ships going to U.S. ports. He advocated the passage of more stringent laws to deal with such individuals.[60] But stowaways continued entering the country in a steady flow. In April 1922 the Baltimore *Afro-American* reported that fifteen young men ranging in age from eighteen to twenty-eight years were caught by officers of a Jamaican steamship en route to Baltimore with a cargo of bananas. In an interview with the men, who were placed in the Baltimore city jail awaiting deportation, the *Afro-American* learned that they had sought to enter the country for the purpose of getting work as there was "no work in Jamaica." According to the *Afro-American* "the highest wages they could get was 75 cents per day, but it was only in rare instances that they could get any work at all."[61] One of the men who had worked as a fireman was married and the father of two children. The others were single and were dock workers. One week later the *Afro-American* reported authorities had discovered twenty-one more stowaways on a Norwegian steamer. They were all laborers seeking work in the United States. An unknown number of illegal immigrant men entered the United States passing as black Americans working on ships.[62]

Stowaways were sometimes treated cruelly when discovered. According to a report in the New York *Amsterdam News*, this was the fate of Jonathan Gibson, a twenty-one-year-old native of Kingston, Jamaica, who had hidden himself aboard the New York–bound *Princess May*. When found, Gibson claimed he had been manacled and forced to remain on deck in inclement weather; the roll of the ship coupled with the constant spray of seawater on his manacled feet caused gangrene and necessitated the amputation of a portion of each foot. Having been hospitalized on Ellis Island for five months, Gibson decided to sue for $100,000 in damages. A Brooklyn federal judge, however, ruled in favor of the *Princess May*, and Gibson failed to recover damages.[63]

If coming to America as a stowaway could be hazardous for men, contractual arrangements African Caribbean women made with white families who sponsored their passage could land them in very uncertain circumstances. One such case involved three Jamaican women who were hired as domestic servants by a family in Douglass, Arizona. According to press reports, one of the women had been mistreated by her employer, a Mrs. Paul, and when she protested Mrs. Paul had her arrested. Although no charges were filed and no hearing called, the woman spent two days in the town jail before being released into the custody of a local African American minister. Apparently press reports of the incident prompted an inquiry by the U.S. State Department, which implicated the Jamaican woman in the incident. But the Chicago *Defender* ran this headline: "Girl Balks against Slavery; Put in Jail."[64]

Thus coming to America could be perilous for those with little or no money or without the protection of family.

For those who did have some money, the emigration process could be less fraught with danger, if not always above board. Bribery of consular authorities in order to obtain visas was not an uncommon practice.[65] Emigrating from one family branch to another, perhaps from parents to older brothers and sisters, provided a buffer against an American setting in which black immigrants faced the double jeopardy of race and foreign status. But not all families saw America as the land of promise for young people. An aunt of novelist Paule Marshall's was "banished" to New York for having "disgraced the family with a child fathered by a pan boiler from British Guiana who came to Barbados every year during the grinding season to work in the sugar factory."[66] Still this aunt paved the way for the arrival of her younger sister, Marshall's mother.

Although Caribbean males outnumbered females throughout the period, roles played by women in helping to settle family members was important.[67] In 1900 Hubert Harrison, who later became the brilliant street orator, came to New York City from St. Croix to join an older sister after the death of his father. Similar circumstances brought the Harlem militant Richard B. Moore to the city. In 1909, after the death of his father, Moore arrived at age sixteen in New York from Barbados with his stepmother, Elizabeth Moore, to join his two older sisters, who had arrived the year before and located jobs. The Moores found lodgings with Elizabeth Moore's sister on West 99th Street.[68] In 1910, W. A. Domingo, later the well-known Harlem radical, editor, and businessman, left Jamaica for Boston to live with his sister who, according to historian Robert A. Hill, ran a boarding house for Jamaicans. He planned to attend medical school but gave up this goal, moved to New York, and found work in the post office.[69] Nevis native Cyril Briggs, later editor of the *Crusader* magazine, joined his mother in New York in 1905 after completing his secondary education in St. Kitts.

Because so little attention was paid in the past to the process of Caribbean women's migration during this period, what little we do know about their patterns of settlement we often learned through the biographies of their better-known male relatives. We do know that many came initially to work as domestic servants and a smaller number worked in the garment industry. Although she had been an accomplished seamstress in Panama, psychologist Kenneth Clark's mother took a job as a sweatshop worker in the garment center. She eventually became a shop steward in the International Ladies Garment Workers Union.[70] Similarly, Kathleen James Moore, the estranged wife of stepladder speaker Richard B. Moore, supported herself and their daughter from her garment-industry job. Kathleen Moore eventually became a sample-maker working with a designer in a dress factory. According to Turner and Turner, "She was able to maintain this more privileged steady employment even during the depression because of her skill and her fair complexion."[71]

A smaller number of Caribbean women came to study in American colleges and universities. Like the writer Claude McKay, Grace Campbell came from Jamaica to study at Tuskegee in 1912.[72] Several Caribbean immigrant women joined the cadre of Harlem intellectuals and street corner radicals.[73]

Those coming to the United States were generally, then, from a selected group. Initially a prospective emigrant had to be able to afford the passage. Panama money—diligently saved—was often used to pay the passage of family members. A majority of male and female immigrants—over 70 percent—were unmarried, as were most southern migrants in the working-age population.[74] Although the first migrant generation was likely to settle with kin once they were in the city, neither Caribbean young people nor southern migrants were likely to migrate with family groups. "Boats from Charleston and Norfolk and the British West Indies bring scores and hundreds of Negro women from country districts or from cities where they have spent a short time at service," noted Mary White Ovington in 1911.[75]

The family support network was very important in the migration process, but large numbers of migrating single women did not have relatives able to assist them. In exchange for a job in household service, agents provided an undetermined number of women with so-called justice tickets. These were boat or train tickets provided in exchange for an agreement to forfeit one or two months' wages. Some migrating women were also the victims of hustlers who lured them into nonexistent jobs and prostitution. Black feminist, writer, club woman, and social service reformer Victoria Earle Matthews set up the White Rose Mission and Industrial Working Girls Home in 1898 to foil the work of these individuals. According to a history of the home, it was the first organization to offer such assistance to women. The Travelers Aid Society, which assisted European immigrants, was organized in 1905 with the support of reformer Grace Dodge. Dodge, reportedly influenced by Matthews's work, stated, "If it's a good thing for colored girls, it is good for all girls." White young women were brought to the White Rose Mission on East 86th Street when Travelers Aid did not have accommodations for them.[76] By 1925 the White Rose Home had moved to Harlem and helped some 30,000 women, mainly from the South but an unknown number from the Caribbean, find temporary lodging and employment. Community workers at the home met trains in Manhattan and ships at Ellis Island and escorted women to their lodgings or to the home if they had no place to go.[77] In 1923 immigrant and native-born social workers and club women organized a similar group, the Welcome Stranger Committee, to help female newcomers find respectable lodging and work.[78] The Welcome Stranger Committee supplemented the work of the White Rose Home by meeting women at Ellis Island and the city docks and accompanying them to their lodging. In 1915 the Danish West Indian Ladies Aid Society (later the American West Indian Ladies Aid Society) was set up in Harlem by a group of Virgin Island women to cater to specific mutual-assistance needs of immigrant women.

If self-help organizations eased the transition of immigrants, their increased visibility attracted negative attention from official channels. On December 31, the Senate amended an immigration bill to add members of the "black or African race" to the list of persons to be excluded from the country, regardless of their ability to meet the requirements of a literacy test. Introducing the amendment, Senator Reed of Missouri stated, "I am not in favor of permitting to come into this country to become part of our citizenship any kind of people except white people." The proposed legislation brought widespread opposition from black Americans, including the NAACP, and was defeated by an overwhelming majority in the House.[79] Booker T. Washington, who had advocated restriction of European immigrants because he viewed them as competitors of black American laborers, opposed the bill before his death in 1915. The African American press in general favored Caribbean immigration while expressing a negative view or neutral position on European immigration. Commenting on the proposed literacy test attached to the bill, Robert Abbott of the *Chicago Defender* editorialized:

> Somehow when the term immigrant is used there crops up in the mind a person below the average in intelligence. While this might fit the vast majority of them, there are exceptions, and fortunately we happen to be the exception. Of the two million immigrants that came to the United States in the year 1914 only eight thousand or thereabouts were Negroes, and these of the highest order of intelligence, hailing from such places as the West Indies, Hayti, San Domingo and Cuba. The immigration bill . . . would not harm us in the least, for the representatives of our race who apply for admission are intelligent enough to pass any examination on fair and equal lines.[80]

Abbott added that those congressmen favoring the restriction of black immigrants "seem to have forgotten that without the services of the West India Negro digging the Panama Canal could hardly have been completed." Calling the proposed legislation an "outrage," the New York *Age* declared the bill an "injustice . . . to the members of the Negro race, not only of other countries, but of this country as well."[81] Educated people in the islands also noted this apparent attempt to exclude their class and feared that they would be "severely handicapped in their desire to acquire professions and study" in American universities.[82]

The Boston *Post*, a white American newspaper, offered this comment: "The exclusion is all the more offensive because it is in no way needed, even if one agrees that the dark peoples ought to be excluded. Only a few negroes enter the United States each year. They come from the West Indies and they are generally useful types of laborers."[83] But by 1924 black immigrants were severely restricted on the basis of quotas.[84] In a report submitted to the Department of Labor and published as an official government pamphlet in 1925, Princeton economics professor Robert F. Foerster proposed a rationale for their exclusion:

> A greater proportion of current immigration is of nonwhite stock than at any previous time in the history of the Republic. . . . Are the race elements involved therein [Latin American and the West Indian] such as this country should today welcome into its race stock? . . . To this question the answer is bound to be negative. . . .

So similar racially to the people of the United States are Immigrants from Europe, especially from northern and western Europe, so well prepared for citizenship and industry, that their members might be substantially increased without creating serious problems for the United States.

[As] one criterion for the immigration . . . [a country] can properly require of its immigrants that they at least equal, if they do not excel, the average of its own citizens in fitness for government, including self-government, and industry. . . . No good ground exists for supposing that the immigrants of countries to the south of the United States would meet the requirements of this criterion.[85]

By 1924, the native African American press was much less adamant in its opposition to the immigration law restricting African Caribbeans than it had been in 1915. In a July editorial, Fred R. Moore of the *Age* voiced almost no objection to the 1924 Immigration Act. Recalling that Caribbean immigrants who had arrived in the "earlier days . . . took their place as valuable assets in building up of the local race community," Moore now felt the new immigrants should follow the "example of the earlier pioneers" and become American citizens. Instead, wrote Moore, they "flaunt their British allegiance" and "[engage in] disloyal utterances."[86] In the NAACP's *Crisis* W. E. B. Du Bois explained the journal's lack of concerted opposition to the bill:

The Nordic champions undoubtedly put one over on us in the recent immigration bill. If our West Indian friends had watched more carefully and warned us, we might have been able to take some effective step.[87]

Despite this excuse, the inattentiveness of the *Crisis* and the NAACP to a law excluding black immigrants revealed the growing ambivalence of key representatives of the native-born African American community toward black ethnicity. As immigrants increasingly identified themselves or were identified as members of ethnic groups, and perhaps only secondarily as members of a racial community, the potential for conflict grew.

Immigrants would soon learn—the American Panama Canal Zone having been a rehearsal—that their identities would be redefined in America. First, segregation was a way of life even in the North for black people in America. For the vast majority of black immigrants, Harlem was to become their community. A reporter for the Baltimore *Afro American* noted in 1921, "They cannot obtain accommodations elsewhere; live here they must. They cannot consult their own convenience by renting an apartment or a room near their work; this is the only portion of the city that stretches out to them."[88] Second, ethnic distinctions were often not understood within native African American society, whose identity was defined almost solely on the basis of race. In Harlem, at the coarsest level a black foreigner became an object of ridicule. In the 1930s a WPA researcher would write, "The West Indians were at the beginning . . . considered as outcast and contemptuously called 'Monkey chaser' and other epithets." "When a Monkey chaser dies he don't need no undertaker," went a derisive Harlem ditty. "Just put him in the Harlem river and he'll float back to Jamaica." This kind of taunting was especially hurtful to schoolchildren, noted Viola Scott Thomas, who arrived as a child in 1920 from Barbados. She recalled being mocked by some black American children because of her accent.[89] Maida Springer Kemp arrived from Panama with her mother in 1917 at age seven and recalled deliberately losing her knowledge of Spanish, "because in a new country, you want to be what you were here. And in the United States, people looked down their noses at foreigners, and my God a black foreigner to boot." But the southern migrant was a newcomer, too, and New York may have seemed just as strange. Maida Springer Kemp adds:

> We were all strangers. The black American, the black foreigner, and we did not like one another, and the white foreigner liked us less and the white American hated all of us.[90]

But for Springer, youthful conflicts were based on visible differences rather than deep-seated, vicious antagonisms: "We fought about our differences, but we weren't very ugly about them." At least for younger newcomers, the initial sting of difference wore off after a few years. As the most obvious distinctions became less apparent, mature immigrants formed their own institutions and settled into family and community life. But competition over the scarce resources of a segregated community as well as cooperation on multipolitical and social levels framed the character of a new historical development in American urban life—African intraracial ethnic community.

The fact that African American Harlem was a relatively new community undoubtedly affected the manner in which immigrants interacted with the native-born African Americans and vice versa. The evolution of Harlem as a black community in New York and the specific residential and demographic patterns that emerged there will be addressed next in an analysis of the unfolding story of the people who made its life so distinctive.

1. These twenty-three women were part of a group of fifty-nine household workers who arrived at Ellis Island aboard the SS *Korona* from Guadeloupe on April 6, 1911. Their final destinations were various cities in Canada, where they had been hired by French-speaking employers. Courtesy of Ellis Island Immigration Museum. Photo by Augustus F. Sherman.

2. African American Harlem real estate pioneer Philip A. Payton, Jr. and his wife, Maggie, and their home at 13 West 131st Street, circa 1907. By 1915, Payton's block was one of the most ethnically diverse in Harlem. Photographs and Prints Division, Schomburg Center for Research in Black Culture, the New York Public Library—Astor, Lenox, and Tilden Foundations.

3. William Derrick, Antiguan native, AME Church Bishop, and leading New York Republican of the pre–World War I era. Schomburg Center.

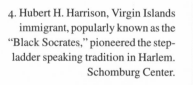

4. Hubert H. Harrison, Virgin Islands immigrant, popularly known as the "Black Socrates," pioneered the stepladder speaking tradition in Harlem. Schomburg Center.

5. Among those at John E. Bruce's grave site in Yonkers (August 7, 1924) are, to the right of Bruce's widow, Marcus Garvey and Arthur A. Schomburg. Schomburg Center.

6. Grace P. Campbell (circa 1920), supervisor of the Empire Friendly Shelter for young women, Harlem Socialist, founding member of the African Blood Brotherhood, and later well-known Harlem Communist was of Jamaican descent. Schomburg Center.

7. Richard B. Moore (circa 1930), from Barbados, was an eloquent stepladder speaker, organizer of the American Negro Labor Congress and Harlem Tenants League, and educational director of the African Blood Brotherhood. Schomburg Center.

8. Jamaican poet Claude McKay and editor Max Eastman (circa 1920). McKay first published his most famous poem, "If We Must Die," in Eastman's *Liberator*. Schomburg Center.

9. 135th Street and Lenox Avenue (circa 1920), a popular site for street meetings, rallies, and parades. Schomburg Center.

10. Fourth UNIA Convention Parade, August 1924, at 135th Street and Lenox Avenue. Schomburg Center.

11. Marcus Garvey in 1921 Harlem Parade. Schomburg Center.

12. Universal Millinery Store, a UNIA Harlem enterprise. Schomburg Center.

13. Jamaican cofounder of the UNIA, Amy Ashwood Garvey, first wife of Marcus Garvey. Schomburg Center.

14. Amy Jacques Garvey, Jamaican, editor of the women's page of the *Negro World*. Schomburg Center.

15. Virgin Islands native and numbers banker Casper Holstein entertaining for "ladies night" at his popular Turf Club in 1923. Schomburg Center.

3

"On to Harlem"

WALKING THROUGH THE pushcart market under the New York Central tracks at 116th Street or the Park Avenue Market, where Caribbean fruits and vegetables were sold, a newcomer in 1930 would have noticed the British Caribbean intonations of vendors and snatches of conversations in French or Spanish or Haitian Creole spoken by black immigrants. And then strolling up one of the main thoroughfares of central Harlem, the same newcomer might not have recognized the Portuguese or African languages spoken by Cape Verdeans or other West Africans. Even some phrasings of Caribbean English may not have been understood by all. "The older [immigrants] spoke in heavy accents understandable only to themselves and their children."[1] People from all of these backgrounds and others—unclassifiable by any existing ethnic terms—were living in the midst of central Harlem by 1915 and on Philip and Maggie Payton's 131st Street block. This chapter uses this heterogeneous block as a focus for examining aspects of the larger multicultural community from 1905, when the block was predominantly white, to 1925, when it was predominantly black.

The intraracial diversity that frequently surprised black and white Americans in 1930 was not a new phenomenon. In 1900 there were 5,000 foreign-born blacks living in Manhattan's scattered downtown African American communities.[2] Many of the features of community life into which thousands of Caribbean newcomers were to later settle had already taken shape on a smaller scale. When black populations shifted uptown to Harlem with the influx of other new residents after 1900, Caribbean immigrants were among them. Subsequent immigrant arrivals made contacts with family members and home people who had been longtime residents of the city. Southern migrants also established residences in these districts. "There was hardly a member in Abyssinian Church who could not count one or more relatives among the new arrivals," wrote Rev. Adam Clayton Powell, Sr.[3]

Even before 1900, there were enough black immigrants in New York to form their own associations. In 1897 Bermudians residing in San Juan Hill formed one of the first Caribbean benevolent associations in the city. By 1913 researcher Gary Ward Moore found that black immigrants had well-established organizations for mutual aid and benefit.[4] Caribbean immigrants who came to America in the late nineteenth and early twentieth centuries usually possessed a sound basic education, often a skilled trade, but little money. "They came to America 'on the strength of a letter and a certificate.'" The certificate attested to their educational competence, and the letter of introduction vouched for their character and good social standing.[5] But while the black immigrants in Moore's study formed their own ethnically based associations, some of them strongly objected to Moore's reference to them as "a group of West Indian Negroes"; they preferred simply to be called Negroes.[6]

This assertion of a racial rather than ethnic identity was typical of the pre–World War I black immigrant groups. But the move to Harlem after 1900 and the expansion of the black immigrant community as part of the Great Migration created a new milieu in which intraracial ethnicity could be nurtured. Still, native-born African Americans and Caribbean immigrants lived in close proximity to one another, mingling on the same block and often lodging together in the same households. Their communities necessarily overlapped while primary social networks formed among people from the same home in the Caribbean or the South. Immigrant and native blacks moved on to Harlem together, constructing opportunities for community solidarity while at the same time contesting old definitions of a racial community.

In terms of its physical expanse, Harlem offered a far greater chance for community building between diverse African American groups than did the Tenderloin or San Juan Hill sections, where blacks and Irish immigrants had engaged in frequent street battles for years. Harlem, on the other hand, was spaciously adorned with wide, tree-lined avenues and some of the finest brownstones in Manhattan, though with limited public transportation. Blacks began settling there in the 130s after 1900, and by 1910 ministers downtown were making "On to Harlem" the text of Sunday sermons. St. Philips Episcopal Church sold its property in the Tenderloin in 1909 and reinvested in Harlem. In 1911 the church made the most important real estate deal of the period—the $640,000 purchase of ten apartment houses along 135th Street between Lenox and Seventh. "The moving uptown of St. Philips P.E. and the Bethel A.M.E. churches made Abyssinian Harlem-minded," recalled Rev. Adam Clayton Powell, Sr. To advance their plans, Powell and other pastors held meetings in Harlem one Sunday afternoon each month, and such meetings, usually conducted under tents, continued until new buildings were bought or built by 1921.[7] Other downtown community groups caught the "On to Harlem" fever. The Bermudian Benevolent Society was holding some of its monthly meetings uptown by 1912, and established the Bermudian Home Club for the purpose of buying a Harlem brownstone as the Society's headquarters. The New York Colored Mission moved its premises from a single brick house on 30th Street to a large structure at 8 West 131st Street by 1915 and served black immigrants and southern migrants.[8]

Philip and Maggie Payton's purchase of the 1887 Victorian Gothic rowhouse on 131st Street in 1903 signaled the beginning of the transformation of the block between Fifth and Lenox Avenues and neighboring streets from an upwardly mobile first- and second-generation Irish and German enclave to a heterogeneous, native-born black American and Caribbean-immigrant community. The transformation of the block reflects the changes in the larger uptown district. From only one family at

No. 13 and a few occupants of just two houses on 134th Street to other blocks in the 130s, the black community expanded rapidly, but in a relatively compact collection of streets and not on the avenues at first. Gilbert Osofsky wrote that "in 1914 Negroes lived in some 1,100 houses within a twenty-three-block area of Harlem." The surrounding streets to the north and northwest and toward Seventh and Eighth Avenues were still occupied by upscale Manhattan whites, who had long been attracted to the area because of its suburban atmosphere. According to Osofsky:

> Few neighborhoods in the entire city at the turn of the century had so disproportionate a number of native Americans or immigrants from Great Britain, Ireland and Germany, including German Jews, living in it.[9]

The genteel residents of central and west Harlem prided themselves on the exclusiveness of the area and had not welcomed Italians and East European Jews after 1900. Although a few blacks had lived in Harlem since colonial times, white New Yorkers never dreamed that it would become a black section. Between 1900 and 1910, as an African American intracity migration shifted from the Tenderloin and San Juan Hill to the central 130s and 140s, there was also a mass movement of Russian Jews from the lower east side tenements to East Harlem and to the blocks to the south around 110th Street. Italians also moved to an enclave east of Third Avenue and south of 125th Street.

By 1920, the two-decade long resistance of white central Harlem homeowners associations crumbled under the weight of the black migration. "This unique community had grown to a city within the City of New York," writes Barbadian Richard B. Moore. "Embracing many thousands, this Harlem enclave then reached from 127th Street on the south to 145th Street on the north and from Fifth to Eighth Avenues."[10] The main thoroughfare ran along 135th Street. By 1930 Jervis Anderson writes, "The word Harlem had become synonymous with black life and black style in Manhattan."

Less than three decades before, in 1905, the Paytons' neighbors on 131st Street were largely white-collar, middle-class American-born, mostly German—including Jews—and Irish. The average first-generation immigrant living on the block had been in America slightly more than twenty years and had acquired considerable economic and social mobility. A historian of Jewish Harlem writes that

> Harlem, Yorkville, and to a lesser extent the new West Side neighborhoods, serve[d] as major safety valves for the thousands of Irish and Germans—among them many German Jews—who had acquired by the 1880s enough economic resources to escape the downtown ghetto for new uptown neighborhoods. Both groups settled in large and almost equal numbers in Harlem. . . . [11]

Although the Payton house, along with a row of other brownstones, had been built in the 1880s, new medium-sized apartment houses were built on 131st Street and surrounding blocks in the late 1890s. "Contemporaries called these blocks 'the best of Harlem.'"[12] Many of the newly constructed buildings were equipped with elevators, maids rooms, and butlers pantries. Seven percent of the households on the block employed female servants, mostly Irish and German immigrants. The occupational profiles of residents reflected the socioeconomic advance of first- and second-generation immigrants. A majority were employed in a variety of what demographers describe as low white-collar occupations—clerks, managers, real estate brokers, bookkeepers, and salespeople. Skilled occupations occupied the next highest employment category. Professionals, merchants, and small shopkeepers made up a significant percentage of the residents and occupied the rowhouses next to the Paytons' No. 13, which had been owned by Ernest Rothschild, manager of a cracker factory in 1900. Similar occupational profiles were reflected in the corner houses bordering the block on Fifth and Lenox Avenues.

A more exclusive residential pattern characterized the neighboring blocks. At 138th and 139th Streets, set back twelve feet from the street, with rear entrances "permitting the business of housekeeping to be kept out of sight," stood the famous Stanford White houses, erected in 1891. These homes later became known as "Strivers Row," the name African American Harlemites gave to the block's up-and-coming black bourgeoisie. "Sugar Hill," located between Convent and St. Nicholas Avenues and stretching north to 155th Street, also afforded some of the most elegant residences in the community.

In the decade between 1905 and 1915, a major ethnic and socioeconomic transformation took place in central Harlem. One of Manhattan's "residential heavens" turned black. Generally, native-born black real estate broker Philip A. Payton is credited with inaugurating the transformation. In a 1911 interview with the Age, he recalled, "My first opportunity came as a result of a dispute between two [white] landlords. . . . To 'Get even' one of them turned his house over to me to fill with colored tenants. I was successful in renting and managing this house, and after a time I was able to induce other landlords to give me their houses to manage."[13]

In 1904 Payton organized the Afro-American Realty Company with undertaker and Texas native James C. Thomas ("the richest man of African descent in New York"[14]); southern migrant businessman James E. Garner; and lawyer Wilfred E. Smith, also a southern native. New York Age editor Fred R. Moore, Emmett Scott, and Charles Anderson became investors, too. Although the company folded in 1908 because of mismanagement and internal dissension, members of the community considered it a "race" enterprise because it had worked to acquire decent housing for blacks in a previously all-white community reluctant to have blacks as neighbors.

The roles played by southern blacks and Caribbean immigrants involved in property management and ownership are valuable to an understanding of black Harlem's origins. One important figure was John B. Nail, a southern migrant and saloonkeeper who had come to New York from Baltimore in 1863, worked as an attendant in white gambling houses, and from his savings opened a cafe in the Tenderloin in the 1880s. When Nail saw the black community moving uptown, he sold his midtown property and invested in five new apartment houses in Harlem. In 1907 his son John E. Nail and North Carolina migrant Henry C. Parker started the successful real estate firm of Nail and Parker. The younger Nail also joined with Caribbean businessman H. Adolph Howell, an undertaker, and others to form the Sphinx Realty Company in 1919. Such business alliances and partnerships between immigrants and native black entrepreneurs appear to have been more common than previously believed. Caribbean immigrant A. A. Austin's Antillean Holding Company was one of the most stable during the period. As white residents continued to leave Harlem between 1910 and 1920, after selling their depreciated property at reduced prices, Nail, Parker, Howell, Austin, and others made significant profits for themselves and their clients.[15]

Other real estate firms, including those of native-born Watt Terry and Montserratan William Roach, honed in on the Harlem market. Both Terry and Roach, unlike Nail, began with almost nothing and grew to become two of the wealthiest black businessmen in New York. Terry, a native Virginian, opened the successful Terry Holding Company in Harlem following profitable speculation in Massachusetts property. William Roach began by cleaning houses and offices around New York. Saving his earnings, he reinvested in Harlem property. In the 1920s he held the controlling interest in the Sarco Realty Company, which purchased the stately Smithsonian apartment house in 1921.[16]

"Millionaire Solomon Riley" was a legend in Harlem. A native of Barbados, he earned his fortune primarily through speculation. According to WPA researcher Theodore Poston's account, when hostile white neighbors compelled him and his white wife to move from their Manhattan townhouse, he rented to black tenants. When his upset neighbors moved away, his wife, acting in his behalf, purchased their property and quickly rented it to other blacks. Riley repeated this pattern again and again on various Harlem streets. The bottom fell out of his investments during the depression, however, and Riley died a relatively poor man in 1935.[17]

Based on survey research, T. J. Woofter's 1928 study of blacks in cities provides a different perspective on this and other popular Harlem success stories. He found that Manhattan blacks owned about two million dollars in property. Investors such as Nail and Parker and organizations such as St. Philips, rather than families, owned most of this property. Few families were able to buy their own homes and less than 1 percent of black families in Manhattan owned their homes in 1920.[18] Woofter pointed out that only business and professional persons and salaried employees had incomes stable enough to enable them to buy. Even these individuals rented to lodgers to help pay the mortgage. Lodging was almost as common on "Strivers Row" as on any other street in Harlem. Both Caribbean and native black homeowners rented to lodgers. "Many [Caribbean] families, after first leasing and then purchasing their property on Hamilton Terrace [in the elite black section known as "Sugar Hill"], quickly became landlords and rented rooms to the now-expanding black population."[19]

Collective economics was a necessary accompaniment of one's material advance in the city. The rotating credit system among Caribbean immigrants—brought to Harlem with migration—was a simple method of accumulating capital by pooling an agreed-upon sum among a small group and rotating the total to each member. For purchasing homes, larger sums were pooled and might require the contributions of the entire week's wages of one or more family members.[20] This system—totally informal and without legal bounds—was based on trust, for after an individual received a "hand," weekly payments continued until all other members had "drawn hands." The degree to which the practice was used to purchase property cannot be determined. Most immigrants probably used this no-interest loan system to survive in the city and to help support relatives at home. Aletha Dowridge Challenor, through her husband, Fred, in Brooklyn, was participating in a rotating credit association while still in Barbados. "Mrs Payne gave me the draw yesterday. She didn't get as many people as she expected and I am sending you $10.00," he wrote her in May of 1910. Fred and Aletha were frequently in "debt" to one or more credit associations.[21]

The Caribbean benevolent societies were another source of immigrant property ownership in Harlem. Benevolent properties, usually three- or four-story brownstones, were purchased through the fund-raising activities of the societies and contributions of members. Income for the societies was generated through the rental of meeting rooms to a wide variety of community groups. One of the earliest such property owners was the American West Indian Association, which was located in a brownstone at 149 West 136th Street. The Bermudian Benevolent Association purchased its brownstone at 402 West 146th Street in 1932.

But the concentration of housing in tenement development rather than single family homes and the speculative land prices in general precluded home ownership by the average wage-earner in Manhattan. In addition to the higher rents African Americans were required to pay, inadequate space remained a major feature of residential life. In 1915, aside from its almost complete racial transformation, a noticeable change in the Payton block from 1905 was the increase in household size. A number of factors accounted for this. Most of the new black residents, whose occupational profiles differed dramatically from the previous residents, could not afford the rents, which were raised and sometimes doubled as buildings became occupied by native and Caribbean blacks. Although African American Harlem offered more desirable housing than the old scattered ghetto communities downtown, blacks were not free to rent anywhere uptown. The nearly 1,700 people residing in the block in 1915 as compared to 1,550 in 1905 is not as great an increase as one might expect. But the greater size of households in 1915 is noticeable in the larger number of extended families and lodgers, in both Caribbean and native black households. The almost universal pattern after 1915 of one of more lodgers per household reflects a dramatic shift in the circumstances of the new residents.

Still, the first black settlement in the Payton block represented the upward mobility of "the better class of Harlem Negroes." The block also represented a mixture of Harlem's elite, bohemia, and working class. The presence of the Paytons, who also owned a country residence in Allenhurst, New Jersey, undoubtedly attracted up-and-coming native and Caribbean tenants to the large, though now somewhat crowded, apartments on 131st Street. Also, the more stable working class would have been among the first to afford new apartments along with higher rents.

In any case, 28 percent (470) of the residents were foreign born in 1915. This number was somewhat higher than their representation in the total African American population. In contrast to the foreign-born German and Irish residents of 1905 who had been in the U.S. an average of 21.33 years, the average foreign-born black resident living on 131st Street had been in America for 10.33 years. Like the native-born black population, they resided mostly in kin-related households or lodged with a family. The foreign-born blacks included not only individuals from the British-held islands, but also from Cuba, Panama, Martinique, West Africa, France, England, Canada, Portugal (probably the Cape Verde Islands off the coast of West Africa), and even China.[22]

Household patterns clearly indicate that more experienced immigrants of African descent facilitated the settlement of more recently arrived relatives and others from their homelands. This contrasted to 1905, when household patterns reflected a far more settled population. In 1915 apartments which had in 1905 accommodated nuclear families and often mature couples in their fifties and sixties now housed more extended families and lodgers. A majority of couples were between ages twenty-five and forty-four.

The occupations of the Payton block's working-age native and foreign-born residents in 1915 were remarkably similar. In those days occupations were not nearly as much as later indicators of social-class standing. A. Philip Randolph, one of Harlem's budding socialist intellectuals, and Lucille Randolph, a former teacher, lived on the block in 1915. He worked as a porter and she as a hairdresser. Even Maggie Payton's occupation was listed as "domestic" by the time of the 1915 state census.[23]

In fact, 355 of Maggie Payton's 131st Street female neighbors were classified as household workers in 1915 (See Appendix, table II-5). Female household worker was the largest occupational category on the Payton block, as it was in Harlem and in most black communities until 1960. The lack of occupational choices reflected the extreme limitations on opportunities for black working women. The labor force participation of the Caribbean immigrant women was very high and little distinguishable from that of native black women. On the Payton block in 1915, eighty-two Caribbean women were employed as household workers, ten as dressmakers, two as laundry workers, and nine others in various service occupations. There were no women on the block, native or foreign-born, working in white-collar or professional positions. Because of their near total exclusion from almost all jobs except domestic worker, black women who did find jobs in other industries considered themselves lucky. A domestic's job, where one could return to one's own family in the evening, was the most sought after job by black women. But a live-in housekeeping job, though not ideal, could be viewed quite practically. Paule Marshall writes about her mother's generation: "Looking back on it now it seems to me that those Barbadian women accepted these ill-paying, low status jobs with an astonishing lack of visible resentment. For them they were simply a means to an end: the end being the down payment on a brownstone house, a college education for their children and the much coveted status these achievements represented."[24] Harlem physician Muriel Petioni, who in 1919 at age five immigrated to New York with her family from Trinidad, also reflects upon the circumstances of her mother's generation:

> In those days there were two possibilities if you came from outside the country: days work or the garment factories. In days work you went up to the Bronx and stood on the street corner to wait for a white woman to choose you to work. You got down on your hands and knees; you didn't use mops in those days. . . . If you were lucky you got a job as a housekeeper. You had to sleep in and you got every other Thursday and Sunday off.[25]

In contrast Maggie Payton's 1905 white female working neighbors were mainly young unmarried women working in a limited number of traditional female jobs, including stenographer, saleswoman, school teacher, dressmaker, and actress. The only white household workers on the block were the live-in servants. The second-generation Irish and German Jewish married women almost invariably did not work outside the home. Female heads of household, whether married, widowed, or unmarried, typically did not work (See Appendix, Table II-1). Black female heads of household invariably reported working outside the home.

But in 1915, the overwhelming number of black employed residents, male and female, foreign born and native, worked in other service occupations—porter, elevator operator, waiter, and laborer. Porter was the most common job category among black men. Ninety-three Payton block residents worked in this occupation, twenty-eight of this number foreign born. A railroad porter's job was considered a middle-class occupation, as was, of course, a post office job (See Table II-5).

Steady work along with the income of a spouse could mean the ability to support one's family in the city. Fred Challenor's letters from New York to Aletha Dowridge Challenor in Barbados are filled with accounts of his search for decent work. In Barbados he had received a very solid elementary school education, as his letters reveal. As customary this basic schooling was followed by training in a trade—in Fred Challenor's case, as a shoemaker. When he arrived in New York he found work in the Miller Shoe Factory but only seasonally and the pay was low. In April of 1910, he wrote: "Work is pretty bright at the factory but I am not making as much money as last year as the job to me now is very tiresome and I am weary with it [I] am trying all the time to get a janitor's position, but haven't succeeded so far but any way shall keep where I am until next month when it's time to go back on the boat."[26] A good job for Fred Challenor would have enabled the family to be reunited sooner. Eventually he did find a steady job as an apartment house janitor. But the strain of the separation apparently taxed the couple's relationship at times. Aletha's friend Addie confirmed that Fred had been "trying to get a place as a janitor & so have you back. I know of three places he has tried for, and hasn't succeeded. . . . You must not lose your confidence in him. Believe what he tells you, never mind what anybody else may say."[27]

While the young Challenor family suffered repeated and frustrating separations during the first years of their marriage, the older Spence couple, natives of Nevis and residents of the Payton block in 1915, were fortunate to have their whole family together. Robert, age fifty-seven, and Emma, forty-two, lived at No. 1 with their six daughters, Eulalie, nineteen; Blanche, eighteen; Emonie, seventeen; Iris, fifteen; Olga, thirteen; and Dora, twelve. Robert Spence, who had come to the country in 1901, had preceded the family by one year. The youngest daughter, Dora, had been born in the States. None except Dora were citizens. Robert Spence's occupation is recorded as butler, and Emma Spence was employed as a domestic. All six daughters were attending school. By 1925, the Spence family had moved away from the block. While no information about the younger daughters could be found, we do know that Eulalie Spence became an author and playwright of the Harlem Renaissance. Like a number of women writers of the period, her work has only recently come to critical attention.[28]

There was an unusually high number of musicians on the block in 1915. Twenty-nine men, all but two native born, worked in this occupation. Their gravitation to this particular block on 131st may have been influenced by Alabama native James Europe, the famous bandleader, who shared an apartment with his wife, Willie, also a musician, and his sister, Ada Ingram, a bookkeeper. The Europes had moved to Harlem from the San Juan Hill district, where he started the famous Clef Club in 1910. For years the Clef Club monopolized the business of entertaining private parties and furnishing music for the new dance steps of the Jazz Age.[29] The orchestra consisted of more than a hundred musicians and dozens of instruments—harp guitar and banjos, mandolins, ten pianos, as well as strings, reeds, and brass. In World War I, James Europe formed the 369th Infantry band famed for its syncopated rhythms that amazed military and civilian audiences abroad.[30]

The household of twenty-six-year-old A. Philip Randolph and his wife Lucille, thirty-one, who occupied an apartment at 48-50 with Josephine Campbell, Lucille Randolph's mother, and one lodger, Andro Faugas, a Cuban-born cigar maker, is an example of social diversity. Although, according to the census, A. Philip Randolph was employed as a "porter" and Lucille as a hairdresser, the couple were well educated. Lucille, a native of Christianburg, Virginia, was a Howard University–trained teacher turned beautician. She had been one of the first graduates of Madame C. J. Walker's Lelia College, a training school for hair preparation located in two elegant brownstones on 136th Street. Asa Randolph, as he was known then, was a Florida native and a graduate of Cookman Institute, where he had excelled in history, philosophy, drama, and public speaking. In the spring of 1911 Randolph worked his way to New York as a dishwasher on the Clydeline steamboat Arapahoe. In the spring of 1914, he met Lucille Green, and in November they were married at St. Philips Episcopal Church, where she was a member.

The Cuban cigar maker lodging with the Randolphs was one of four immigrants engaged in this trade and residing on the Payton block in 1915 (see table II-5). New York's Cuban and Puerto Rican cigar makers were often politically active among anti-imperialist, pro-independence immigrant circles and became members of the Cigar Makers Union, one of the few unions interested in the welfare of foreign workers, according to Bernardo Vega. A considerable number were also active in the Socialist party. They helped create the tabaquero tradition in New York, where in the larger shops in Puerto Rico and also in Tampa these skilled artisans forged virtual working-class universities. The workers "were proud of their trade and revolutionary in thought and action." This may have been largely due to the institution of factory readings. Bernardo Vega wrote:

> The institution of factory readings made the tabaqueros into the most enlightened sector of the working class. The practice began in the factories of Vinas & Co., in Bejucal, Cuba, around 1864. . . . Emigrants to Key West and Tampa introduced the practice into the United States around 1869. . . . In Puerto Rico the practice spread with the development of cigar production, and it was Cubans and Puerto Ricans who brought it to New York. It is safe to say that there were no factories with Hispanic cigar workers without a reader. Things were different in English-speaking shops where, as far as I know, no such readings took place.[31]

The connections between the Cuban and Puerto Rican tabaqueros and the Harlem Socialists remains unclear, but there were close connections between them as part of the larger uptown Socialist party movement. The Latino cigar makers were the second largest skilled group on the block.

Whether the Randolphs and their lodger may have become acquainted through their political affiliations is not known. Caribbean-born lodgers on the block generally roomed with someone from their homeland. Still, there are enough census examples of immigrants lodging with natives to show the proximity with which diverse ethnic groups shared the limited space in Harlem. High rents and the massive flow of newcomers between 1920 and 1924 encouraged lodging as a way of life in better than 50 percent of homes. A 1927 Urban League study found at least one lodger per household.[32] While some families may have taken in lodgers for profit, others did so to meet the rent or to provide friends and relatives with a place to live in the city.

In 1925 the basic household patterns observed on 131st Street were still evident, although there was a near complete migration of residents from the block. This may have indicated upward mobility for earlier residents, the deterioration of the block, or both. (The Randolphs moved to Seventh Avenue and then finally to the elite Dunbar Apartments.) Lodging was still a feature of many households. Over a quarter of the residents were lodgers in 1925 (see Table IV). A typical lodging household oc-cupying an apartment in No. 67 were John E. and Irene Smith. He was a native of St. Kitts and she of Jamaica. They had come to this country more than twenty years before. John worked as a janitor and Irene in household service. Lodging with them were more recent arrivals from the Caribbean: Cuban-born tailor Justine Hacabarra; wife Rosa, who was not employed; and their daughter, Doris, a dressmaker. Mildred Brown, twenty-one, also a lodger in the Smith household, had been in the country since 1909 and also worked as a dressmaker. None in the household was a natural-ized citizen. The mixture of cultures was not unusual. Many Cuban and South American–born black immigrants had family or social ties in the British-held is-lands. Another pattern reflected in this household was the similarity in occupations. Groups of workers often lived together. It is not clear from the available data if these two families worked in the garment industry or for themselves.

The New York Colored Mission, with buildings at No. 8 and on East 130th Street, was a social-service organization aiding immigrants and natives in their search for work. It maintained an employment bureau in addition to temporary housing and meals for migrants. Most available jobs were in domestic work, but by the mid 1920s the agency reported the availability of more factory jobs. In 1927 the mission reported receiving over 500 applications for factory work from Caribbean immigrants. Though it began as a religious mission in the 1870s, by the mid-1920s the agency functioned on the settlement-house model, socializing children and adults in middle-class values. According to an article in the Urban League's Opportunity, "the Junior Sewing Classes have been given their instructions in neatness, order-liness and decorum, while they have learned to ply the busy needle." The mis-sion also provided a sewing class for adults and a nursery school for working mothers. In addition, boys and girls clubs—Clover Leaf, Comrade, Athletic Club, Blue Bird Social—provided activities for neighborhood children. Muriel Petioni, whose family lived at No. 26, recalled spending many hours at the mission.[33]

In 1925 Charles Petioni, a night-school pre-med student, and his wife, Rosa Allen Petioni, occupied a "railroad flat" a half-block from the mission with their daughters, Muriel and Marguerite.[34] Also living in the household and described in the census as "lodgers" were Edith Mitchell, Rosa Petioni's sister, her son, Eric, and Inez Cole, also a lodger. The family took in lodgers, according to Muriel Petioni, to help pay the rent and to help with the expenses of her father's night-school edu-cation. The Petionis had been in the country less than ten years but were all naturalized citizens. The Mitchells had arrived only two years before. According to the census, the adult women were all engaged in "housework." The Petionis' and Mitchells' advance in America illustrates the determination of immigrants to over-come racial barriers, but their background in Trinidad also equipped them with essential skills to help overcome obstacles in the American setting. Muriel Petioni recounted the experience of young people in her parents' class and generation:

Children were given a free sixth grade education. This was usually very well grounded in the British system so students were very well prepared in the primary grades. If you were bright or had money you went to the next category—secondary school. Some received scholarships. Most were trained in a trade.[35]

Rosa Allen, who had been born in British Guiana, the daughter of a Chinese father (born in Hong Kong) and a South American Indian mother, migrated with her family to Trinidad as a young girl. She had been apprenticed as a dressmaker, as was the practice among many young women of her class. Before migrating to New York, she worked in Waterman's Department Store in Port of Spain.

Charles Petioni had attended secondary school and worked as a newspaper reporter in Port of Spain. His anticolonial articles got him fired, and he was told by a superior that he would never find work again in Trinidad. Already married to Rosa Allen and a father, Petioni left Trinidad in 1917 determined to seek an independent occupation so as to always be in a position to express his political views without fear of losing a job. When Petioni arrived in New York "he had never lifted anything heavier than a pen." He found work first as a stockman in the shipyards, then as an elevator operator, and later a porter. He began attending pre-med classes at night and was joined by his family in 1919. Rosa Allen Petioni found work as a finisher in a downtown sweat shop:

> Because it was well-known that this was where you could go. So they just went . . . there. And they were glad because a lot of people could not keep up with the pace. And many people dropped out. . . . People came and went all the time. . . . I don't know if it was ever difficult to get a job if you could keep up with the pace. It was piece work and you had to complete a certain number of garments for them to keep you.[36]

Black women accounted for less than 2 percent of the International Ladies Garment Workers Union in 1929 and were practically unknown as cutters or operators—the key crafts. Most served as finishers at the lower end of the wage scale.[37]

Rosa Allen's employment in this and other jobs helped support the family and enabled Charles Petioni to complete his studies at City College and later Howard University, where he completed his medical degree in 1925. He next returned to Harlem and set up his medical practice at No. 26. Rosa Allen Petioni then quit her job in the garment factory and went to work as Petioni's receptionist. The lodgers moved on to their own apartments, and Petioni used the first two rooms of the flat as a waiting room and an examining room. Eventually the Petionis moved from the flat at No. 26 to a brownstone at 114 West 131st Street, where one floor was used as offices, another two as living space, and a fourth as space for tenants, usually friends and relatives from Trinidad. The household became a center of political and social activity as well. Petioni emerged as an outspoken leader of the Caribbean and Harlem community. Both of the Petioni daughters attended college, Muriel becoming a prominent Harlem physician and Marguerite a psychiatric social worker. Muriel and Marguerite's half-brother also became a physician.

Edith Mitchell eventually found a job with the Pennsylvania Railroad, cleaning cars as a maid. For a variety of reasons, including access to unionization and standardized hours and wages, black women engaged in this work considered it much better work than domestic service. She later worked as a volunteer in hospitals during World War II and finally became a practical nurse, an occupation representing upward mobility for black women. As a single parent she worked to send her son, Eric, to medical school. He later became a physician.[38]

The possibility of finding a better job and thereby improving one's own material condition or those of one's children was a primary motivation behind most newcomers' decision to migrate to the city. But while wages were an improvement over those at home, jobs were by no means easy to come by. Upon arrival in New York, Caribbean immigrants immediately confronted America's unique definitions of race. This was nowhere more apparent than when seeking employment commensurate with one's training or background. On the surface race and racial discrimination appeared to be the great equalizer. A former clerk could find himself working side by side as a laborer with someone considered his inferior at home.[39] But the struggle to maintain and elevate one's status, perhaps at the cost of racial solidarity, may have contributed to the conflicts between natives and immigrants. In her commentary on the immigrant women in Brown Girl, Brownstones, Paule Marshall writes:

> In terms of their relations with black American women it seems to me from what I observed as a child that the West Indian woman considered herself both different and somehow superior. From the talk which circulated around our kitchen it was clear, for example, that my mother and her friends perceived of themselves as being more ambitious than black Americans, more hard working. . . . [40]

In addition to their own preoccupations with class distinction, white American society often reinforced the distance these women sometimes perceived between themselves and other black women. In Brown Girl, Brownstones, a white woman speaks of her Caribbean household worker in these terms:

> I've never been able to get another girl as efficient or reliable as Ettie. When she cleaned, the house was spotless. . . . And she was so honest, too. I could leave my purse, anything, lying around and never worry. She was just that kind of a person. . . . I've always told my friends there's something different, something special about Negroes from the West Indies. Some of the others are . . . well . . . just impossible.[41]

"With this kind of insidious divide and rule encouragement," Marshall adds, "it is no wonder that even in the face of the racism they inevitably encountered, these women sought to escape identification with those who were considered the pariah of the society." "If only we had our own language," Marshall reported her mother saying—

something which would have clearly established that they were "different, foreign, and therefore perhaps more acceptable."[42]

On 131st Street immigrants from the same region tended to cluster in the same buildings. For instance, in 1915 many immigrants lived at No. 26, but by 1925 the Petioni family was the only immigrant household recorded in the census of that year, though other immigrants still resided on the block. While all may not have eventually moved to a brownstone as did the Petionis, it can be assumed that they did move from the "railroad flat" to more desirable apartments. Middle-class status, symbolized by ownership of a Harlem brownstone, took years to achieve on the salaries of service workers.

Skilled workers or ones with education, like the Petionis, could move ahead faster or at least have realistic expectations that their children would. This was possibly the aspiration of Moses and Rose Holder, who lived with their four children on the Payton block at No. 32 in 1915. The Holders had been in the United States eight years but had not become naturalized citizens. Moses Holder, a native of Trinidad, was a "master carpenter" and was apparently well educated, as his daughter later described him as a "bona fide teacher." Rose Holder, whose occupation is listed only as "domestic," was also a skilled craftswoman who made baby bonnets for the department store that later became B. Altman's, according to a recorded account by her daughter.[43] In 1925 the Holders no longer lived at No. 32. In fact, none of the residents—the three native-born and one Caribbean households—still resided there. The household workers, musician, post office clerk, piano maker, butlers, and so on had apparently moved on to better circumstances.

The Holders' oldest child, Lenon, who was nine in 1915, became a teacher of history and art and also a talented craftswoman. As a 1938 bride, Lenon Holder Hoyte moved to No. 6 Hamilton Terrace on Sugar Hill. Described as one of the first black immigrant "pioneers" of the previously all-white Hamilton Heights area, Holder Hoyte later founded Aunt Len's Doll House and Toy Museum in the basement of her home.

While having a skill could afford black newcomers with social mobility at least for their children, Caribbean as well as southern migrant men met stiff competition in the building trades in New York. Charles Zampty, a native of Trinidad who came to New York City in 1928, could not find a job as a carpenter, a trade he had practiced extensively as a skilled artisan in the Panama Canal Zone. In proportion to their numbers in the population, more Caribbean men than native blacks were employed in this trade, according to Herbert Gutman's larger sampling of 1925 Harlem occupations.[44]

When unable to find work in the trades, some immigrant men formed their own small businesses. Having worked in Panama and having acquired a small savings, C. Lisley John established his own business and became a founding member of the St. Vincent Benevolent Association.[45] John was married to the well-known Harlem community activist and radio personality Alma John, a native of Philadelphia. Jamaican immigrant Tyrell Wilson found that his skill as a tailor did nothing to assure his employment in New York City. His ambition to work his way through law school was dashed by the lack of a job that would pay tuition and support his growing family. While working in various occupations, Wilson became an activist during the 1920s and later set up with other immigrants and southern blacks a rural all-black community in Gordon Heights, Long Island.[46]

An analysis of the African American residents, native born and immigrant, reveals a striking similarity in housing, occupational, and other household characteristics during the years 1905 to 1925. But perhaps the most revealing aspect of the residents' experience in Harlem cannot be determined from the data alone. As the attractiveness of 131st Street declined, residents moved away from the block. Though their whereabouts in 1925 could not be traced here, one factor influencing mobility appears to have been the possession of both skills and education. While working, perhaps for all their lives at menial occupations, the first urban generation native born and immigrant, if educated themselves, could realistically hope their children would move up in the social ladder. But as these examples show, possessing skills and education did not afford many of even the most qualified first-generation immigrants mobility in fields where their race alone blocked their advance in America. St. Vincent native Hugh Mulzac, the first black person in United States history to become licensed as a ship's captain in 1918, could find work only as a steward, second mate, or radio operator. For him, being prevented from doing work for which he was trained "deprived life of its most essential meaning."[47]

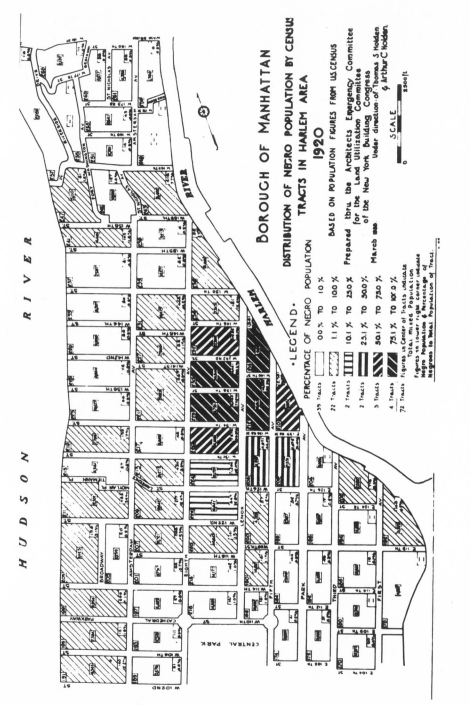

African and Caribbean American population in Harlem, 1920. Source: Slum Clearance Committee Reports, 1934

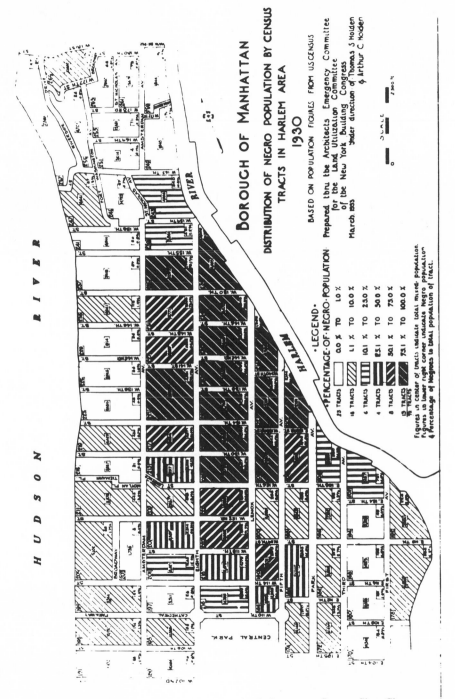

African and Caribbean American population in Harlem, 1930. Source: Slum Clearance
Committee Reports, 1934

4

Churches, Benevolent Associations, and Ethnicity

IN ITS FIRST three decades, the evolving Harlem community was comprised of a myriad of social networks linked together by churches, benevolent and fraternal societies, and lodges. It was largely because of these networks that one observer claimed that "inside of six months" immigrants and southern migrants became "pretty good New Yorkers."[1] In 1921 a writer in the *New York Evening Graphic* observed that "churches are far more important than cabarets. . . . The influence of the church is not waning. . . . The church is the social center of the colored race."[2] Alongside and often in cooperation with the church, other voluntary groups promoted the special interests of their members through what can be characterized as homeland societies—more than thirty in number. These were groups formed to maintain contact and preserve traditions of immigrants from the same town or region. There were smaller numbers of these associations among migrants from states along the American southeastern seaboard.[3]

Harlem residents in general also developed a large variety of lodges and social clubs. "Social clubs and secret lodges are legion. And all of them vie with one another in giving dances, parties, entertainments and benefits in addition to public turnouts and parades."[4] These associations added interest and vitality to community activity while bringing together influential people to mediate community problems and advance its goals. It is significant that most men in the Harlem community—native or foreign born—who rose to positions of influence at this time were likely to be members of one of the major lodges or fraternal orders. In the words of playwright Eulalie Spence's character T. J. Kelly, an up-and-coming young man in Harlem paid "dues in a club, two Societies and a Lodge."[5] Membership usually conferred a large, automatic constituency for anyone aspiring to leadership. Women's participation in fraternal orders—often women's auxiliaries—also conferred prestige, if not power. Other female-run associations, carried along in the wake of the larger national black women's club movement, sought to elevate the status of black women in the city. Ethnically based women's associations, such as the American West Indian Ladies Aid Society, somewhat reminiscent of the Dorcas societies of the nineteenth century, were insurance associations providing sick and burial benefits and also offering charitable and social-service relief.[6] The activities of all these

56

groups reveal not only the nature of ethnicity in Harlem, but also the context in which disparate social units functioned.

Churches were among the fastest growing institutions shaping Harlem's development as a black community. NAACP executive and poet James Weldon Johnson counted 160 churches in 1930.[7] Their numbers had quickly increased as migratory waves rapidly expanded New York City's black population in the first three decades of the century. The most popular congregations doubled and tripled in size throughout the period as they quickly increased their financial base in Harlem. For migrating young women, especially in an age of considerable religious awareness, such an affiliation assured parents of a daughter's respectability in a city of many vices. Figures released by the Greater New York Federation of Churches in 1929 show a black community church membership of 62,633. Approximately two-thirds of this number were female and nearly one-half Baptist. The number did not include members of storefront churches.[8] The report also indicated that in Harlem traditional Caribbean faiths accounted for less than 7 percent of the total.[9] Because of their historic importance in the United States as institutions controlled by their communities, churches were the premier ethnic institution among native-born African Americans in the city, but perhaps less so in the beginning among Caribbean immigrants in New York.

Some early immigrant Anglicans sought affiliation with white Episcopalian denominations. Aletha Dowridge and her close relatives and friends from Barbados attended Brooklyn Heights Holy Trinity Episcopalian Church at first but were required to sit in a separate section. They later joined Brooklyn's historic black St. Augustine Episcopalian. The rector (between 1896 and 1943), George Frazier Miller, a native of South Carolina, was a well-known Socialist. Miller officiated at Aletha Dowridge and Fred Challenor's wedding in 1907. But the Dowridge-Challenors felt unwelcomed at the predominantly native-born black St. Augustine and later joined with cousin Letty Murrell a newly organized Christ Church Cathedral, located at Atlantic and Classon Avenues. This church, headed by Barbadian Rev. Reginald Grant Barrow, served the Caribbean-immigrant community. It later became affiliated with the African Orthodox Church.[10] This pattern may have been followed by other immigrant families, especially members of the Anglican Church, which did not have its counterpart in the United States.

Although several New York black churches had long traditions in Manhattan (since 1796 for African Methodist Episcopal "Mother Zion," 1808 for Abyssinian Baptist, 1809 for St. Philips Protestant Episcopal, and 1819 for Bethel African Methodist Episcopal), it was the more recently formed churches which first served the needs of southern migrants and Caribbean immigrants. In the Tenderloin and San Juan Hill, these were Mount Olivet Baptist, St. Marks Methodist Episcopal, St. James Presbyterian, Union Baptist, St. Cyprian Episcopal, and St. Benedict the Moor Roman Catholic. With the exception of St. Cyprian and St. Benedict, all of these congregations later moved on to Harlem. Union Baptist was first housed in a storefront downtown, and its pastor, the Reverend Dr. George Sims, a Virginia native, gathered "the very recent residents," mostly southern migrants, to build a new church. Union Baptist, Mt. Olivet, and other churches revived the tradition of southern preaching and were known as "shouting" churches.[11] Here the newest migrants were made to feel at home. While migrants—mostly female in the case of American-born blacks—bolstered the careers of black clergy, some clergymen played significant roles in incorporating specific ethnic groups—southern and Caribbean—into the larger African American community.

John H. Johnson, Sr., a native of Virginia, became pastor of St. Cyprian Episcopal Church, a stronghold of Caribbean immigrants in San Juan Hill. Although St. Philips Episcopal Church was located in the area, according to one account the immigrants sometimes frequented all-white Episcopalian churches. In an attempt to avert integration, the Protestant Episcopalian Mission Society supported financially the formation of St. Cyprian in 1905. In addition to servicing the new black immigrants, St. Cyprian served the black community in ways that St. Philips did not.[12] It became the stronghold of working-class immigrants and the surrounding mass-based community. Its community house on West 63rd Street provided a training gymnasium for many of the early black prize fighters. The church's Parish House was a well-known social center for native black and foreign-born New Yorkers, not all of them Episcopalian. Dances were held twice a week, and "large groups attend[ed] and it [was] difficult to maintain order."[13] The Parish House also maintained a playground for the black children of the area. After the move on to Harlem, St. Cyprian remained as the outstanding social center among seven blocks of poorer blacks between 59th and 65th Streets. According to the researcher W. T. Woofter, in 1928 the section still represented "the area nearest the poverty line to which the poorer migrants flock." But when the African American community shifted uptown, some better-off Caribbean immigrants joined St. Philips.[14] Other second-generation black immigrant members of St. Cyprian changed their affiliation to its sister church in Harlem, St. Martin's, located at 230 Lenox Avenue and founded by John H. Johnson, Jr. in 1928. St. Martin's became the bastion of the Caribbean middle class in Harlem, and Johnson remained pastor of the Church until the 1950s. By the mid-1930s St. Martin's claimed 1,200 members and a Sunday school of over 500 children. According to one study, fully 75 percent of the congregation was of Caribbean descent. "The most prominent lawyers, realtors, politicians and men of medicine are active members of the Church." Harlem's first municipal judge, James Watson, was one of these.[15]

Like his father, John H. Johnson's position as pastor of St. Martin's served to link the Caribbean parishioners with the larger Harlem community. Johnson Jr. organized the Citizens League for Fair Play in 1934 as part of the Jobs for Negroes Campaign. He became a series of "firsts" in New York City by becoming the first black chaplain of the police department; first black to serve on the Borough President's Advisory Board, on the Board of Managers of the Mission Society, and as Trustee of the Cathedral Church of St. John the Divine; and first black president of the Standing Committee of the Diocese of New York.[16] Johnson's role as head of a largely professional Caribbean congregation has considerable significance for our understanding of the importance of class and position rather than ethnicity per se in determining the avenues of influence in the community.

If American-born black ministers served as heads of important, predominantly Caribbean immigrant congregations, the well-educated male immigrant also found opportunities in historically black denominations in the United States.[17] The African Methodist Episcopal (A.M.E.) and the A.M.E. Zion Churches quickly attracted talented Caribbean immigrant ministers. The connection was in part due to the establishment of these denominations in the Caribbean during the nineteenth century. A.M.E. minister William E. Ferris provided an interesting account of these ministers' affiliations with African American denominations:

> In September 1900 the Bishop of the New England Conference of the A.M.E. Church was a West Indian, the presiding elder was a West Indian, the secretary of the conference was a West Indian, the pastor of Ford Chapel, Newport, Rhode Island, the second largest A.M.E. Church in New England, was a West Indian, and the pastor of the much sought after Church in Greenwich, Connecticut, was a West Indian. Prior to that time the A.M.E. presiding elder in New Jersey was West Indian. Toward the close of the first decade of the Twentieth Century, Dr. Yearwood of British Guiana was popular as a pastor in Hartford, Connecticut, and Dr. R. R. Ball, a Canadian, was popular as a presiding elder and then pastor in Hartford. At the same time a West Indian was the highly respected pastor of a Baptist church in Cincinnati, Ohio. West Indians held regal sway as Episcopalian ministers all the way from Boston to Palatka, Florida, between 1890 and 1920. The most brilliant example was Dr. George Alexander McGuire. They were even sought after in Presbyterian churches.[18]

The most distinguished of these ministers in New York was Bishop Derrick of the A.M.E. church. Derrick, a native of Antigua, was pastor of the historic Bethel A.M.E. and bishop of the eastern conference until his death in 1913. A Republican and a Booker T. Washington supporter, Derrick was a source of political influence for the pre-Harlem downtown African American community as well as a leader within the small immigrant community.[19]

The African American church was the main avenue in Harlem through which Caribbean immigrant males gained influence in an earlier period, but in the twentieth century the migrations ushered in a larger urban milieu in which to rise. Politics, journalism, business, and other professions offered limited outlets for the ambitions of an educated male-immigrant elite. After 1900, Caribbean clergy increasingly turned to the growing black immigrant community as a base for leadership.

Charles Douglass Martin, a native of St. Kitts, established Harlem's first branch of the Moravian church on West 134th Street in 1908. While relying on his mostly African Caribbean church membership as a base, Martin developed close ties to the African American community. Deeply committed to a study of the African past, he became a member of the pioneering Negro Society for Historical Research, established in 1911. One of the Society's founders, popular journalist John E. Bruce ("Bruce Grit"), in turn became a member of Martin's Moravian congregation.[20] Martin was also active in the American-based race struggle. In 1917, as one of Harlem's leading ministers, he helped to spearhead with W. E. B. Du Bois the famous Silent Protest Parade down Fifth Avenue in which 15,000 black New Yorkers denounced the rising tide of violence against African Americans in a dramatic muffled-drum march. When Martin's church dedicated its new location at 124-6 West 136th Street in 1921, the leaders of Harlem's predominantly native-born black congregations were present to share in the celebration.[21]

As the Caribbean community grew after 1900, other congregations emerged, ministering to the specific needs of the newer immigrants. By the 1930s WPA researcher Robinson counted four Episcopalian, one Wesleyan, one Catholic, a number of Moravian, and a Jamaican Baptist church,[22] which were predominantly black immigrant. Caribbean immigrants also affiliated with other congregations, including Seventh-day Adventist, Presbyterian, and storefront churches. These churches also helped maintain links with "home" and, as Robinson observed, helped to

> conserve the island culture, facilitate adjustment and help to prevent personal demoralization by organizing such ceremonies as the Rockland Palace Coronation. Islands-type harvest festivals, Christmas and New Year celebrations, Emancipation Day ceremonies (August 1) help soothe the nostalgia for the homeland and assist the churches in financing themselves. This was most strikingly expressed by one church which printed the entrance to an affair in English shillings.[23]

Caribbean immigrant churches perpetuated island traditions such as those relating to weddings and funerals. At a typical wake "food, drink and continuous dancing goes on for three days." Elaborate weddings were a sign—sometimes misleading—of the social standing of the families involved: "formal attire, strict etiquette . . . from 200 to 500 guests are a minimum." Robinson noted that the second generation, who were more likely to marry native-born African Americans, tried to modify these traditions. Ideally, a community of relatives and friends promoted marriages between people from the same Caribbean country. At a Seventh-day Adventist Church, Tyrell Wilson's married future sister-in-law, on the lookout for a suitable Jamaican husband for her sister, detected his Jamaican accent, observed his behavior over several Sundays, and introduced the pair, who were later married.[24]

The smaller Caribbean immigrant parishes, while carrying on these traditions, had less economic influence than similarly situated native African American churches, but their pastors were often politically active. The Harlem Congregational Church, located at 250 West 136th Street, had a membership of 150 mostly Caribbean immigrants in 1921. Its pastor, Wesley S. Holder, a native of British Guiana, was an activist in the African American community and a member of the National Equal Rights League. One newspaper account described him as a "thoroughly educated and cultured man, trained in Western College, Bristol, England." But Holder's parishioners were barely able to support a church. Their economic status affected their ability to worship freely, he said. Many found it necessary to work on Sundays, and others were literally "too tired out" to come to church regularly.[25] Like a number of other Harlem pastors, Holder attempted to establish business enterprises among his parishioners and others. In 1907 he was affiliated with the West Indian Trading and Development Company.

The Jamaican-born pastor Ethelred Brown, faced with similar economic hardship at his Harlem Community Church, pointed out that "Negroes, however intelligent and cultured, are poor, because in America they are elevator men and porters."[26] Early in the depression, during the worst of times, Rev. Paul E. West of the predominantly Virgin Islander Lutheran Church of the Transfiguration, 74 West 126 Street, found it necessary to solicit the financial support of the American West Indian Ladies Aid Society: "Our Congregation could not be worse financially; we are trying all legitimate means to raise funds in order to meet our obligations."[27] In general the class and economic composition of immigrant and native churches was quite similar. While the leadership of some churches may have been middle class, the vast majority of the members were unskilled and service laborers who were, according to John H. Johnson, Jr., the most active church workers "and almost unbelievably generous and self-sacrificing in their attempts to improve the community."[28]

The manner in which most black Americans conducted their religious services challenged and broadened the cultural experience of some middle class from the Caribbean used to the more staid Anglican and Catholic services. Harold Cooke Phillips, an immigrant from the British-held Caribbean, noted in his 1921 Columbia University study of Harlem Churches that on his first visit to predominantly southern migrant Metropolitan Baptist, "it was in many ways a revelation. There was a spirit of absolute informality between the preacher and his audience."[29] Immigrants with other cultural backgrounds were equally amazed at the cultural performances in American black churches. Puerto Rican Arthur Schomburg said, "I attended the Baptist Church where, for the first time, I heard spiritual songs. Every society of the church was begging for money; women were jumping up and down and shouting; the doors of the church were locked and I did not know what the ultimate religious performance would be, except that it was new to me."[30] The emotionalism of the black American churches caused uneasiness in some Caribbean and American-born black intellectuals. E. Ethelred Brown said "Our colored ministers must . . . cleanse their religious meetings from the over-emotionalism which dangerously borders on fanaticism."[31]

Brown was not alone in his criticism of the African American church. The socialist *Messenger* editorialized that "the Negro church has failed." This deficiency was due, in the opinion of the editors, to the fact that the black church had been "converted into a business and the ruling characteristic of a business is that it is run for profit." Stepladder speakers would later target St. Philips, formerly number one on the honor roll of black business achievement, as one of Harlem's worst slum-lords.[32] The native-black church was the most important symbol of the collective financial potential of small-wage earners, even if not all in the community agreed on what its role should be.

In 1914 Howard University sociologist Kelly Miller provided a valuable portrait of the black minister's role. "The Negro minister often transacts a greater volume of business than any other member of the race in his community," he wrote. "By virtue of his confidential relation to his membership the minister often becomes their financial adviser. He inculcates the spirit of economy and thrift—advises the inexperienced men in his congregation to start bank accounts and directs them in the purchase of property."[33] Miller's assessment did not specify the role female members played in the economic success generally of some black churches and their male preachers. But women's management of a profusion of fund-raising church committees and their historic participation in church-related self-help organizations provided the necessary foundation for real estate and other business projects like those sponsored by Metropolitan Baptist. The church's emphasis on independence had a special appeal for female wage-earners, especially live-in domestic workers with "every other Thursday and Sundays off."[34] Women's roles in male-led African American urban churches deserve further study, but their majority presence and impact on the predominantly native-led Harlem churches distinguished these institutions from several important Caribbean immigrant churches. Ethelred Brown's Harlem Community Unitarian Church congregation rarely if ever numbered over one hundred members, though Brown himself was one of Harlem's major religious and intellectual leaders. The membership rolls of the Community Church show many more men than women. The Church was never able to purchase its own building and, until Brown's death in 1951, held services in rented space. Theology scholar Morrison-Reed suggests that the reasons lay in the limited appeal of the Unitarian denomination among American blacks:

> Who was drawn to [Brown's Harlem Community Church]? We know there were initially the left-wing radicals, many Jamaicans, but only a few black Americans. On a number of occasions Brown mentioned people who had forsaken organized religion until they found the Harlem church. The overwhelming impression is that people came for political and intellectual reasons.[35]

Morrison-Reed continues: "This church was an institutional anomaly, for church is traditionally a women's haven." Five of the fifteen original members were women, but the peculiarity of its ongoing membership perhaps prevented Brown's Community Church from becoming a "viable religious community."[36] Brown himself was probably better known as a political leader and Harlem radical, a stepladder Socialist and a major figure in the Jamaican independence movement in New York. He also had cordial relations with black American leaders, including Adam Clayton Powell, Sr. and Adam Clayton Powell, Jr., and over several decades was frequently invited to preach at Abyssinian Baptist Church.[37]

Though his congregation was not large, Brown's career in Harlem requires some attention here because of his views on an alternative religious thought and his link to other activist movements. Upon his arrival in 1920, Brown observed "men and women who had long since outgrown intellectually and morally the fundamental teachings of the older churches." In the same year he formally organized his church in the Lafayette Hall on 131st Street and Seventh Avenue. Referring to the church's teaching as "religious liberalism," he credited stepladder intellectual Hubert Harrison with stirring up religious skepticism on the streets of Harlem and having attempted unsuccessfully to organize "the Liberal Church of Harlem." Upon Harrison's death in 1927, Brown renamed his church for this influential community figure and teacher.[38] The founding members proved to be a remarkable group of Harlem community activists. Among them were Richard B. Moore of Barbados, Grace Campbell and W. A. Domingo of Jamaica, and Frank Crosswaith of the Virgin Islands.

Brown emphasized the importance of a worldly mission and was particularly critical of Harlem preachers who focused primarily on the hereafter. His usual sermons stressed the here and now and, using biblical texts, he reinterpreted traditional outlooks. He often claimed, "Jesus has been represented by some of his mistaken followers as meek and lowly, meaning by that he was a soft spineless person incapable of being angry and of showing his anger. I do not so conceive Jesus . . . he was encompassing in his denunciation of hypocrites, of unworthy leaders of his people, of those who prostitute the temple to a business exchange . . . and he was capable of showing forth his wrath in dramatic fashion."[39]

During the 1920s Brown was a frequent speaker at political forums around New York City and one of the Socialist Speakers Bureau's stepladder orators during political campaigns. On one occasion, when he was out of work as an elevator operator, he recalled how his Socialist associations developed:

> The Socialist Party of America discovered me during those hard weeks of job hunting, and strangely, Mr. Hunt, Field Secretary of the A.U.A. [American Unitarian Association], was the unconscious help to the discovery. One place that he did send me was the Socialist Headquarters at the Bronx . . . only to discover . . . that the position to be filled was that of a part-time janitor at $20 a month. As I expressed my disappointment I met the Executive Secretary of the Socialist Party, who then and there hearing that I was a Socialist in good standing promised to try and find me a position suited to my intelligence and training. He did find such a place in June when I got a speaking appointment on probation. On July 1, at his orders I quit the elevator job and became a Socialist campaign speaker.[40]

Another immigrant churchman, Dr. George Alexander McGuire, the organizer of the African Orthodox Church, also made a departure from traditional religious teachings. McGuire was born in Antigua and educated at the Nisky Theological Seminary in the Virgin Islands. He immigrated to the United States in 1894 and became a priest of the Protestant Episcopal church. He was well known among African American Episcopalians and became the first black archdeacon in charge of "colored work" in Arkansas. But throughout his affiliation with American Episcopalians, McGuire sought more independence from the national body and for his growing black congregation at St. Bartholomew in Boston. While in Boston, McGuire also attended Jefferson Medical College and became a physician. Perhaps this career move was an attempt to establish his own financial independence while he fought the white Episcopalian establishment for more black autonomy within the church. Eventually McGuire settled in Harlem and initiated a "new movement among Negro Episcopalians." He formed the Church of the Good Shepherd in November of 1919. A *Negro World* report claimed that seven other black clergymen had joined the movement and that the Good Shepherd served as a mother church. In 1920 the nationalist-oriented movement became known as the African Orthodox Church, drawing its first members from Marcus Garvey's UNIA. The AOC retained much of its former Episcopalian ritual, but it was highly race conscious. McGuire promoted the idea of a black Christ and stressed that should Christ visit New York City, he would have to reside in Harlem because of his color.[41] Kelly Miller observed that the idea of a black Christ had a powerful mass-based appeal.

The AOC spread to congregations throughout the Caribbean and had at least one branch in South Africa. Garvey scholar Tony Martin writes that AOC members were active in anticolonialist struggles in these regions. Like those attracted to Brown's Harlem Community Church, the appeal of the AOC was largely political and intellectual but also had black-nationalist appeal that attracted many more converts to it. Its retention of Episcopalian rituals made the movement less attractive to large numbers of American-born southern migrants. Marcus Garvey realized this when he distanced the UNIA from open affiliation with a particular church or denomination:

> The UNIA endorsed at its recent convention all churches under Negro leadership. It does not ally itself with any particular church, but as heretofore it has endorsed Methodist and Baptists of the Negro race, so now it endorses this new movement among Negro Episcopalians which has resulted in the formation of the African Orthodox Church.[42]

In 1921 McGuire, a member of the UNIA, ran into difficulty with Garvey over McGuire's attempts to recruit AOC followers from the UNIA membership lists. The matter was resolved by 1923, and McGuire returned to the UNIA in 1924. In his capacity as the chief architect of the UNIA's religious ritual, McGuire compiled and published the *Universal Negro Ritual.*

Congregations of the foreign born, native black, or both played crucial roles in stabilizing the lives of Harlem's long-term residents and newcomers. Here the nuances of Harlem's ethnic and class character were also evident in the formation of church congregations and their specialized roles within the community. Gender ratios in the Caribbean community appear to have had observable influence on the slower manner in which its organized religious community developed. But if Caribbean churches had comparatively little political and economic position relative to American black churches, other kinds of voluntary organizations made deeper inroads in the formation of community in Harlem.

In addition to the church, Harlem's fraternal and benevolent associations claimed the membership of a large cross-section of the Caribbean and black American communities. Membership in these associations provided practical mutual aid but also helped to establish an individual's social position and identity in a large, impersonal city. In Harlem, it was often commented, *everyone* belonged to something. An examination of these social networks helps us to learn more about intraracial ethnicity there.

Mutual benefit and relief societies based on place of origin had their roots in late nineteenth-century migrations from the south and the Caribbean. Although the basic purpose of these societies was to provide sick and death benefits for members, acquiring social distinction was an important built-in feature. Many of the early societies restricted their membership to men, prompting the formation of female groups or auxiliaries.[43]

Curiously the northern migration also prompted the formation of an exclusive association based on one's nativity in New York. The Society of the Sons of New York, founded in the 1880s, drew its membership from the "cream" of New York African American society. According to one account, southerners from comparable backgrounds could become associate members but could not take part in the deliberations of the group. The society was made up of prosperous head waiters, real estate speculators, politicians, cooks, and professionals. A Society spokesman said membership had been carefully selected to include only men who satisfied "the most delicate taste of gentleman-like tone and behavior" and to exclude "all vulgarity and every trace of ungentleman-like deficiency."[44] New York women of comparable social standing formed the Society of the Daughters of New York. According to its public pronouncements, this group banned together for "love, mutual protection and elevation."[45]

While the Societies of the Sons and Daughters of New York were clearly organized to reflect status already achieved and to guard against the encroachment of newcomers, the homeland associations organized among southern migrants and Caribbean immigrants helped stabilize life in an evolving community and then promoted upward mobility in it. No official channels—state based or federal—were available to aid either immigrants or southern migrants in their adjustment to the city. In his August 23, 1929, letter to the editor of the *New York Age* the British Pro Consul, Walter F. James, pointed out how beneficial he believed benevolent societies had been:

> There are in New York many West Indian Societies by names peculiarly adopted to each of the West Indian Islands, Bermuda and Bahamas. These societies promote the general interests of West Indians and many acts of the most

beneficial charity have originated with these institutions, which in addition afford counsel and assistance to strangers upon their arrival, leading them to prosperity to the benefit of the individuals and the ultimate aggrandizement of their adopted country.[46]

Southern migrants' benevolent associations were formed among individuals migrating from the same state. The Sons and Daughters of Florida's club song captured one of its goals:

Glory! Glory!
We are trying to find each other as we travel
    through the North.
And we mean to carry out our aim regardless
    to the cost.
We hope that they will join us and not a one
    be lost
As we go marching on.[47]

There was often more than one association from the same state or island and many of these are still functioning today. The Florida association was formed in 1918, and because many Caribbean immigrants first settled in Florida before coming to New York, the association was comprised of Caribbean and southern migrants. The South Carolina Club was created when twenty-two people met at a party in 1918 and discovered they were all migrants from different towns and cities in South Carolina.[48]

One uniform characteristic of benevolent associations, southern and Caribbean, was their restriction of membership to those born—or having resided a specific number of years—in a particular locality. Although critics of the benevolents accused the associations, especially those of Caribbean immigrants, of promoting self-interest ("clannishness") over that of the community, regulations about membership requirements among southern associations showed a similar tendency. WPA researcher Odette Harper recorded this story about the induction of the first president of the Women's Auxiliary affiliated with the United Sons of Georgia:

All the officers had been elected. And the elaborate affair which was the Installation Ceremony, food and speeches in abundance and the members resplendent in snow white silk frocks, had come and gone. The group settled down to its business of collecting dues and socializing, when somehow rumor leaked that the Grand Worthy Madame President was not a native Georgian. She had been born on the boundary line of Georgia. Indeed she had spent her childhood playing on Georgian soil. But actually the house in which she had been born and lived was in the southernmost county of the state of South Carolina. Immediately action was taken and the lady was disgraced and ousted.[49]

In addition to eligibility for sick and death claims, the ousted president would have held considerable prestige among people from her home communities and also served as the liaison with scores of other similar community organizations and groups. She also chaired the executive committee which carried out many of the financial obligations of the society. In the 1920s the United Sons and Daughters of Georgia was said to be the wealthiest organization of its kind in New York.[50]

By 1930 Virginians were the largest southern-migrant group in Harlem. Ten years earlier in November 1920, the Sons and Daughters of Virginia was organized, opening membership to any New York black resident who was a Virginian "by birth or parentage," provided he or she met with other requirements of membership. During the first year of the association's existence, membership grew to 600 and reached its peak of 1,110 in 1927. Picnics and outings as well as regular educational and literary forums were held. Like all other homeland associations, the Virginia association paid death claims and sick benefits.[51]

Ira Reid noted that the foreign-born black groups tended to organize on the basis of three main ideas: 1) mutual benefit and relief; 2) economic and political adjustment in the United States; and 3) the perpetuation of desirable conditions in their homelands. A category not mentioned by Reid was organizational activity that provided a vehicle for self-improvement through educational discussions and debates of various issues. Reid noted that leaders in the first two categories tended to be individuals who had most successfully come to terms—one way or other—with New York's economic, social, and political conditions. Success in these fields automatically conferred prestige on homeland interest groups in which individuals served as the "titular if not the functional leaders." Immigrant organizers of benevolents were also often naturalized citizens—business people or professionals.

The Bermuda Benevolent Association was formed in 1897 by organizers Clarence W. Robinson and George L. Joell, entrepreneurs in the San Juan Hill district. They sent invitations out to forty Bermudians known to be living in the New York area. The first meeting was held at 131 West 32nd Street, near the site of what was later to become Gimbels Department Store. According to an association history, "The wisdom of including women in the membership was soon recognized." The organization's records indicate that female Bermudians were prime movers within the early association, although the key leadership positions remained male dominated. One woman, Annie Joell, became president but served only one month, from April to May 1901. During the first years of the organization's existence, Rosinia Campbell made her home at 250 West 17th Street available for monthly meetings. She also hosted educational meetings and debates and other special occasions for the association.[52]

The constitutions and bylaws of Caribbean benevolent and native-black benevolent associations were quite explicit. Strict procedures for the conduct of meetings, election of officers, and initiation and acceptance of new members were outlined in the booklets printed and distributed by each society. An "investigating" or admissions committee received all applications at regular meetings and conducted an inquiry into the backgrounds of candidates for membership. A report was submitted at the next meeting. Very carefully worded guidelines relating to the handling and transfer of funds were stated in the constitution. In this regard any member whose dues in arrears exceeded a stated amount was required to forfeit his or her membership.

According to the bylaws of the Bermuda Benevolent Association, when a member in good financial standing became ill and desired to claim a sick allowance, "such member shall cause due notice of this desire in writing to be forwarded to the financial secretary accompanied by a certificate from an authorized medical practitioner stating that member is unable to follow in employment and giving the nature of the complaint." A limited economic safety net was thus available in needy times. A member was eligible for sick or death benefits only after having been a member in good standing for one year. In the event of death, the member's beneficiaries received a stated amount to help defray funeral expenses. But any member who was arrested and convicted of any crime was investigated by the executive committee and, upon its recommendations, suspended or expelled. If expelled no member "shall be reinstated."[53]

As was the case with all such societies, members of the Bermuda Association were required to be of Bermudian birth or parentage or part of the immediate family of a Bermudian and in good health. Any person who had lived continuously in Bermuda for ten years was also eligible. Persons whose reputations reflected "distinction upon the Association" could become honorary members.[54] Membership in the Association never exceeded 250—in part because of careful screening of new members—although the Association's records indicate membership drives were held periodically. In 1898 an initiation fee of two dollars was required and an assessment of twenty-five cents in monthly dues.

The Bermudian Association, like other such groups, performed an important service in a period when insurance companies rarely extended coverage to blacks.[55] Helena Benta of the Montserrat Progressive Society noted, "Disappointments, illusions and new hardships are rife, and until new adjustments are made the immigrant suffers untold misery. Benevolent organizations of the various island groups have grown out of these experiences."[56] The benefit program was financed through the assessment of dues and fees. Upon the presentation of a doctor's note, members were eligible for three dollars in sick aid and increments each week during an illness. Members could also expect a visit from the "sick committee."

Members appear to have conformed unfailingly to social etiquette when they received sick benefits. Records of the American West Indian Ladies Aid Society (AWILAS) as well as those of the Bermuda Association are filled with thank-you notes from members who had received benefits and visits. Cornelia Jackson wrote to the Ladies Aid Society, "Allow me to thank you for the kind remembrance you so cheerfully sent to me. I greatly appreciate same. . . . I am greatly improved. . . . Wishing you all health and prosperity."[57] Such notes indicate the high level of literacy of most members as well as the etiquette expected of middle-class status.

Prosperity was an underlying goal of all of the benevolents, and the Grenada Mutual Association, formed in 1926, appears to have quickly attracted members. By the mid-1930s it claimed a membership of 425 native Grenadians, a significant number from so small an island. No doubt the Great Depression encouraged cooperative economic efforts. The association charged a membership fee of one dollar, monthly dues of forty to fifty cents, and a tax of fifty cents and provided each member with health and death benefits. Upon the death of any member, one hundred dollars—a very helpful sum for the times—was paid to relatives to assist with funeral expenses. The association held annual affairs and regular musical, literary, and educational functions. It also collected funds to help educate poor students on the island.[58]

Other activities promoted by Caribbean homeland associations regularly brought older and more recent immigrants together at social, educational, and charitable functions. Among these were annual boat rides, picnics, and Thanksgiving programs to which other Caribbean associations were invited to purchase tickets. Aletha Challenor joined the Sons and Daughters of Barbados to find suitable social outlets for her three daughters. Violet Murrell also found the association an important social outlet for picnics, bus rides, and trips to Niagara Falls.[59] Educational forums and musical and literary programs were organized for the mutual improvement of the members and invited guests. Once the Bermuda Association purchased a home on 146th Street, it established its own library. As members became more established, the Association also included charitable programs, including scholarships for students in Bermuda and contributions to community charities in New York. While the Bermudians promoted home traditions, the organization also solidified its links to the larger African American community by purchasing lifetime membership in the NAACP.

As Reid has suggested, cooperative financing was a basic reason for the widespread existence of immigrant (and southern migrant) benevolents. Many things not possible for the individual were made possible together—loans for mortgages, political influence, and general welfare.[60] The Bermuda Benevolent Association began granting mortgages to its members after a forty-year reputation of service to the group. Benevolents were thus significant in not only providing mutual aid to their members but by playing an important role in advancing economic stability in the larger Harlem community.

The financial resources of several associations were aided by contributions of some of their more established or wealthy members. The Trinidad Benevolent Association was founded by Harlem physician Charles Petioni. Petioni also formed the more explicitly political Caribbean Union, which promoted cooperation between the various associations, solidarity with progressive black American causes, and independence for the Caribbean. With economic stability as one of its primary goals, the Montserrat Progressive Society was established in 1914 with businessmen William Roach and Joseph Sweeney and journalist Hodge Kirnon among its founders. A stated purpose was to unite the people from the island of Montserrat in New York, "to assist in uplifting them socially, morally and intellectually, to care for its sick, and those in distress, and to bury its dead." In 1925 the Society had 750 members, contributed $1,200 in sick benefits, and owned a meeting hall at 207 West 137th

Street valued at $13,000.[61] Another prominent Montserratan, Helena Benta, a secretary of the Montserrat Progressive Society, was a frequent public speaker in Harlem and an advocate of unity among the Caribbean organizations in their benevolent work as well as in their collective political interest in the Caribbean. She became an organizer of the West Indian Federation and gave talks on the role of women in the development of West Indian nationhood.[62]

In Harlem Caribbean women may have had more opportunities for leadership than at home, although here as in the native communities men dominated the public arena. Still, benevolent associations provided women with a variety of leadership opportunities. In 1915 a group of women from the then Danish West Indies (now the U.S. Virgin Islands) felt women's interests special enough to form their own organization—despite the presence of several other Danish West Indies benevolents in New York. A group of women connected with the organization known after 1917 as the American West Indian Ladies Aid Society (AWILAS) became Harlem leaders. Male-led Virgin Island Associations frequently communicated with AWILAS for assistance with women's problems. A typical referral was this undated note sent by Ashley Totten, head of the Virgin Islands Industrial Association:

> [A request] comes from a girl of 13 years, Lavinda Urcila March. Her mother's name is Lavinda Cumberbach. She is without support in the islands and [has] not heard from her father since 1919. The name of her father is Archibald Egthebert March, last address II West 137th Street. Perhaps someone in your society might help us to locate him.[63]

This young woman and her mother, like an unknown number of other Virgin Island women, may have been the victims of abandonment experienced after the exodus of many Virgin Island men from the islands following the passage of the Volstead Act and the 18th Amendment to the U.S. Constitution in 1919, prohibiting the "sale or manufacture of intoxicating liquors. . . ." The manufacture of rum and other alcohol products was a primary industry and employer of black men. Rumrunners from the Virgin Islands would continue to make some profits from illegal sales during the prohibition era of the 1920s but with little benefit to the black population. It is not clear if the Ladies Aid Society was able to help this family.[64]

But in general the Society's records provide evidence of the complex nature of voluntary association among Caribbean women. While the Society maintained a constitution and bylaws like other benevolents and conducted its business by the strict guidelines of most fraternal orders, the leaders of the organization were involved in radical political activity as well as reform movements in the Virgin Islands and in New York. Elizabeth Hendrickson, president of the Society in 1924 and again in the 1930s, was a well-known street corner speaker, involved in rent and landlord struggles of the Harlem Tenants League in the 1920s.[65] The Tenants League was a militant group which attempted to organize residents against unfair treatment— exorbitant rents, increases, evictions, and so on.

The AWILAS was still functioning in the 1950s and was stridently anti-imperialist; it had relationships with similar pro-independence groups during the 1920s and after. During the 1920s AWILAS officers—Redalia Matthews, Antoinette Reubel, Sylvania Smith, and Estelle Williams—were connected to other political movements, particularly of Virgin Islanders in Harlem. The Society participated as part of a network of Harlem community organizations with which the fledgling Brotherhood of Sleeping Car Porters and Maids, led by A. Philip Randolph, sought to cooperate. This link was no doubt facilitated by Ashley Totten, a Virgin Island Pullman porter and a Brotherhood organizer. In the 1930s the International Labor Defense of the American Communist Party also solicited the political support of the Society, probably through Elizabeth Hendrickson, who was by then affiliated with Communist-led activities in Harlem.

Few organizations of this type combined mutual aid with such active politics. The UNIA probably comes closest to this model. The local New York UNIA began with many features of the mutual aid and fraternal orders and at first almost no political agenda. Many native-born and immigrant Harlemites were attracted to the organization because of its provision of sick and death benefits as well as its political program, which matured.

But the vast majority of benevolents, one researcher has argued, performed little function in Harlem's community life beyond their cultivation of self-interests.[66] This perspective needs some revision. Benevolents, while primarily concerned with the needs of their members in New York, also tended to reflect broader charitable concerns, according to their means, not always limited to their own islands. In 1902 the Bermuda benevolents sent ten dollars to Martinique for relief after a volcanic eruption.[67] In 1927 the St. Lucia United Association collected three hundred dollars to send to victims of a fire that nearly destroyed the town of Cantrice, St. Lucia. Other associations—including the Grenada Mutual Association and the Montserrat Progressive Society—also sent money to Cantrice. A common practice among the benevolents was collecting and sending bundles of clothing home to needy families and friends. Some associations became especially well known for their philanthropic outreach. The work of the Virgin Islands Congressional Council was abetted by its wealthy president, Casper Holstein. Holstein had numerous business interests, including being the most successful numbers operator in Harlem during the 1920s. The Virgin Islands Congressional Council sent thousands of dollars in charitable contributions to the Virgin Islands and other Caribbean locations.

If the benevolent organizations helped institutionalize ethnic presence in Harlem while serving the needs of a larger Caribbean community at home and abroad, other kinds of voluntary associations provided opportunities for interaction between native-born and immigrant groups. In all major African American communities the lodge and fraternal order were popular social anchors for the average nonprofessional middle-class as well as a haven for professionals. Like the benevolents, fraternal orders (Prince Hall Masons, Odd Fellows, Elks, Order of Eastern Star, etc.)

were class-defining institutions. One scholar of fraternal organizations has noted that these orders and the "middle-class churches have formed an environment conducive to the creation, maintenance and protection of a self-conscious, socially cohesive black middle-class community."[68] With several exceptions, membership in these orders tended to de-emphasize one's ethnic background while promoting racial solidarity, self-help, and self-reliance.

Fraternal orders organized and maintained almost exclusively by black immigrants were mainly those based in the British-held colonies of the Caribbean and thus unfamiliar to African Americans. For instance, the Ancient Order of Shepherds, the Mechanics, and the Free Gardeners were all run by Caribbean Harlemites. In some cases black immigrants found, though ethnically mixed in their homelands, these orders were racially segregated in the States. Such was the case of the Lebanon Foresters, a group consisting of black immigrant men from different Caribbean countries who had worked on the Panama Canal and who had an active chapter there. In 1918 they applied for membership in the white New York body and were turned down. They formed their own organization in 1923.[69]

But Caribbean immigrant professionals especially joined native-black-run fraternal orders. Memberships were proudly announced as part of an individual's credentials or list of accomplishments. For instance, in 1927 the *West Indian American* saluted physician Aubrey L. Magill in its "biography of distinguished men." Magill arrived in America from Jamaica in 1894 and became a citizen in 1905. He had received his M.D. degree from the University of McGill, Canada, and practiced in New Haven, Connecticut, before establishing a practice at 236 West 139th Street on Strivers Row. Magill was married to Jane Mason of Augusta, Georgia, and his biography noted, "The fraternities claim him also, being a 32nd Degree Mason, a member of the [Knights of] Pythias, St. Luke [Independent Order of St. Luke], Ancient Order of Foresters and past Exalted Ruler of Elks."[70]

The Elks were the largest and most powerful fraternal order in Harlem. Membership conferred on an individual access to social, economic, and political influence. The largest order, Manhattan Lodge No. 45 was located at 266 West 139th Street—"a large and imposing structure" with club rooms, assembly hall, and offices. The lodge claimed its own symphony orchestra and band. Its public events included frequent concerts in Harlem parks and public schools. Its membership, according to WPA researcher Baxter Leach, was about 2,000. Another Elks lodge, the Monarch, owned its headquarters at 245 137th Street. The other Elks, the Imperial Lodge, and the Henry Lincoln Johnson Lodge No. 630 had similar holdings. The Henry Lincoln Johnson Lodge had a heavy Caribbean membership. According to Leach, the Elks had combined resources valued at over one million dollars by 1939.[71] The other fraternal orders, the Pythians, Odd Fellows, and Masons, "by pooling their resources have made themselves a power to be reckoned with in . . . community life. . . ." Most of the orders had "ladies auxiliaries" which ran their own affairs and raised their own money as well as funds for the general body.

Caribbean immigrant professionals, while maintaining membership in their own fraternities, often made strategic gestures in joining the American-based orders. Marcus Garvey, whose UNIA had many features of the fraternal orders and drew upon them for membership, became a Mason himself under the influence of John E. Bruce.[72] Many UNIA activities, including elaborate neighborhood parades, were modeled on those of fraternal orders. Other Harlem notables, including municipal judge James S. Watson, were affiliated with the Masonic Order. Although some immigrants selected lodges in which their groups were heavily represented, fraternal lodges generally reinforced social and political links with the larger African American community. Bibliophile Arthur Schomburg was a high-ranking officer in the Prince Hall Masons and, during the 1920s, considered one of their most distinguished members. He traveled widely as the Grand Secretary of the Prince Hall Grand Lodge of the State of New York and became an associate editor with John E. Bruce of the *Masonic Quarterly Review*. In the 1920s he was better known nationally among African Americans as a fraternal leader than as the founder of the now famous library of black materials that bears his name.[73]

Virgin Islander Casper Holstein was a founder of New York's powerful Monarch Lodge, and in 1929 he nearly gained presidency of the national organization. The 1929 convention was the first at which longtime president J. Finly Wilson faced an effective challenge. Holstein received widespread support from native-black New Yorkers as well as from influential native blacks in other cities. Oscar De Priest of Chicago, the first African American congressman since Reconstruction, supported Holstein's candidacy.[74] Although Holstein was head of the powerful Monarch Lodge in New York, when he ran for president of the national organization, his opponents publicly questioned whether a Caribbean immigrant could become head of a historically African American organization. This was one of the few times Holstein's background was raised as a political weapon against him. The real issue, however, appears not to have been Holstein's foreign birth at all, but the fact that as national president of the Elks and as a powerful and wealthy numbers operator, he could obviously wield influence his rival could not match. His Caribbean birth then became a tool of the opposition, used to split his support among the predominantly native-born membership, and he was defeated.[75] Yet Holstein's attempt to become national head of the Elks was a shrewd political move at a key point in his career as one of the leading businessmen in Harlem.

Churches, benevolent associations, lodges, and fraternal orders comprised the first line of urban accommodation for Caribbean immigrants and southern migrants in Harlem. In important ways they helped to fix Harlem's social, economic, and political agenda by dealing with individual needs from the cradle to the grave. The smaller associations became the training ground of new leaders, who may have found leadership roles in the larger community impossible to acquire at first. Churches and fraternal lodges, through their leaders especially, bonded the newer Caribbean community to larger African American Harlem, although this connection was not always smooth. Certain individuals, such as the Revs. John H. Johnson, Sr. and Jr., Ethelred Brown, Elizabeth Hendrickson, Helena Benta, Charles Douglass Martin, Arthur Schomburg, and Casper Holstein, provided crucial bridges between Harlem's multiple communities.

Churches, benevolents, and fraternal orders were also class- and gender-identified institutions. Individual affiliations with churches, such as St. Martin's or Metropolitan Baptist, tend to illustrate ways in which class was sometimes more significant than ethnicity in distinguishing Harlemites from one another. Gender was also more important than ethnicity as a factor determining the influence of the black church in Harlem. And there is little question that Harlem's many voluntary associations carried multiple traditions forward as they also helped to assimilate newcomers into an emerging community. Even in the 1990s benevolents formed before 1920 still hold regular meetings, though their influence is far less significant than in an earlier era. However, other forms of organization, particularly in the field of politics, highlight far more intense struggles over the limited economic and political resources of the early twentieth-century community. While the voluntary associations illuminate methods of group accommodation and community building, the more public political arena perhaps best illustrates the challenges faced by black ethnic diversity in Harlem.

Politics and the
Struggle for Autonomy

DEMOGRAPHICALLY, HARLEM was a predominantly black section of Manhattan more than a decade before the community could claim any significant direct representation in the political councils of the city. The period between 1900 and 1930 saw a gradual movement in the allegiance of black voters from the Republican to the Democratic party. But the real challenge for African American Harlem lay in gaining political autonomy for the community.

Competition for political space was keen in an environment where individual loyalties and favors were the key bargaining chips. Internal antagonisms as well as shifting alliances among Harlem's native-born and Caribbean immigrant professionals were commonplace. Such a situation often encouraged the subordination of community clout to battles for personal power and control. In an observation about local politics in his 1940 *Harlem: Negro Metropolis*, writer Claude McKay noted:

> White leaders and sub-leaders directly represented their people in the Tammany organization and therefore felt responsible to them. But the Negro people were represented by Negro "leaders" who in turn were represented by white leaders in the Tammany organization. And so the Negro leaders did not feel directly responsible to the Negro people who made their appointments possible. In Tammany politics as in Republican it was the same old chronic sickness of indirect representation, the eternal tapeworm in the belly of Negro life.[1]

A system of patronage based on personal loyalty, manipulation, and rewards had operated in the old downtown black communities and continued to do so well after 1900 in Harlem as the black population migrated uptown. During the height of the black migration, Ohio native Charles W. Anderson, a close associate of Booker T. Washington's, headed the black Republican clubhouse located on 53rd Street in San Juan Hill.[2] For his loyalty in delivering the black community's votes to white Republican candidates, Anderson rose with Washington's support from a low-level job in the office of internal revenue to the post of Collector of Internal Revenue for the Second New York District in 1905. This was the highest-ranking federal appointment of any African American in the United States.

As head of New York City's black Republican political club, Anderson controlled access to every "colored" government job from post office clerk to janitor. James Weldon Johnson became a close friend of Anderson's and described him as

> an astute politician, keen in his study of men and the uses to be made of them. A versatile man, more than an ordinary orator. . . . A cool calculating player in the hard game of politics. . . . On friendly terms with Theodore Roosevelt, Elihu Root, Chauncey M. Depew and other Republican leaders.[3]

Anderson asked the multilingual Johnson, the writer, musician, educator, and lawyer, to become the first house manager of the 53rd Street Club. He later obtained an appointment for Johnson, as U.S. Consul to Venezuela (1906–1908) and Nicaragua (1909–1912). It was through men like Anderson that the educated elite could rise to a few cherished positions of responsibility. Johnson's diplomatic career ended with the Democratic victory in 1912. But he moved on to become a field secretary of the NAACP and its first African American Executive Secretary in 1920, a position he held until 1930. Anderson's influence declined somewhat after the Roosevelt-Taft era and the death of Booker T. Washington, but he remained head of the local club and a force in local politics until 1930.

But after 1915 it was Ferdinand Q. Morton, a native of Mississippi, who commanded the most important political influence in Democratic-controlled New York City, as head of the United Colored Democracy. As Civil Service Commissioner for the City of New York, he was in charge of dispensing colored jobs on the public payroll. He was also a member of the NAACP and a source of political influence for Dr. W. E. B. Du Bois.[4] Morton was born in Mississippi in 1881 and educated in the public schools of Washington, D.C., Phillips Exeter Academy, and Harvard. According to Du Bois, Morton determined to enter politics as a Democrat while still a student. He received his first appointment as an indictment clerk in 1910 while serving as the "right hand man" of UCD head Robert N. Wood.

Men such as Morton and Anderson, backed up by the migration of a more substantial black electorate, were able to improve the political position of blacks within the constraints of the patronage system. They wielded their limited influence in ways that had not been possible before. Earlier, in spite of impeccable credentials, old New York political hopefuls like James D. Carr, a native of Baltimore and Phi Beta Kappa graduate of Rutgers and Columbia University Law School, could not get decent political jobs. In 1897 Carr's nomination for a position as an assistant attorney general was turned down by the U.S. Attorney in New York and an African American messenger was hired instead.[5]

Memory of these years led Du Bois and others to view the influence of powerful men such as Morton as beneficial to the race. According to the NAACP *Crisis* editor, when Morton joined the UCD in Harlem, the organization consisted largely of men contented with "janitorships" and small jobs supplemented by bribes on election day. Coming to the defense of Morton during a challenge by insurgents in 1925, Du Bois pointed out to *Crisis* readers:

In 1910 there was not a single colored policeman in New York. The race had no representation either in the State or municipal legislative branches. The only positions held by Negroes were in the Street Cleaning Department, with the exception of school teachers, not regarded as political. Today there are fifty or more Negro policemen. Hundreds of Negroes are holding positions as clerks, stenographers, typists, investigators, parole officers and court attendants. The race has representation in the Corporation Counsel's Office and District Attorney's Office. An alderman and a member of the State Legislature are Negro Democrats, and the party that gets the black vote in Harlem has to fight for it desperately.[6]

While Du Bois regarded Morton as a "strong, skillful, courageous man," he admitted that the UCD leader had not attempted to stop all gambling, bootlegging, and prostitution in Harlem. "Morton has no illusions about politics." But he had limited vice and "tried to protect those who wish to be decent." Despite Du Bois's optimism, the Harlem community as a whole received little political advantage from the positioning of men such as Morton.

But the access gained by Morton and the UCD to Tammany's patronage, however limited, was virtually the only avenue through which ambitious young black men could rise. Women had even fewer, if any, political opportunities in this system.[7] The jobs described by Du Bois, including those of clerks, typists, and stenographers, were mainly held by men in these years. Though they maneuvered to various levels, it was very difficult for newcomers, including Caribbean immigrants, to penetrate the system. The Democratic party, however, seeking to build a larger following, at times appeared to offer wider opportunities for newcomers, and key Caribbean immigrants and southern migrants steadily joined its ranks. They learned quickly that when they supported the Republicans—the party of Lincoln— the turnover in largely token black leadership was not geared for a transfusion of new blood.

In 1898 a small group of African American Republicans, including Caribbean immigrant W. R. T. Richardson, Americans Edward "Chief Sam" Lee, Caleb Simms, and others, with the support of Tammany established the first black Democratic political club in New York, the United Colored Democracy. The UCD, in a deal with Tammany, promised to deliver black votes—crucial in close elections—"in exchange for one colored man in at least every department in the city government."[8] A few professional jobs were included in the agreement. Tammany leader Croker, for instance, appointed the disgruntled former Republican James D. Carr to a position in the office of the Corporation Counsel. But most Tammany patronage, as Du Bois correctly pointed out, was in the form of traditional "colored" jobs.

Until approximately 1910 loyal black Republicans regarded black Democrats as mere traitors and "outlaw brothers" to the black community.[9] During local political campaigns, mobs in San Juan Hill knocked Tammany Hall supporters from their stepladders and wagons, pelted some with rotten cabbage and fruit, and ran others from the street corners.[10] However, a small group of blacks who broke with the Republicans laid an early foundation for an alternative source of political influence in the city. Coincidentally, it was through Tammany that some Caribbean immigrants gained access to patronage and limited influence. Antiguan native John W. A. Shaw assumed the leadership of the UCD after 1900 and for his loyalty received an appointment as Deputy Tax Assessor for Queens, the highest position ever held by an African American in the state. After Shaw's success "respectable elements of the race" began to regard the club as a legitimate source of political influence, according to columnist Edgar M. Grey. But the UCD remained a segregated club down to its final demise after 1930, when amidst scandal Ferdinand Q. Morton was stripped of his appointment powers.[11]

At the beginning of the century, black immigrants and native-born blacks generally cooperated with one another to gain recognition for the race in both political parties. Though native blacks dominated the leadership slots in the segregated political clubs of both parties and held almost all of a very limited number of electoral offices before 1930, key Caribbean naturalized citizens played important political roles in the larger African American pre–World War I community. In the first decade of the century, as in the nineteenth century, Caribbean-immigrant professionals remained too small a presence to represent a separate ethnic group and were inevitably merged into the native African American talented tenth. They regarded themselves as representing the interests of a racial, not just an ethnic/immigrant community.

An important example was influential immigrant Republican William Derrick, the presiding Bishop of the New York Diocese of the AME Church and pastor of Bethel AME, one of the oldest and largest predominantly native-born black churches in the city. In 1908 he served as chairman of the board of trustees at the Ohio-based Wilberforce University, the oldest black college in the United States, founded in 1856. Born in Antigua in 1843, Derrick immigrated to the United States before the Civil War. Like many of the early Caribbean immigrants, he was educated in America. As an AME minister, he followed a common avenue to leadership through the AME ministry. At the turn of the century, Derrick became a Committeeman-at-large of the New York State Republican Committee, a handpicked "colored" position. In this capacity he was expected to voice the concerns, within reasonable limits, of black Republican voters. But while the position carried prestige in the black community, the title had very little power. According to the *Age*, the influence of the Committeeman-at-large was "largely a matter of his own personality exerted upon the members and officers of the committee."[12] Charles W. Anderson later occupied the position, but by 1929 Harlem voters elected their own committee members.[13] From the standpoint of the community, *Amsterdam News* columnist Edgar M. Grey believed such positions were "destructive to political progress."[14]

The first black immigrant to run for New York State Assembly was Adolph Howell. Howell, a funeral director by profession, was one of the city's most successful black businessmen. Like other early black Republicans and all Caribbean politicians, his ties to both the immigrant and native-born black communities were important to his success. He was an influential member of the Sons and Daughters of Barbados, a benevolent society, but was also, according to historian Holder, "an active member of every black fraternity in New York" and a member of the Urban League's executive board.[15]

Among Caribbean immigrants the pioneer black Democrat was W. R. T. Richardson, who immigrated to the city from St. Kitts in 1884. He became a naturalized citizen in 1892 and throughout his life was a staunch supporter of naturalization among fellow immigrants. He ran a citizenship school in the Tenderloin district on West 40th street in the 1890s and, according to the *Amsterdam News*, was responsible for many Caribbean immigrants' becoming citizens and no doubt influenced their party affiliation. Among the prominent Harlem residents Richardson mentored were well-known physicians York Russell and E. E. Rawlins and businessman Adolph Howell.[16]

By the 1920s the group Richardson nurtured represented a significant Caribbean talented tenth in their own right.[17] They joined the ranks of the colored Democrats in steady numbers and increasingly criticized the appointment powers chiefly controlled by Ferdinand Q. Morton and the UCD. Moreover, Harlem voters began shifting party affiliation to the Democrats throughout the 1920s, and the drive for autonomy focused increasingly on elimination of the Jim Crow UCD. By the 1924 elections, even the Republican *Age* editorialized that "the Republican leaders had good reason to fear the disaffection of [the African American] voters in the past campaign. There were many reasons why their allegiance to the party had weakened and for the feeling that the time had come to make new alliances." The *Age* continued: "it would not take many more campaigns to sever the tie that binds [with Republicans]. It has worn looser and looser with each succeeding campaign."[18]

Another important development affecting the political atmosphere in Harlem was the right of suffrage won by New York women in 1917. The Woman Suffrage Party estimated that abut 15,000 African American women resided in Harlem's four assembly districts and were eligible to vote. Led by Mary K. Lewis and female step-ladder speakers such as Helen Holman, Harlem women had been extremely active in the campaign for woman suffrage in New York State. Their victory helped to shift traditional alliances in Harlem politics. The *Age* noticed that "colored women are preparing to take an active part in politics. They have begun to form political clubs and are taking politics with zest and enthusiasm."[19] Although the *Age* correctly predicted that with black women's votes, the 21st Assembly District would "send an assemblyman to the State Assembly," carving up Harlem districts the year women became eligible voters undoubtedly postponed the impact of electoral politics.

It was not until the mid-1930s that African Americans elected a black Democratic district leader. From the formation of the first black political club in 1898, the black community got its services and patronage indirectly through the segregated United Colored Democracy. The operation and control of the Tammany machine by white bosses frustrated Harlemites who wanted more democratic and direct representation by members of their own community.

Meanwhile Harlem became more aware of its ethnic diversity. Early political alignments had often formed on the basis of race. But since Derrick's period the ethnic character of Harlem had changed. Between the outbreak of the World War in 1914 and the Immigration Act of 1924, thousands of Caribbean immigrants had arrived in Harlem. Their immigration peaked in the latter year just before their numbers were severely restricted by legislation. An immediate impact of this immigration was an increased visibility of Caribbean people on Harlem streets. And this visibility often appeared to solidify in the personalities of a highly politicized group of mostly foreign-born black radicals speaking from Harlem street corners.

The growing immigrant population also made the growth of new businesses possible. The import and export of island products based primarily on a Caribbean clientele gained steady entrepreneurial attention among blacks. Also, new ethnic-based organizations, such as the West Indian Protective Society, were formed. The Protective Society was organized in 1916 by Samuel Duncan, who originally immigrated from St. Kitts by way of Bermuda. He arrived in New York in 1900, was employed as a porter, and became a naturalized citizen in 1908. The Protective Society maintained offices at 178 West 135th Street and a branch office on St. Felix Street in Brooklyn. According to its promotional material, it maintained accommodations for new arrivals and out-of-town visitors and a club room and recreational center for members and friends. Annual dinners and receptions were held on Empire Day and La Fete Nationale Francaise. To distinguish itself from the somewhat rigid membership requirements of the benevolents, a brochure advertised: "We are not a Sick and Death Benefit Society! No Doctors Examinations!" The Society made no open challenges to colonial powers, and its literature announced that the organization provided a liaison to the various consular representatives of Great Britain, France, the Netherlands, and Denmark. The Society's labor bureau promised to "endeavor . . . to place members of the Society in profitable employments in Domestic Service, in offices, and in several industries throughout the country." Its relief bureau also claimed to "afford assistance to indigent persons." The officers of the West Indian Protective Society were all prominent immigrants, including James Watson, later the first municipal judge from Harlem; physician A. St. Clair Jones; lawyer John B. Thorne; and ministers Charles Martin and Jedidiah Edmead. Mrs. Jane Adams, the only female officer, served as a field agent. Samuel Duncan, the head of the Society, became an advocate for immigrant interests in local politics.[20]

A rising tide of nativism reflected in the larger American society and shared by some in the black community also helped influence a quickened consciousness of ethnic identity among immigrants. The postwar period ushered in an intensity of anti-foreign propaganda across the nation. The favorable attitudes with which Caribbean immigrants were earlier received by members of the African American community also shifted, though one must be careful here. Harlem's ethnic antagonisms were peculiarly tied to blacks' racial subordination in the United States. Nevertheless, even some black contemporaries shared the observation that "there was a casual [causal] connection between the American attitude toward foreigners in general and the American Negro's attitude toward the West Indian Negro."[21] Edgar M. Grey noted that native blacks had done almost nothing to welcome Caribbean immigrants or to incorporate the immigrants into the community. "In all the years in which the native American Negro has had contact with the West Indian resident of Harlem, no attempt by him has been made to organize any Americanization campaigns among the immigrant. The Negro American has confined his assistance to the immigrant to lip service." Grey felt that the average immigrant had no way of learning of the "longing and strivings of the American Negro."[22] William Ferris said he witnessed a rise in antiforeign attitudes among native African Americans in 1919, which, he noted, was the same period in which anti-Jewish, Catholic, and black sentiments were publicly expressed. The "Red Scare" focused its attacks on foreign-born Socialists, as well as native-born radicals. Marcus Garvey's presence in Harlem also disturbed African Americans who hoped to channel the new urban masses into the political mainstream. In the summer of 1920, at the end of the Universal Negro Improvement Association's month long convention, Fred R. Moore's New York *Age* reprinted a story from Philadelphia's white-owned *Public Ledger* describing Harlem as a "model densely settled Negro district, the best housed, best behaved Negro city in the world." It then added:

> Into this satisfied, settled, luxury loving, civilized black city, which already possesses a profound community feeling, has come an intruder, a man from the British West Indies. He is Marcus Garvey, the Black Moses. . . . [23]

The negative reaction of influential members of the black press to what it saw as Garvey's intrusive foreign status and the uncertain feelings such bias evoked in the Caribbean community is important to understanding Harlem's ethnic dynamics. The point here is that the presence of the UNIA leader helped to focus ethnic awareness in ways not so apparent before his organization galvanized such spectacular appeal in Harlem. Garvey was not solely a leader of Caribbean immigrants; he attracted large numbers of black Americans, including politicians who in the early years tried to use the organization's constituency for their own purposes. Although Garvey and his organization promoted internationalism and were enthusiastically supported by wide segments of the native-black community in Harlem, William Ferris also noted that "the Garvey movement, by marshaling the West Indians en masse, made manifest the characteristics in which the West Indians differed from the American Negroes."[24] Garvey and the controversies surrounding him helped to shift the nature of traditional politics to encompass ethnic as well as racial concerns. Still it is important to keep in mind that in Harlem the more fundamental battle was over political space and the economic rewards it afforded, areas which Garvey's leadership challenged on the local as well as the national scene.

Although many Caribbean immigrants joined with native organizations to cement their identification with African Americans, these same individuals also maintained affiliations with exclusively Caribbean organizations to ensure a continuing connection with that community.[25] W. R. T. Richardson's citizenship school and Samuel Duncan's West Indian Protective Society both sought to promote the interest of immigrants. Edgar M. Grey organized the Foreign-born Citizens Political Alliance in 1919 to promote awareness and participation in politics. The West Indian Committee, organized in 1928, promoted business development, naturalization, and social welfare among black immigrants. Its advisory board included individuals who had important economic stakes in the community and who were dependent upon native-born as well as immigrant support for the success of the businesses they represented. They were involved in real estate, insurance, jewelry sales, photography, the laundry business, and so on.[26]

The committee tried to stimulate employment opportunities among immigrants and also to serve as a clearinghouse for inter-organizational problems. In the interest of promoting cordial relations with native blacks, naturalization was encouraged as an appropriate step to enhance political power for the entire community. At one of its meetings, prominent physician Dr. Charles A. Petioni urged immigrants to remain in the United States and become citizens. Still another representative from the Jamaican Benevolent Association emphasized cooperation, even naturalization, but not complete cultural amalgamation with Americans, black or white. In April 1928, the committee held a meeting at Abyssinian Baptist Church—the topic: "Should West Indian Citizens [*sic*] Become Naturalized?"[27]

The status of numbers of Caribbean immigrants in Harlem produced tension between themselves and natives bent on improving their circumstances in the United States by all available means and particularly by exercising voting privileges so blatantly denied them throughout most of the country. The presence of unnaturalized Caribbean immigrants had long been a subject of contentious editorializing and debate on the part of *Age* editor Fred R. Moore and others. According to Moore, only a negligible number of Caribbean immigrants were qualified to vote. "No special cause is assigned for their reluctance to forswear King George and pledge support to the flag under which they have elected to sojourn," he commented. Such a refusal to naturalize, in Moore's opinion, could not be excused "in a period of stress and warfare as at present."[28] Just before the fall elections in 1923, William Kelley of the *Amsterdam News* criticized both native blacks and immigrants for their voting negligence. "If American-born Negroes and West Indians living in Harlem would become voters a colored man could be sent to Congress with ease."[29] In fact Harlem did not elect its first congressman, Adam Clayton Powell, Jr., until 1944. The reasons were far more complex than Kelley suggested and lay primarily in the long struggle required to gain control of the community's districts and the nomination process. Meanwhile the Harlem newspapers sizzled with the citizenship debate. In 1926 Edgar M. Grey, using statistics gathered by the League of Foreign-born Voters (a white national organization) claimed that only 1,126 foreign-born persons of African descent were registered voters, but even if all those who qualified for naturalization became eligible voters, this number would not appreciably change Harlem's electoral strength. "For twenty-five years the native American Negro has told the world that if these West Indians would only become citizens his political troubles would be over. This is all nonsense." Grey noted correctly that far larger numbers of native-born blacks remained unregistered. Coming down hard on people such as Fred R. Moore, Grey noted, "He has mouthed the phrase, 'Why don't you West Indians become naturalized citizens,' after each failure on his part to make any appreciable showing at the polls: he has compensated for his own bad showing by abusing the 'monkey chaser.'"[30]

Throughout the controversy Tammany neglected to engage in major citizenship drives among black immigrants or registration drives among native black voters. This tactic contrasted with the manner in which the machine courted and relied upon rapid rates of naturalization and voter registration among white immigrants. In any case, for average black immigrants, Harlem's subordinate position in New York politics and the second-class status of generation after generation of American blacks were not convincing arguments for immediate naturalization. Ira Reid noted in *The Harlem Immigrant* (1939) that Caribbean newcomers quickly observed the fictional nature of "American democracy" as it applied to African Americans.[31] Citizenship was therefore often regarded as a practical move, to obtain jobs or to otherwise establish economic or social position.

A majority of black immigrants made much slower moves toward naturalization. Some were circumspect in their approach to the INS, which was not known for its reputation of fair treatment. Others, like Fred Challenor, who had "simply got off a boat" in Brooklyn and walked to lodgings with Constance Payne on Adams Street were afraid that their entry might not be deemed legal. Because he worried about his status, Challenor did not visit Barbados until after he raised his children to adulthood and became a naturalized citizen. Others felt that they had more rights as foreigners than native blacks had as citizens. "When you are a foreigner away from home you have rights." This attitude was often viewed by black Americans as unnecessarily condescending. Claude McKay put it this way about Caribbeans from the British-held islands: "West Indians are incredibly addicted to the waving of the Union Jack in the face of their American cousins."[32] Edgar Grey posited another reason for the lack of enthusiasm for naturalization:

> When the West Indian immigrant arrives in New York he seeks others of his countrymen with whom to reside and to associate. He is in a new environment as far as location is concerned, but he is still at home as far as contact and ideals are concerned. . . . It takes about five years on average for a West Indian to read an American newspaper or magazine for any other reason than to find a job or to locate a flat or rent a room. . . . [33]

Moreover, Grey added, it was impossible for the "green immigrant" to find lodgings in the homes of well-informed African Americans. He or she attended church and social gatherings with other immigrants and was therefore "entirely cut off" from association with those of native stock who might be in a position to impart to the newcomer "benefits, racial and personal, which may be derived from the fact of American citizenship." Although Grey did not consider the fact that immigrant institutions were precisely those entities through which the "green" newcomer became adjusted to New York, he made a valuable point about the alienation of the average Caribbean immigrant from the native black mainstream.

While Grey saw Americanization as a way the American black community should incorporate black foreigners, Jamaican journalist Wendell Malliet did not agree. His experiences as a black man in America and his study of the race problem led him to oppose "Americanization" on the basis of prevailing ideas of racism and discrimination. Malliet also believed in the superiority of the British justice system. In one of his newspaper articles he told African American readers that "the true administration of justice is one of the fundamental principles of British institutions, under the genial influence of which I was born and reared." But in his *Pittsburgh Courier* series, Malliet wrote that Caribbean immigrants could become naturalized citizens "without being in sympathy with the institutions of the country or desiring to assimilate American ideas, customs or characteristics." Black immigrants should cooperate to the fullest extent with their "colored American cousins in their fight for Liberty, Justice and Equality."[34]

The complex nature of the issue surrounding citizenship is illustrated by the case of Virgin Island immigrants. The *Negro World* reported the proceedings of one of their first mass meetings, held in June 1922 and called to protest the political status of thousands of Virgin Islanders living in America. While the Virgin Islands were a possession of the United States since 1917, the Virgin Island people could not apply for citizenship and were therefore literally "Outcasts . . . neither citizens, subjects nor aliens."[35] Harlem Virgin Islanders vigorously protested this status and demanded American citizenship. For them citizenship held out a promise, however distant, of fuller participation in their own affairs at home as well as in New York City politics. A major source of contention was the presence of U.S. Marines and the administration of the islands by white, often segregationist, Americans. In the 1920s street speaker Elizabeth Hendrickson and Ashley Totten organized the Virgin Island Protective Association primarily to channel dissent against the American mistreatment of residents in the islands.[36] Citizenship status would enable Virgin Islanders in New York to have more direct impact on politics at home. On the other hand, for the average Anglophone and Francophone black immigrant, American citizenship could mean very little and even a decline in status as just another member of the black American masses.

Economic motivations for becoming citizens were very strong during the depression. The local branch of the UNIA reported a steady increase in requests for legal advice on the naturalization process. The organization's records reveal applications for citizenship were somewhat more complicated than "foreswearing allegiance to King George." A sizable minority of prospective citizens feared deportation on the basis that their immigration had not been legal. The INS repeatedly met the UNIA local's attempts to intercede on behalf of applicants with inordinate delays and bureaucratic red tape.[37]

Despite the complex issues the average immigrant faced in becoming a citizen, the growing number of Caribbean-male professionals—lawyers, doctors, and businessmen—longtime naturalized citizens made their mark in Harlem politics. Their first major challenge, to ouster Ferdinand Q. Morton and dismantle the segregated UCD, gained broad-base support in the community. Fed up with the iron hand Morton wielded over the ambitions of black Democrats in the 1920s, a group of insurgents, mostly Caribbean with African American allies, began demanding direct access—by virtue of potential votes and influence—to the white district leaders, thus bypassing handpicked collaborators.

In 1925, Caribbean immigrant Thomas Dyett, a respected Harlem attorney; longtime Democrat W. T. R. Richardson; immigrants William H. Austin, Frank Seaton, and others voiced public opposition to the segregated UCD and demanded the right to join the regular Democratic clubs. Supported by white district leaders in the 19th and the 21st districts who recognized the growing strength of the dissidents while seeking to guide it, the insurgents succeeded in integrating the district clubs. They also organized their own club, the Ramapo Democratic club, which held its meetings at the American West Indian Benevolent Association headquarters. However, a few key Caribbean leaders retained their affiliation with the UCD throughout the controversy. Others, such as James S. Watson, an assistant corporation counsel and a Morton supporter, astutely straddled the fence, retaining membership in the UCD and also joining the Cayuga Club.[38]

These and other Caribbean professionals—having been among Harlem's first black Democrats—were thus among the first to become members of the regular political clubs with direct access to white district leaders. Historian Holder described developments this way:

> Between 1930 and 1935, a West Indian Democrat was made a city marshall, another was selected as a presidential elector [Godfrey Nurse], and a third was given [elected to] a seat on the Democratic State Committee. These positions were considered very important in the black community. In the same period, moreover, four West Indian Democrats were appointed assistant district attorneys, while others secured less prestigious political appointments. All of these West Indians, however, owed their jobs to the largesse of the white Democratic politicians who headed the clubs in which they were members and who ran the political affairs of the 19th and the 21st Assembly Districts.[39]

Despite their importance in the electorate, women were not the beneficiaries of Tammany's largesse. "There are no women officers or sachems in Tammany," noted McGoldrick in 1928. "There are none on its important committees." A few women became members of Harlem's political clubs, but their roles continued to be supportive and the more important jobs were held by men.[40] But the fact that Caribbean men, disproportionately when compared to American black men, were receiving increased recognition granted by forces outside the community's control rankled some in Harlem's native African American professional class. "It was natural that the exclusive tenth among the native-born would be a little resentful!" noted Claude McKay.[41] Another contemporary, lawyer Hope Stevens, a native of the Virgin Islands, described the atmosphere more bluntly: "In those days the hostility was so thick you could cut it with a knife."[42]

Rise in district politics could mean important rewards. The nucleus of a district club was a group of public-job holders who could number as many as six hundred (ranging from elevator operators to janitors to clerical workers). In addition, in the white-controlled clubs, twenty or more club members held important elective or better-paying appointive positions. All city-job holders were required to belong to the club, and it was through the clubs that any professional could expect to rise.

For years almost all "colored," mostly menial, city jobs were distributed by white district leaders on the basis of votes "delivered" by black bosses during local elections. As Harlem emerged a few jobs were professional positions and competition was keen. This practice of doling out favors obviously encouraged in-fighting between competing groups. Claude McKay noted in *Harlem, Negro Metropolis*:

> There is a sharp struggle for place and elbow room between the educated West Indians and the native-born Negroes. . . . The educated American Negro is brought up in the old tradition of special protection and patronage for the talented members of his group. He regards the West Indian as an outsider, who should not share in the special patronage. . . . The educated native Negroes resent the aggressiveness of the foreign-born Negroes, especially in politics.[43]

The subordinate political position of Harlem affected ethnic rivalries and contributed to feelings of powerlessness that often frustrated and exacerbated relations between native black American and Caribbean groups. Such groups understood that the focus of political power lay in the hands of district leadership, in which Tammany held an "unambiguous distribution of authority." Throughout the 1920s district leaders in Harlem's 19th and 21st assembly districts in both parties continued to be white males. Historian Thomas Henderson correctly points out that the political impact of Harlem's population growth was deliberately stunted by a 1917 redistricting. Harlem's two major political districts, the 19th and the 21st, were created to divide the community into two sections and thereby dilute its growing political strength. The line between the two districts ran along 136th and 137th Streets, splitting the black community in half. To the west, a heavily black district was incorporated into the 13th assembly district. On the east side, a heavily black area was placed together with the predominantly Jewish and Italian 20th assembly district. Based on these artificial district lines, the Harlem community, at a crucial point in its development, could not exercise political autonomy. Some observers, including the editors of the *Age* and the

Amsterdam News, frustrated with Harlem's lack of political clout in contrast, for example, to Chicago's south side, blamed the African American community itself. Although they pointed to dissension between Caribbean and American blacks as a major source of political weakness, a more likely explanation was the deliberate gerrymandering of Harlem's assembly districts.[44] Henderson notes that:

> Minority status for Black Harlem had been assured as early as 1917, when the two parties in concert had gerrymandered the Harlem community, setting up district boundaries which remained unchanged for more than twenty years. . . . [T]he gerrymandering of Harlem was the keystone to the longevity of the system of subordination. By including White areas in the 19th and 21st A.D.'s, the gerrymander prolonged the rationale for White district leadership and for the segregated clubs, . . . until the decade's [1920s] end, when the expansion of the Black community encompassed almost the entirety of both districts. Only then did Black protests become weighty enough to have the segregation of the clubs ended.[45]

Predominantly African American groups like the Harlem Lawyers Association as well as the insurgents critical of the UCD tried to correct this situation. But the lack of local autonomy kept their ambitious and expanding professional classes battling over political crumbs, while the most serious grievances of the community were neglected. As late as 1933 the *Amsterdam News* reported that when the 21st assembly district's population was almost 70 percent African American, only two black appointees in white leader Thomas F. Murray's 21st assembly district held city jobs paying three thousand dollars or more per year. In contrast, more than thirty whites from the district held such municipal positions.[46]

A major source of higher-paying jobs were those controlled by the Harlem Hospital administration, which had been the site of a partisan takeover by Tammany in the 1920s. All hospital appointments and promotions were controlled by Tammany, and Morton dictated the fate of black physicians at the public facility. Black doctors in Harlem, as elsewhere in the country, had long-standing grievances over appointments to hospital staffs where they could treat their patients. Caribbean physicians, many of whom were insurgent Democrats, felt especially slighted by Morton. This issue drew the concerns of Caribbean and key native black physicians closer to the grievances of the larger community, which complained of the hospital's treatment of its black patients. The facility was known in the community as the "morgue" or the "butcher shop." African American nurses were segregated within the hospital's facilities, as were black physicians.

Moreover, Morton blocked a proposal by the Julius Rosenwald Fund to survey medical conditions in Harlem and possibly establish a private hospital where black physicians could care for patients. In 1930 the *Age* editorialized that the head of a segregated political organization's denunciation of the proposal as Jim Crow, "while he upholds a separate organization in politics, appears to be a trifle inconsistent." The Manhattan Medical Society, backed by Morton, rejected the proposal as "uninvited, uncalled for and unnecessary." Morton was supported by at least one key immigrant doctor, Aubrey Maynard, and the well-known African American surgeon Louis T. Wright, who, though a board member of the NAACP, had not complained about the hospital's policies. But both the *Age* and the *Amsterdam News* denounced Morton's handling of the Harlem Hospital affair. The UCD leader and others like him were increasingly criticized for their "hat in hand" politics. Such men, in the view of the *Amsterdam News*, "don't give a rap about the progress of the Negro in the medical profession, or the welfare of the Negro patient and public so long as they themselves are taken care of."[47] Ultimately the Harlem Hospital controversy led to demands on the part of the broad spectrum of Harlemites for direct representation and assertive leadership within the Democratic party.

One Democrat, Caribbean-born physician Conrad Vincent, who had been appointed to the Harlem Hospital staff by Tammany in 1925, was ungrateful enough to lodge a public complaint on behalf of black hospital staff about the deplorable conditions at the hospital. Rejected by the NAACP, which supported Morton in the *Crisis*, Vincent sought out young, charismatic, assertive maverick Adam Clayton Powell, Jr. Powell, defiantly bypassing all local bosses, took the Harlem Hospital case directly to Mayor John O'Brien. Ignoring the young minister's complaint, O'Brien allegedly told Powell to "go on back to Harlem, boy, and don't fan the flames."[48] Instead Powell returned to Harlem and used Abyssinian Church as a base for a massive community protest against hospital conditions. At least in the Harlem Hospital case, Tammany was forced to capitulate to a new populist Harlem politics. Caribbean insurgents such as Vincent, in allying themselves with community issues and choosing the popular young Powell as spokesman, made an important political gesture. And Powell emerged as the new-age Harlem politician with vital links to insurgent Caribbean Democrats.

While the Harlem Hospital controversy built into a community movement between 1925 and 1933, the black electorate continued to live a more broad-based reality in hopes of selecting race candidates who would promote their interests. At the same time, Harlem's Caribbean and native-born professionals publicly positioned themselves for political openings. In 1930, Harlemites elected Jamaican-born lawyer James S. Watson as the community's first municipal judge for the newly created 10th judicial district. By this time Harlem's black electorate was overwhelmingly native-born, and even the gerrymandered districts contained a majority of black residents. In any case the creation of the 10th district guaranteed the election of two black municipal judges. Watson and native-born lawyer Charles Toney were elected to the two posts over two native-born black Republican candidates.

But Watson's nomination for the post was not obtained without—in the words of the *Amsterdam News*—"childish bickering" among members of the Harlem Lawyers Association. According to a reporter from the paper, during a July meeting in 1930, native-born attorney Cornelius W. McDougald nearly disrupted the session when he learned Watson had been nominated for the position. He allegedly accused the "West

Indian element" of controlling the selection process. Apparently McDougald's name and others had been placed in nomination along with Watson's at a previous meeting, but Watson had won though only seven out of the some fifty lawyers present were of Caribbean descent.

Watson was well placed for the nomination. He had powerful connections to both the UCD and to the white-controlled Cayuga Democratic Club. His ties, like those of earlier politicians, were linked to the white political structure as well as to diverse groups in the black community. He was a member of a host of lodges and fraternal orders, Alpha Phi Alpha, an African American fraternity, and the Executive Board of the New York Urban League. Watson's campaign literature omitted any reference to his Caribbean birth or affiliations. (He was a member of the Jamaican Benevolent Association and numerous other Caribbean-based clubs.) A brochure did inform voters that he had been "trained and educated in New York, giving him a thorough knowledge of, and sympathy with, the problems of the citizens of Harlem."[49]

Watson had arrived in America from Jamaica in 1905 and became a naturalized citizen in 1912. He studied law at City College and New York Law School and after receiving his law degree was admitted to the bar in 1914. Watson opened his office in Harlem in 1920 and in 1922 received an appointment in the office of the corporation counsel of the special franchise tax division of New York City. He served as municipal judge for twenty years.[50] Watson's broad-based support symbolized the growing strength of a Democratic black electorate.

Once Harlem was demographically African American, the battleground for a hoped-for autonomy focused on the struggle for a black district leader for Harlem's two key districts, the 19th and the 21st. The Republicans elected the first black district leader from Harlem, native-born Charles W. Fillmore, from the 19th district in 1929. A representative on the state committee was also elected in this year. For the first time as well, an African American woman was elected to the state Republican committee. But the Republican party's decline in Harlem was already in evidence, and these gains made little difference in the local political arena.[51]

The real battle for the Democratic leadership of Harlem's 19th and 21st districts, and for the political jobs they controlled, began in the early 1930s. Political hopefuls still complained that a majority of patronage jobs went to whites in districts that were 80 percent black. Furthermore, native blacks excoriated leaders Martin Healy in the 19th and Thomas Murray in the 21st for favoring Caribbean immigrant politicians with the few black positions available. Native-born lawyer Louis Lavelle attacked Healy for his "mean prejudice and hatred against native-born American Negroes."[52]

In the meantime Caribbean immigrant politicians sought out opportunities to push ahead. Shifting alliances formed between key native black politicians and immigrants who sought greater autonomy for Harlem in the districts. Two insurgent clubs, the Ramapo, headed by native-born assemblyman William T. Andrews, and the Beaver Democratic, headed by Barbadian-born restauranteur Herbert Bruce, formed and worked outside the control of white bosses. Their aim was to take over the 21st assembly district altogether. The coalition, supported by both the *Amsterdam News* and the *Age*, eventually threw its support behind Bruce, whom they believed to be untainted by "white influences." He became Harlem's first black Democratic district leader in 1935.

But the noncitizenship status of foreign-born Harlem residents remained an issue, especially among the community's professionals. The Citizens Welfare Council of Harlem, a community organization comprised of several prominent African American leaders, organized "for the promotion of better community life." It was headed by native-born physician Charles A. Butler and attorney Myles A. Paige. In its list of thirteen objectives, the first was "the naturalization of all foreign-born citizens" and its last "a strict adherence to the teachings of Jesus Christ." The Citizens Welfare Council also engaged in a struggle to secure "positions in Institutions run by the Government."[53] It is not clear from available evidence what accomplishments this apparently short-lived organization made in pursuit of its stated objectives. But this latter objective suggests that an important aspect of the controversy was over competition for political appointments. In the 1930s the ethnic nature of the competition was full-blown. The Foreign-Born Citizens League published a letter allegedly written to officials by native-born attorney Louis Lavelle, a Democratic state senator. Lavelle made clear his objections to the appointment of prominent physician Dr. Godfrey Nurse, a native of British Guiana, as Collector of Internal Revenue, the position held for years by Republican Charles Anderson. "The native-born American Colored person has a superior claim upon and to the institutions of these United States of America as against some foreigner who arrived here, as it were (metaphorically speaking) night before last, the ink on whose citizenship papers is not yet hardly dry."[54]

Similarly the statements of other black community groups indicate that competition over the scarce economic and political resources of the community was a source of considerable tension. The North Harlem Community Council, with which native-born attorney Miles Paige was affiliated, passed a resolution sent to other community councils in the city calling for the enforced naturalization or enforced deportation of "large numbers of foreigners in our communities of the City of New York . . . who have not responded to the necessity of supporting the government which affords them the comforts and luxuries of life, and enables them to support their families in other lands. . . ."[55]

In response, Caribbean political organizations proliferated in the 1930s, their aim to organize foreign-born voters. The Negro Foreign-Born Citizen League was formed in the early 1930s. Its purpose was to organize voters of foreign extraction into a "militant political organization" to protect the rights and privileges of its members. Its organizer and executive director, H. S. Boulin, had also served as a field organizer of the West Indian Protective Society. The League claimed to be a "nonpartisan" organization of foreign-born colored voters. Its letterhead publicized its goal "to unite the 15,000 foreign-born voters in Harlem."[56] Whether such a constituency of registered voters existed at the time cannot be determined, but it is clear that significant moves toward political organization on the basis of ethnicity and not race alone had begun to take place.

Between 1900 and 1930 the control of the local political clubs was largely restricted to Harlem's most economically stable citizens, whether native born or immigrant. The regular political parties were not outlets for divergent political ideas. Political mobility remained largely a matter of individual initiative and contacts. Political leaders, especially Caribbean, were often financially secure and Americanized. Herbert Bruce, a redcap for many years, helped finance the Beavers Democratic Club after he became a successful restauranteur. But despite the growing number of black elected officials, the masses of black Harlemites, both immigrant and native born, were not the beneficiaries of any notable community-improvement projects. Overcrowded conditions, inadequate health care, deportations, high rents, dilapidated rat- and roach-infested housing, police graft, prostitution, and racketeering plagued the community on a daily basis. Other issues, including those of color and class, the need for labor organizing and consumer power, as well as the unrealized dreams of a new urbanized population were to be addressed by a different kind of politics.

6

Stepladder to Community

FROM WORLD WAR I through the 1930s, the unclaimed terrain of the Harlem street corner became the testing ground for a range of political ideologies and a forum for intellectual inquiry and debate. The open-air arena claimed other adherents as well—barefoot prophets, musicians, healers, and traders—competing for the souls and pocketbooks of the urban masses. Space does not permit the treatment of all of these groups here, but on any day of the week, including Sunday, homebound Harlemites emerging from the subway at 135th Street and Lenox Avenue would most likely encounter congested sidewalks and the well-toned voice of the street orator, often of African Caribbean descent, positioned atop a stepladder and surrounded by crowds of listeners.

Farther west on Seventh Avenue, between 137th and 138th Streets, other stepladder speakers (or "soap boxers") often espousing competing ideas, drew street audiences, too.[1] The meetings attracted larger and larger street crowds by the mid-1920s, and Harlem police often arrested speakers on charges of "obstructing traffic." "This street talk was virile and unconventional . . . unchained, free even daring," wrote an unidentified reporter from the African American New York *News* in 1926.[2]

The early radicals, the group who came together around 1917, those who invented the Harlem street corner speaking tradition were self-educated, mostly Caribbean immigrants. The mentor among them, Hubert Harrison, and a slightly younger Richard B. Moore, Frank Crosswaith, W. A. Domingo, Grace Campbell, Elizabeth Hendrickson, Marcus Garvey, and native migrants A. Philip Randolph and Chandler Owen and others articulated the urban generation's most urgent discontents and aspirations.[3] The street corner became the most viable location for an alternative politics and the place where new social movements gained a hearing and recruited supporters. Here a speaker did not have to be concerned with losing favor with political bosses or offending sources of influence.

After 1930, the street corner meetings retained their vitality and became an even more popular forum for airing public grievances. But in this decade a new breed of speaker was emerging. Claude McKay noted that "these soapboxers were rough men of the people whom educated Harlemites considered amusing or dangerous, according to the speaker's choice of subject."[4] One woman speaker, Louisiana native Audley Moore, recalled in an interview that "none of the churches would let us in with our kind of talk. . . ."[5]

Indeed the street corner provided an alternative to Sunday service, where uncon-
strained attacks upon black established leaders, landlords, and business people, not
to mention the deity of Jesus Christ, were not likely topics of discussion. On the
street corner, individuals, even those unknown to the community, who had a superior
facility with the spoken word, wit, and a worthy topic could earn the respect of
tough-minded Harlem working folk. "It is here where the West Indian shines," noted
a WPA researcher.[6]

Influential activist women, among them Audley Moore (Queen Mother Moore)
and Bonita Williams, of African Caribbean descent, were to make their mark here as
well. But even in this initially most untraversed of political spaces, women had fewer
opportunities to articulate their own viewpoints, though women's issues, such as birth
control, were among the topics raised. Socialist Helen Holman became well known in
Harlem for her street corner speeches in favor of woman suffrage before the 1917
New York law was enacted. In the broader realm of activist politics, women were
often the liaisons between leftist organizations, speakers, and bedrock community institutions.[7] They were also financial backers of important social movements growing
out of the street corner tradition.

Why did such a politics emerge? In what ways did Harlem's immigrant radicals
diversify and shape the direction of racial politics in New York City? And what has
been the legacy of the ferment they helped create?

The restricted political space and the narrow political objectives of Tammany-
controlled machine politics account in part for the appearance of a growing radical voice among the new black, urban generation as it had been among white, particularly Jewish, immigrants. In addition the proliferation of new ideas, particularly
after World War I and the questioning of old values, including religious-based assumptions, influenced the young immigrant intellectuals. The appeal of socialism
had been compelling enough for 94,000 Americans who voted for Eugene Debs
on the socialist presidential ticket in 1900. The Bolshevik Revolution's overthrow of
an undeserving elite; the rising discontent of Third World colonial peoples of color;
and the growing sense of an internationalism evident in contacts between dispersed
Africans from the colonial dependencies as well as American blacks were factors
making a less provincial politics imaginable. The Harlem orators sometimes collaborated and shared platforms with Jewish Socialists or Communists from stepladders
on Wall Street, Hanson Place (across from the Long Island Railroad) in Brooklyn.
Stepladder forums sprang up also in Chicago and other major urban black centers
across the North. But Harlem street corners nurtured the most active marketplace of
ideas.[8]

Although some radical organizations made it possible for speakers to earn a partial income from their open-air lectures, the audiences who heckled and challenged
some speakers helped mold, promote, and sustain the tradition. Ultimately the stepladder tradition was shaped not by organizations, but by the personality, skill, and
ability of the speakers. Street audiences were drawn to the oratory of the individual
speakers rather than to the organizations they represented, although the UNIA during

its heyday is a possible exception to this. To the same unknown New York *News* reporter, indoor talks were "platitudinous, artificial, and lack[ed] courage." Moreover, "a fellow who is burdened with the weight of a church, a school, a lyceum or some other institution is afraid to say some of the things which [Hubert] Harrison said boldly on this street corner [137th and Seventh Avenue]. The indoor talks are generally limited, muzzled, tongue tied."[9]

The open-air meetings were not just political forums; they became the university of the streets, Harlem's first adult education centers. Speaker Audley Moore claimed, "That's where I got my Ph.D., on the street corner." Listeners could get an education in "everything from the French Revolution, the history of slavery, to the rise of the working class."[10] The New York *News* reporter made this rare observation about a summer 1926 Hubert Harrison street meeting:

> The Age of Pericles and Socrates in ancient Athens had nothing on the present age of Harlem in New York. Coming out of the "movies" between 137th Street and 138th Street on Seventh Avenue, we saw one of the biggest street corner audiences that we have ever met in this block, which is famous for street corner lectures, and the subject was "Evolution." This was not a selected audience but the "run of the street," and their faces were fixed on a black man who stood on a ladder platform, with his back to the avenue and the passing buses and his face to the audience who blocked the spacious sidewalk. . . . And what was he talking about? . . . The theory of evolution, and its illustration in different lines of material and biological development—the Darwinian science of the evolution of life, and the Marxian philosophy of the evolution of capitalism—and a possible development from capitalism to a state of communism.[11]

The reporter claimed he had "never seen a more attentive audience on a subject of this magnitude," as double-decker buses, autos, and clanging fire engines passed by. The listeners' serious absorption was broken only when Harrison "bore down on the fixed, immovable and unprogressive science of the pulpit." At these times there seemed to be "smiles and bits of merriment." Contemporaries believed that it was such meetings that inspired the New Negro movement of the Harlem Renaissance, though later scholars rarely make this connection. Immigrant street speaker Frank Crosswaith recalled in 1926 that "Negro Harlem had never before witnessed such inspiring spectacles as those intensely active nights when . . . thousands of dark-skinned individuals of both sexes and all ages [stood] motionless for four and five hours drinking the message of the 'New Negro.'"[12]

Not all Harlem residents thought the street speakers were inspiring, however. For "the best people of the community"—some in the black middle class and the pulpit—Harlem business people, and the police, the street meetings were a source of constant irritation. In 1916 the editors of the *Harlem Magazine*, which represented the interests of those who tried to stem the tide of the black "invasion," termed the intersection at 135th and Lenox, where "self-appointed orators" held forth nightly, "bug house corner."[13]

But if credit is given to one individual for establishing the open-air forums both as political and educational institutions in New York City as well as in Harlem, it would be Hubert Harrison, a brilliant scholar and biting social critic. A man of stocky build, dark complexion, and booming voice, he was known around New York as the "Black Socrates."[14] Even before World War I, Harrison, a Socialist, was speaking with other Socialists in Madison Square Park, 96th Street off Broadway, and other locations. As a young immigrant Richard B. Moore was particularly impressed, as was Florida native A. Philip Randolph, both of whom later became two of Harlem's most magnetic street speakers. But before newer Harlem residents got to know Harrison's biting rhetoric, he had already earned his bricks and bats from mainstream native-born African American leaders.

Soon after he graduated with honors from De Witt Clinton High School, Harrison ran into trouble with the New York arm of Booker T. Washington's Tuskegee Machine. While holding a much-coveted colored job as a postal clerk, he sought direct involvement in the African American race struggle. As a speaker for St. Benedict The Moor Lyceum in San Juan Hill and a contributor to the New York *Sun* and New York *Call*, Harrison came to considerable public notice. In his New York *Sun* articles, he made his position against the accommodation views of Booker T. Washington quite clear. As the Tuskegee sage's emissary in New York, African American Republican Charles W. Anderson kept close tabs on Washington's critics. In a September 1911 note to Washington he wrote:

> Do you remember Hubert Harrison? He is the man who wrote two nasty articles against you in the New York "Sun." He is a clerk in the Post Office. The Postmaster is my personal friend, as you probably know. Harrison has had charges preferred against him and I think he is liable to be dismissed from the service. If not dismissed, he will get service punishment. Can you see the hand? I think you can. Please destroy this that it may not fall under another eye—unless it is Emmett's [Emmett J. Scott, Washington's personal secretary]. I will attend to Harrison. It he escapes me, he is a dandy.[15]

By the end of October, Harrison had lost his job. "I'm sure you will regret to learn that Mr. Hubert Harrison has been dismissed from his position as clerk in the New York Post Office," Anderson wrote Washington on the thirtieth.[16] Harrison never again worked in a similar job and made his living from his lectures and the sale of his books. He struggled to make a livelihood for his large family until his death from an attack of appendicitis in 1927.

Shortly after his dismissal from his post office job, Socialist party leaders in New York approached Harrison, who had been a member of the party since 1909, with the proposal that he be "made a paid speaker and organizer for Local New York for special work in negro districts."[17] Although the Socialists' poor record on civil rights was known to Harrison, he had arrived at his own independent political position, and their offer provided remuneration for the work he was already doing. Between 1911 and 1915 he actively tried to recruit African Americans into the party.

Feeling the young Harrison no longer a threat to Washington after dismissal from the post office job, Charles Anderson gleefully observed, "He is now stomping for the Socialist Party. . . ."[18] In the pre-war years, Harrison was one of the party's leading speakers, taking his soap box to the very site of capitalist power on the corner of Wall and Broad Streets, between the Stock Exchange and the office of J. P. Morgan. Here the young Henry Miller, noted novelist/essayist, said he received an education at the "foot of Harrison's soapbox."[19] Harrison provided a rationalization for his ideas in a 1912 essay, "The Black Man's Burden," which appeared in the *International Socialist Review* and later in his 1917 publication *The Negro and the Nation*. He located racial injustice within the structure of the capitalist system. Blacks were "the most ruthlessly exploited class in America . . . hanging on the ragged edge of the impending class conflict." He believed socialism was the means by which the working classes could be empowered.

Harrison was an early proponent of workers' struggles, and he was involved with IWW leaders Elizabeth ("Rebel Girl") Gurly Flynn, William ("Big Bill") Haywood, and Morris Hillquit in their leadership of the 1913 New Jersey silk-mill strike. It was Harrison who brought the Socialist movement to Harlem and encouraged the careers of the up-and-coming native-born and immigrant radicals. He helped establish the Harlem School of Social Science and the Modern School.[20]

But the Socialist party was not Harrison's main source of inspiration. During and after his Socialist party period, he maintained ties with a small group of native African American and African Caribbean scholars and bibliophiles, among them the Puerto Rican Arthur Schomburg and African American journalist John E. Bruce, who had in 1911 formed the Negro Society for Historical Research. This group of self-trained historians devoted themselves to reconstructing the history of people of African descent, mainly through their far-ranging collection of books and materials on Africa and the African diaspora. Their private libraries and bookshops became the reference tools of street speakers. For instance, the Rev. Charles Martin, a native of St. Kitts, maintained a library on the second floor of his brownstone on 134th Street and made it available to lay historians. Schomburg maintained an extensive library in his home on Kosciusko Street in Brooklyn. Family members reported that "there were bookshelves all over the house, even in the bathroom." He was also a supporter of Marcus Garvey and loaned him books from his collection and translated letters and documents for him.[21]

Harlem book dealers, like the street speakers, became freelance educators in history, philosophy, religion, and politics. Book dealer George Young was a Pullman porter who, according to Richard B. Moore, owned the first African American bookshop in Harlem at 135 West 135 Street. "In Young's Book Exchange, known then as *The Mecca of Literature Pertaining to Colored People*, there was . . . an astonishing array of material [about Africa] and her dispersed descendants." Moore began collecting himself in 1918, "having been led into the field by Hubert Harrison."[22] In the 1940s Moore opened his own bookshop, the Frederick Douglass Book Center, on 125th Street.

Harrison's and other speakers' involvement with research societies devoted to Pan-African topics was a crucial distinction between themselves and others who also spoke from street corners. In addition, the Caribbean scholars led by Schomburg provided an important international perspective to the study of the black experience. Schomburg's biographer notes that "to Schomburg the United States was merely a part, albeit an important one, of the wider American nexus, and he regarded himself as an historian of that greater southern land mass which also was America." Harrison, Moore, and others reflected this same perspective in their lectures.

By 1915 Harrison had severed ties with the Socialist party over disagreements with party leaders about the party's lack of a position on African American civil rights. He objected to the view that the grievances of the black masses were no different than those of white workers. Refusing in "this crisis of the world's history to put either socialism or the Socialist Party above the call of [his] race," Harrison moved his stepladder permanently to Harlem, where black grievances as well as his trademark liberal arts lectures became the focus of his street discourse.[23]

After years on street corners in Union Square, Wall Street, and in Harlem, the New York City Board of Education hired Harrison to give a series of lectures in 1923. But according to several contemporaries, Harrison had never been recognized by the "Negro leaders" and had never been mentioned in W. E. B. Du Bois's *Crisis*.[24] In a WPA biography of Harrison, Jamaican journalist and popular historian J. A. Rogers wrote that Harrison's "plainspokenness brought him many enemies among the leading Negroes, one of whom was Dr. Du Bois. . . ." Claude McKay recalled that Harrison had a "personal resentment against the NAACP and nicknamed it the 'National Association for the Advancement of Certain People.'"[25] Harrison apparently was never admitted nor sought admission to the inner circles of African American leadership. When he was hired as a lecturer by the Board of Education, William Pickens wrote an article for the *Amsterdam News* in recognition of the first black to be hired for such a position. Concerned that Harrison be elevated from the "obscurity" of the street corner, Pickens added that Harrison "ought to be a lecturer in some great American University," perhaps Columbia. In response Harrison dashed off a note to Pickens, thanking him for his "goodwill." "I can only hope that the other 'big Negroes' who have known for years what you have but recently discovered may not jump all over you."[26]

His ability to mingle with the masses was a quality his supporters admired in him. Few barriers appear to have existed between Harrison and his native African American audiences. Upon his death in 1927, African American newspapers memorialized his unique contributions. In the view of the Boston *Chronicle*, a Caribbean-owned newspaper, he did Harlem a great service that was not fully appreciated. "He belonged to none of the uplift organizations because he refused to be fettered by any policy but his own, which was to dig out the truth and proclaim it on the highway without fear."[27] Journalist Hodge Kirnon noted in the *Negro World*, "No trace of the Brahmin spirit was to be found in Harrison. He lived with and amongst his people; not on the fringe of their social life. He taught the masses and he drew much of his inspiration from them."[28] Nor did Harrison underestimate his audiences, the *Pittsburgh Courier* editorialized:

> To those who have little faith in the ability of the common man and woman on the street to appreciate "deep" subjects . . . it was a revelation to see Hubert Harrison, mounted on his street corner ladder and surrounded by a crowd of several hundred Negroes, discussing philosophy, psychology, economics, literature, astronomy or the drama.[29]

The *New York Times* added that on his stepladder platform throughout the city Harrison influenced "countless thousands" of whites as well.

Although after 1917 Harrison carried on his stepladder discourse primarily as a freelance lecturer, others who saw an opportunity in the open-air forums were increasingly affiliated with organizations, which often absented a street speaker from his or her audience. These were as divergent as the Socialist party, the Communist party, and Marcus Garvey's UNIA. Between 1916 and 1930, individuals and organizations of national prominence emerged from an initial grounding in street corner politics.

Florida native A. Philip Randolph, who later became head of the Brotherhood of Sleeping Car Porters and Maids, the first African American national labor union, began his public career at the corner of 135th and Lenox Avenue in 1916. When Randolph, the son of an AME preacher, arrived in the city in 1911, he sought out opportunities for intellectual exchange among young people and found that, with the exception of the Epworth League of the Salem Methodist Church, most churches "allowed no secular interests to intrude upon their study of the Bible."[30]

After giving up on an acting career, Randolph discovered that with an academic diploma he could attend City College for free.[31] During this period he developed a friendship with Ohio native Chandler Owen, who was a political science student at Columbia University and whose iconoclastic views he admired. He withdrew from the Epworth League and formed his own political study group with Owen, while honing his speaking and debating skills at City College. During the fall of 1916 the pair, largely due to Randolph's gifts as a speaker, became "the most notorious street corner radicals in Harlem exceeding even Harrison in the boldness of their assaults on political and racial conditions in the country." Although Harrison had left the Socialist party, he praised Randolph and Owen as "two brilliant young leaders."[32] They set up their stepladder on weekday nights and "if other soapboxers wanted to hold on to their audience, they had to be careful not to hold their meeting too close to where Randolph was preaching."[33]

But Randolph's sporadic employment could hardly have sustained his political activities without the active support of his wife, Lucille Green Randolph, a successful businesswoman and protégé of black hair-products millionaire Madame C. J. Walker. "Chandler and I had no job and no plan for the next meal. But I had a good wife. She carried us," Randolph later acknowledged.[34] Jervis Anderson,

Randolph's biographer, notes that Lucille Randolph's financial backing was crucial in the launching of the two soapboxers' monthly magazine, the *Messenger*, in the fall of 1917.[35]

Having proved themselves on the streets, the *Messenger* editors also helped launched the 21st Assembly Branch of the Socialist party. The Harlem Socialist Club was composed of a group of outspoken, largely immigrant young men and one woman, Jamaican Grace P. Campbell. The men included street speakers Barbadian Richard B. Moore, Jamaican W. A. Domingo, and Virgin Islander Frank Crosswaith. After starting the *Messenger*, Randolph and Owen apparently were not among the regular speakers. In 1917–1918, according to Richard B. Moore, aside from himself the list of Socialists included the following: W. A. Domingo, Otto Huiswoud, Rudolph Smith, Frank Poree, Anna Jones, Elizabeth Hendrickson, Frank Crosswaith, Herman Whaley, John Patterson, Victor C. Gasper, Thomas Potter, and [John] Ramsay.[36] Others, including Ethelred Brown, were added to the list after 1920.

This group also formed a study seminar known as the Peoples Educational Forum, which met every Sunday afternoon at Lafayette Hall on 131st Street and Seventh Avenue. The meetings' format included a lecture and a discussion afterwards, which also perhaps served as a warm-up for street oratory. Moore characterized these meetings as "intellectual battlegrounds" where a speaker would have to be prepared "to battle for his ideas."[37] Joyce Moore Turner points out that by 1921 the Socialists were rotating their stepladders from nine different sites, several of them in Harlem:

> On the same evening Moore, Ethelred Brown, and H. Leadett would be speaking at Lenox Avenue and 128th Street, while Domingo, John Patterson, and Frank Poree were holding forth at Lenox Avenue and 133rd Street.[38]

A favorite assembly spot of course was 135th Street and Lenox because of the expansiveness of the sidewalk and the avenue. Turner and Turner continue:

> Once the stepladder was hauled from a fellow socialist tailor or cigar shop on 135th Street, the comrades assembled for a street meeting put a standing question to one another: "Well, what shall it be tonight? Shall it be propagate straight socialism or shall we talk Negro-ology?" They were prepared to discuss the meaning and significance of socialism or to deal with the problems and suffering of the Afro-American people and the potential solutions to those problems. Since the Socialist Party had not been able to come to grips with the "Negro Question," there remained two separate topics rather than an integrated approach.[39]

The younger group of Caribbean immigrants may have been drawn to the Socialists by the early example of Hubert Harrison. The party's educational programs, including the Rand School of Social Science, also attracted young people. But their own consciousness of class contradictions and the exploitation of colonial systems combined with the brunt of American racism would have appealed to these young intellectuals. Joyce Moore Turner notes that in relationship to the Socialist party, "the

Harlem group . . . had little connection with headquarters and developed their study group and educational forum according to their own ideas."

Clearly it was their independence of thought and the aggressive, daring style of the speakers, rooted in the black oral tradition, which appealed to Harlem audiences.[40] The Socialist party itself failed to address key complaints of the black masses, including racism within Socialist-led unions. A major disadvantage was the absence of a mass-based, black-controlled community organization where grievances and aspirations could be addressed.

Hubert Harrison, now advocating "race first" and black self-determination but not rejecting Socialist theory, was the first of the soapboxers to attempt such an organization. In 1917, in the wake of the antiblack East Saint Louis Riots, he issued a call for a mass meeting to protest lynching and disfranchisement. Over two thousand Harlem residents attended the meeting held at the Bethel AME Church on June 12. "It was made clear that the 'New Negro Movement' represented a breaking away of the Negro masses from the grip of the old-time leaders—none of whom was represented at the meeting." A number of "new" leaders were present, however, including Marcus Garvey, who spoke on behalf of his Jamaica-based UNIA and gave his endorsement to the movement. A new organization, the Liberty League, was formed with Harrison as its president and editor of the new publication the *Voice*.[41] Though his street corner speeches are lost to posterity, the *Voice* and Harrison's book *When Africa Awakes*, largely a collection of his articles, remain sources of his ideas.

In his lectures Harrison confronted directly one of the key class grievances of the Harlem masses: the promotion of light-skinned African Americans over those of darker skin in public and private life. He openly condemned the practice, particularly as a criterion for selecting leaders. "So long as we ourselves acquiesce in the selection of leaders on the ground of their unlikeness to our racial type, just so long we will be met by the invincible argument that white blood is necessary to make a Negro worthwhile."[42] Statements like this could be interpreted as an assault on African America's "Talented Tenth" and "representative Negroes," over half of whom were light complexioned. His continued criticism of African American leaders on other grounds, including an article in the *Voice* entitled "The Descent of Du Bois," could hardly have induced the *Crisis* editor to have reviewed his work in the NAACP's monthly journal.

But stepladder speakers such as Harrison continued to focus their discourse on issues of immediate concern to the community. Among these were questions of the use of violence or self-defense, high rents and high prices, and police brutality. The increase in violence against African Americans, much of which occurred in centers of recent African American migration, was a grievance which found its effective response in Harlem street and mass meetings. A series of race riots between 1917 and 1921 and scores of street clashes between migrating blacks and mostly working-class whites not only challenged any expectation of a nonracial urban proletariat, but helped to usher in a new era of black militancy. While established leaders cautioned restraint and trust in the judicial system, Harrison was now joined by other young immigrant street speakers who urged blacks simply to defend themselves and their property.

One incident took place on May 30, 1917, when a crowd estimated at two hundred tried to free a black man arrested in Harlem.[43] Just four days earlier, blacks in San Juan Hill had battled white residents and police after officers had shot into the store of a well-liked black immigrant grocer, wounding him and a small child.[44] Following this episode Harlemites were enraged when a white police officer struck the Rev. Dr. George Sims, pastor of Union Baptist Church, with a nightstick during an unrelated street disturbance. Sims had previously led a citizens protest of the San Juan Hill shootings.[45] Still another incident occurred on July 4, two days after the bloodiest day of the East Saint Louis Massacre. Police ordered twenty-five members of the all-black Fifteenth Regiment to move from a street corner. When police arrested one of the soldiers who questioned the validity of the order and refused to move, black residents and other soldiers attempted to rescue the prisoner. At the height of the disturbance, two thousand people had gathered, according to the New York *Times*, most of them fighting with knives, clubs swinging and bricks flying in the air.[46]

The day after the Fifteenth Regiment incident, Harrison called a meeting at the Metropolitan Baptist Church. The New York *Times* printed its report of the meeting directly beneath its story of the soldiers' riot to demonstrate the connection. According to the *Times*, Harrison told an audience of a thousand cheering Harlemites: "We intend to fight, if fight we must . . . This thing in East St. Louis touches us too nearly. We must demand justice and make our voices heard."[47]

The 1917 East Saint Louis race riot, or "massacre" as Harlem soapboxers preferred, the bloodiest of the century up to that time, touched off an intensity of community feeling in Harlem and around the United States. Reports that white mobs had driven thousands of blacks from their homes and had shot, burned, and hanged scores of others shocked Harlemites. On the surface, both established and emerging black spokesmen in Harlem were as one in their outrage and calls for a community response decrying such savagery. A coalition of leaders, including Hubert Harrison, W. E. B. Du Bois, black ministers, the NAACP, and the Urban League, organized the silent protest parade and marched down Fifth Avenue to midtown Manhattan on July 28, 1917. However, the masses of New York blacks in skirmish after skirmish before and after the July 28 march demonstrated that they were in no frame of mind for silence and were inclined to test the effectiveness of any coalition of black leaders. Self-defense became one of the major issues separating urbanized African Americans from the counsel of old-line leaders.

Fred R. Moore had a revealing exchange with Harrison over the issue of violence after the East Saint Louis riot. He wrote in the New York *Herald Tribune*: "The representative Negro does not approve of radical socialistic outbursts such as calling upon Negroes to defend themselves against whites." In the *Age* he advised, "No man, or woman, either, for that matter, is a friend to the race, who publicly advises a resort to violence to redress wrongs and injustices to which members of the race are subjected in various sections of the country at the present time." To this Harrison wrote a stinging reply: "Now, although the *Voice* seeks no quarrel with the *Age* we are forced to dissent from this cringing, obsequious view which it champions. And we do this on the ground that cringing has gone out of date, that the *Age*'s view does not represent any influential or important section of Negro opinion."[48] Spurred on by Harlem's expanding boundaries and the restless post–World War, mass-based community, a series of new organizations and publications emerged, sharing connections to the stepladder tradition.

Harlem's 21st assembly district Socialists Club provided a third party alternative to the Democratic or Republican platforms, and Harlem's leading black politicians found themselves in direct competition with the growing presence of irreverent, young Socialists. The presence of the black Socialist party candidates was particularly irksome to those who hoped to elect the first black candidates from the 21st and the 19th assembly districts. A reader wrote the *Crusader* to complain about the magazine's support of black Socialist candidate Rev. George Frazier Miller, who ran unsuccessfully for Congress in 1918. In the opinion of the writer, a Republican, Miller's and others' candidacy on the "defeatist Socialist party" ticket served only to split the black vote and ensure the election of a Tammany Democrat. "Does this not conclusively show that you think more of your Socialism than you do of race representation, more of party than of race rights?"[49] In view of the party's lack of a position on civil rights, the reader's point could not be set aside easily. Harlem voters ultimately chose the Democratic party by 1930, but in the meantime, from 1917 and throughout the 1920s, Harlem street audiences helped shape political alternatives.

In these years the race's "representative Negroes" faced new challenges, if not a lapse in influence. One highly publicized incident occurred the year before, in October 1917, when Theodore Roosevelt came to the Palace Casino to speak on behalf of mayoral aspirant John P. Mitchell, a Fusion candidate. Rev. Adam Clayton Powell, Sr. chaired the meeting, and other distinguished Harlem "Old Guard Negroes" were on the platform. By prearrangement, the supporters of the Socialist mayoral candidate, Morris Hillquit, strategically placed throughout the audience, hissed and heckled, nearly disrupting the meeting altogether. Characterizing the hecklers as "soapbox orators" who made themselves "obnoxious," the *Age* fumed about the incident in its next issue: "Even Roosevelt was insulted by these ruffians. . . . They insulted everybody, even the prominent ministers who spoke." But Socialist street orator Frank Crosswaith had a different recollection of the incident: "Roosevelt's speech was literally drowned out in a turbulent sea of cat-calls and hoots. The 'New Negro' was out of control and could not be defeated."[50] Actually the Socialist candidate lost the election, but the party gained significant recognition in Harlem, polling nearly a quarter of its votes according to an undisputed *Messenger* estimate.[51]

Black Socialists attracted considerable support from Harlem street audiences as well as in the polling places. Numbers of new black women voters may have been impressed with Grace Campbell, who ran for State Assembly from the 19th district in 1920 and received a quarter of the ballots cast. A native of Jamaica, Campbell was known for her pioneer social-service work among young black women. She worked as a parole officer for the city of New York from 1921 to 1924 and set up the Empire Friendly Shelter, a home for unwed mothers and a forerunner of the Katy Ferguson Home in Harlem. According to Richard B. Moore, Campbell used much of her own salary to start the shelter.[52] She may not have been a regular stepladder speaker, but she was a well-known public speaker, and her activities were carefully watched by federal agents. An FBI informant reported that in a 1920 campaign speech, she "made a few remarks on the need of women waking up to the fact that they are being driven to prostitution and other evils by the low scale of wages. She promised to work hard among the women, not only of her race but all of the women."[53] Despite the paucity of information available to researchers about her life and activities, Campbell obviously helped influence the direction of Harlem radicalism. In 1923 an FBI informant's report described her as a "prime mover of the African Blood Brotherhood" (ABB) in Harlem.[54]

The ABB was formed in 1919 by Nevis native Cyril Briggs, who had immigrated to the United States in 1905. Among the founding members were Harlem stepladder speakers and African Caribbeans Grace Campbell, Richard B. Moore, W. A. Domingo, and Arthur Reid. Briggs himself was not a public speaker, due to a speech impediment.[55] He worked as a journalist for the *Amsterdam News* from 1912 until 1918, when he was forced to resign after refusing to have his editorial columns censored. With the financial backing of several Harlem businesspeople, Briggs launched the monthly magazine *The Crusader* in August of 1918. The *Crusader* and Randolph and Owen's *Messenger* were important repositories for stepladder speakers' ideas.

The ABB was a secret fraternal order whose aim was armed self-defense, the struggle for equal rights, and self-determination. It was one of the first Harlem-based organizations to affiliate with the new American Communist Party. Briggs and most of the ABB charter members, including Moore and Campbell, became Communists. Membership in the ABB remained relatively small nationwide, though chapters were set up in major urban centers. Campbell's involvement and apparent leadership role in this predominantly male self-defense organization need further investigation. ABB recruits included native-born World War I veterans as well as workers in the building trades—plumbers, electricians, and bricklayers. The federal government charged that in the Tulsa riot of June 1921, when white mobs attacked the black community, the local chapter of the ABB played a leading role in the armed resistance of black neighborhoods.[56]

Just after the Tulsa riot, ABB speakers in Harlem passed out fliers inviting "every Negro tired of lynching and peonage, jim crowism, and disfranchisement to come out and hear our plan of action to remove these injustices which we suffer with others. You have nothing to lose but your chains. You have your liberation to achieve." "Our aim," W. A. Domingo said from a stepladder platform, "is to allow those who attack us to choose the weapons. If it be guns, we will reply with guns."[57] This very practical notion about self-defense was simply a reflection of what African Americans had demonstrated in Tulsa and elsewhere between 1917 and 1921.

If these years witnessed the most militant performances on Harlem streets, by 1921 very clear ideological differences had taken shape. Communists, Socialists, Nationalists, freelancers, and educators provided street audiences with an eclectic menu, usually at agreed-upon street corner locations. Disputed spaces occasionally resulted in street fights, though just as often the ideological battles took place in newspapers, magazines, and journals. By 1922 disputes reflected ethnic antagonisms as well as ideological differences.

One of the speakers who became involved in such disputes was W. A. Domingo, who arrived in New York in 1912 from Boston, where he had spent the last two years. In Harlem Domingo resumed his political activities and journalistic interests which he had begun while still in Jamaica. He landed a job as a post office clerk and organized the Jamaica Benevolent Association in 1917. Between 1912 and 1916 Domingo met and formed a close political association with Randolph, Owen, Moore, Campbell, and other Socialists. Later he joined the Socialist Speakers Bureau and took part in the Peoples Educational Forum. Unlike most of the other Caribbean Socialists, Domingo did not join the Communist party. At some point in the early 1920s he left his post office job and started a business as a successful importer of Caribbean foods, mostly fresh vegetables and fruits. Of all the Harlem radicals, Domingo was probably the most financially secure. The stereotypical description of a Harlem radical as "an over-educated West Indian without a job" never applied to him.

While he still had his post office job, Domingo came to work for Marcus Garvey as the first editor of the *Negro World*, which Domingo used in part to spread Socialist ideas. The two parted in 1919 over Domingo's editorials, which were not in keeping with the program of the UNIA. Domingo also claimed he refused to write editorials and make street corner speeches in support of Garvey's Black Star Line.[58] When Garvey arrived in New York in 1916, he sought out Domingo, whom he had known in Jamaica. Apparently Domingo helped Garvey make contacts for his fledgling organization and perhaps helped to set up some initial speaking engagements. Garvey eventually became one of Harlem's most popular street corner speakers before the organization moved to Liberty Hall, but his first speaking date was a disaster. According to an account written by Domingo, Garvey arranged a lecture at St. Mark's Church Hall in May 1916.

> Shaking like an aspen leaf and with a tremor in his voice he started to deliver his oration. He hadn't gone very far when the audience began to vent its disgust by whistling and hooting. . . . He looked around in affright and pulling a manuscript from his pocket began to read. The more he read the great[er] was the din created by the audience.

Despite the sympathy of several supporters Garvey apparently could not continue and in his nervousness lost his balance and "fell off the stage and lay prostrate on the floor."[59] But Garvey—perhaps ill on this occasion—apparently recovered quickly. A. Philip Randolph, who claimed to have presented Garvey to his first public forum on 135th and Lenox Avenue in 1916, gave a conflicting account of the speaker's abilities. "Garvey got up on the platform and you could hear him from 135th to 125th Street. He had a tremendous voice."[60] James Weldon Johnson reported that Hubert Harrison's 1917 meeting was "Harlem's first real sight of Garvey, and his first real chance at Harlem. The man spoke and his magnetic personality, torrential eloquence, and intuitive knowledge of crowd psychology were all brought into play. He swept the audience along with him."[61] By 1919 the UNIA leader had established himself as one of the most exciting street corner speakers in the community. His emphasis on economic nationalism and race pride appealed to listeners. Furthermore, Garvey appeared to have a concrete program in the Black Star Line and the Negro Factories Corporation. The UNIA's community connections with local churches and with the fraternal orders, plus the pageantry and regalia of its activities, attracted broad-based audiences to Garvey's stepladder. John E. Bruce, a Garvey supporter, claimed "his street corner audiences were larger than those of the Socialist orators on the other corners a few blocks away, and they stayed longer."[62] Bruce became involved in the movement after hearing Garvey speak from a street corner.

By 1920, criticizing Garvey from the street corner must have required tact and possibly police protection. Garvey supporters threatened at least two preachers from the relative safety of their pulpits. Toward the end of August 1920, the *Age* reported an incident in which the nationally known Baptist minister Rev. Charles S. Morris of Norfolk, Virginia, had to be escorted to his lodgings by police when he spoke against Garvey during a revival meeting at the Abyssinian Church tent, located on the future site of the new 138th Street structure. The Abyssinian meeting coincided with the UNIA convention being held at Liberty Hall just next door. According to the *Age*, the demonstration against Morris became "so violent and the threats so earnest" that he had to be taken to his stopping place on 134th Street by an alternate route. However, Morris's host, Abyssinian pastor Powell, Sr., refused to exit by this route. Instead he walked through the crowd, ignoring the insults.[63]

Garvey's loyalists may have been devoted to the image of an early militant UNIA leader who, like other stepladder speakers, demanded equal rights in America. But by 1921 he retreated politically, making some alliances which were interpreted as reactionary by many both in and outside the stepladder community. His highly publicized meeting with the Grand Wizard of the KKK in the summer of 1922 set off an explosion of criticism from a variety of fronts. All of the 1917 radicals—including the Caribbean Socialists and Communists—who had earlier been associated in one way or another with the organization in Harlem denounced Garvey as a "demagogue" or charlatan. But native black critics also labeled him as a "foreigner" and his followers as "ignorant West Indian Negroes."[64] A series of vituperative public exchanges between native and foreign-born radicals ensued and will be explored more fully in chapter 7.

Harlem's nationalists, many of them Garveyites, created their own stepladder discourse. After Garvey's incarceration in 1925 and subsequent deportation in 1927, nationalist street speakers emerged as community leaders in their own right. Their Harlem-based street meetings focused much of their rhetoric on local issues. Jamaican St. William Wellington Grant, head of Harlem's local Tiger Division, claimed Lenox Avenue between 133rd and 135th Streets as UNIA territory. The Garveyites often appeared in paramilitary dress, carrying parade muskets and sabers and advocating a militaristic approach to black nationalism. A number of violent confrontations with Communists, the Harlem police, and even the rival Garvey Club occurred during their open-air meetings.[65]

Meanwhile, the stepladder meetings were increasingly connected with larger organizational movements. The labor organization was one of the most important outgrowths of the street meetings. Barbadian Moore and Virgin Islander Crosswaith were two of the better-known speakers who became worker advocates. Moore was also active in the Communist party's International Labor Defense and the Negro Labor Congress, but Crosswaith strictly avoided any Communist affiliation. As the activist head of the Harlem Tenants League, Moore was instrumental in using strikes to halt huge rental increases and to improve housing conditions in the 1920s. The strikes were aimed at both white and black landlords whose names he cited on the stepladder. Moore's Harlem Tenants League met each Monday evening at the 135th Street branch of the public library until library officials, unnerved by the militant tone of the meetings, refused to allow any further gatherings. Undaunted, members moved to another location, vowing to "make the rent gouging landlords squirm." The League targeted St. Philips Corporation and black millionaire Watt Terry in their campaign against Harlem slumlords.[66] Moore was a skillful orator, and audiences often came to street corners just to hear him. When fellow Communist Harry Haywood first heard Moore speak at an indoor meeting, "he brought the house down with an impassioned speech. . . . I had never heard such oratory."[67]

Frank R. Crosswaith was also one of the most polished orators in any setting. He traveled widely and became the most recognized stepladder speaker outside of Harlem. "In Chicago, in Saint Louis, in Denver, and in San Francisco his great booming voice is known even as it is on the corner of Seventh Avenue and 137th Street."[68] Born in Frederiksted, St. Croix, Danish West Indies, in 1892, he came to New York City as a teenager, enlisted as a sailor in the U.S. Navy, and later worked as a porter and as a garment worker. He aspired to go to law school, but involvements in the labor and Socialist movements in Harlem cost him his job and his plans. In 1917 he took to the street corners. Always smartly attired—boutonniere in his coat lapel, white scarf about his neck, clothes faultlessly pressed—he was known as "a Negro Debs."[69] According to the *Amsterdam News*, during the campaign season

Crosswaith, who frequently ran for political office on the Socialist ticket, nightly drew the largest outdoor crowds.[70]

In Harlem Crosswaith organized the elevator operators, elevator constructors, mechanics, barbers, laundry workers, and motion picture operators. Politically, Crosswaith distinguished himself from some stepladder speakers by his willingness to work with mainstream labor and black establishment groups. He was a general organizer of the International Ladies Garment Workers Union and was instrumental, with the NAACP and Urban League, in increasing black women's numbers in that union, particularly after 1929. In 1925 he organized the Negro Labor Committee in order to get more black workers into predominantly white labor unions.

But while Crosswaith was willing to make alliances with black establishment organizations, he readily excoriated black as well as white landlords who exploited residents. In support of tenant organizing he wrote that "certainly it is utterly absurd to claim because Negro landlords are securing exorbitant rents from Negro tenants and are growing wealthy that fact should be the yardstick by which the race's progress should be measured. . . . Social and economic progress never comes through a parasitical class as such."[71]

One of the lasting labor outcomes of the street corner brigade was the formation of the Brotherhood of Sleeping Car Porters and Maids. Pullman porters approached A. Philip Randolph, who helped launch the organization on August 25, 1925. Virgin Islander and porter Ashley Totten talked to Randolph about leading the new union because Randolph was not a porter and subject to dismissal by the Pullman Company. Pullman porters also knew Randolph by reputation as a street corner speaker and editor of the *Messenger*. Porters were among the most reliable agents for the magazine. There is a suggestion also that Totten approached Randolph to head the national union because he was an American-born black whose right to leadership would not easily be challenged by anyone biased against the leadership of foreign blacks.[72] Moreover, the labor union, comprised of many native blacks and immigrants living in New York and elsewhere on the East Coast, was a good example of intragroup cooperation and was hailed by all sectors of the community. Crosswaith later claimed that in the union's "fierce but fascinating fight, the question of birthplace plays no part in one man's estimate of the other."[73]

But street speakers were perceived as a growing threat to some in the community. By the mid-1920s arrests, and therefore threats to street orators' First Amendment rights, increased. In September of 1926 police arrested Richard B. Moore on charges of "speaking without a permit" and disturbing the peace. In addition to his work with the Harlem Tenants League, Moore also headed a group which had been distributing handbills in Harlem calling upon residents to fight police "terrorism." On the evening of Moore's arrest, a crowd of two thousand gathered to hear the stepladder veteran and his comrades speak in front of the Lafayette Theater in support of striking motion picture operators. When Moore refused to stop talking upon police orders, officers drove an automobile into the crowd. No one was reported injured, but Moore and his companions stood their ground and were taken to jail and fined ten dollars each.[74]

Supporters viewed Moore's arrest as not only a violation of free speech, but part of the general atmosphere of police suppression of the community. A meeting of five hundred gathered at Liberty Hall in protest. The *Amsterdam News* reported that before the Moore incident, a group of Harlem citizens met at Abyssinian Baptist Church to draft a letter to the mayor requesting that street speakers be barred in Harlem. This action was believed to have been motivated by an attempt to prevent speakers from criticizing political candidates in the coming election. Hubert Harrison charged Harlem politicians with using their office to protect "crooks and criminals" while failing to protect law-abiding residents.[75] Socialist A. Philip Randolph, who had parted with Moore over the issue of Communism, nonetheless editorialized in the *Messenger* that "things are coming to a pretty pass in Harlem when a man or woman is hustled off to jail on some trumped charge of disorderly conduct or blocking traffic."[76] Communist community leader and school teacher Williana J. Burroughs, who, with Grace Campbell and others, formed a committee in support of the street meetings, sent out letters urging residents to preserve the gatherings at all costs, describing them as "the chief agency for spreading the leaven of improvement."[77]

The story of Harlem's female activists, immigrant and native, awaits a fuller investigation, but there are indications that they, like women in other African American movements, were key organizers behind the more public performances of male colleagues. But they also participated in predominantly or exclusively female groups. Williana J. Burroughs, Hendrickson, and Campbell were involved in a network of Harlem community organizations. Hendrickson's work with the American West Indian Ladies Aid Society and the Virgin Islands Catholic Relief Organization has already been mentioned. Although Campbell, Audley Moore, and others became active in the Communist party during the late 1920s and early 1930s, their concerns appear to have been rooted in the practical needs of the community. This approach, rather than a commitment to party dogma, brought Grace Campbell into conflict with male leadership in the 1930s. According to a Claude McKay account, Campbell favored the establishment of cooperative stores run by working-class Harlemites as a solution to unemployment and to establish community control of commercial development. When introducing the proposal to a Harlem audience, "Miss Campbell made a simple, earnest speech and the audience was moved. But when she had finished speaking, Comrade leader James W. Ford took the floor and declared that real Communists could not support their own comrade's scheme because it was not Communist enough!"[78]

Audley Moore, seldom modest about her own considerable abilities, asserted that although "I was little people, I was enthusiastic about my freedom and I could organize. That was the reason the Communists found it hard to deal with me, because I was such a great organizer. I was the best organizer they ever had."[79] Moore, whose politics shifted from the Garvey Movement to the Republican party and then to the Communists, claimed she inducted a reluctant Adam Clayton Powell, Jr. into the activism. As an initiator of the Harlem jobs campaign, Moore sought a committee of "respected Harlem leaders" to negotiate with Harlem's business community. "I went to [Powell] and asked him would he head my job campaign. He said, 'Oh, I'm too busy.' 'Oh, Reverend Powell, you don't have to do a thing, just say, "yes." I'll organize the committee, if you say you'll head it.'" Moore claimed she got Rev. William Lloyd Imes to co-chair the committee and Arnold Johnson [probably John H. Johnson] to serve as secretary. Powell made Moore captain of the picket line. Once initiated, Moore claimed, "You never saw anybody develop so quickly in the struggle as Adam Powell did."[80] Moore also claimed she inaugurated the Association of Colored Women's Clubs, an organization of middle-class women, of which she was a member, into labor consciousness. "Under communist influence" she got them to establish a labor committee, "a thing they'd never thought of before."[81]

The speakers who took to the streets after the mid-1920s were perhaps less polished than the 1917 radicals. These speakers "knew their audiences like a rent party piano player knew his dancers," wrote Harlem writer Wallace Thurman.[82] The passage of time saw an increase in African American leaders' complaints about the influence of stepladder speakers. This objection to "soapboxers" grew throughout the 1920s, when street meetings often became violent and individuals McKay characterized as "rough men of the street" took up the tradition. In 1928 one *Amsterdam News* reader wanted such speakers, whom he characterized as "enemies of the race," removed from the streets:

> Can you use the influence of your newspaper to drive from the sidewalks of Harlem the crop of ignorant stepladder orators that has infested it? As one stops to listen, one hears the most ridiculous misstatements of facts of history and government, of science and geography, of art and literature imaginable. Yet these impostors are able to attract audiences. If the audience, as well as the would-be leaders and orators, would avail of the evening high schools in and near Harlem, they would easily secure truthful information.[83]

Crosswaith identified the critics of stepladder radicals as the "best people of the community"—politicians, preachers, and landlords. "As the radicals relentlessly pressed forward, the old and contented crowd became desperate. Frantically they raised the false alarm of 'foreigners.'"[84]

But the popularity of the tradition carried over into the 1930s, and while federal and local authorities continued to keep an eye on their gatherings, during the depression Evangeline Pollard claimed that stepladder speakers were "the nearest thing to leadership the Harlem community seems to have."[85] As leaders they continued to function most effectively outside traditional forums. The new breed included the flamboyant, turbaned, emerald-robed organizer of the Jobs for Negroes Campaign American-born Sufi Abdul Hamid. Jamaican Arthur Reid and southern migrant Ira Kemp were partners and organizers of the grass roots Harlem Labor Union. Kemp and his mentor Reid made quite a pair on Harlem streets. Reid, master of inflammatory invective, had an "unfailing talent for arousing Negroes to action." A native of Macon, Georgia, Ira Kemp was "a redoubtable soapbox orator who inveighed against landlords and high rents, the sale of rotten meats in Harlem, police brutality, and the prevalence of prostitution in certain sections of the community, and many other evils in the Negro district." While meetings flourished on 135th Street and Lenox and 137th and Seventh in the 1930s, open-air gatherings were increasingly staged in front of white-owned businesses targeted as discriminatory in employment or otherwise a "menace" to the community. In addition an entirely new thrust in stepladder oratory revolved around the Italian occupation of Ethiopia in 1936.[86]

We have seen that stepladder speaking linked the immigrant speakers to the native-black community, who could accept or reject their discourse on the spot. But speakers' connections to Harlem's Caribbean community are important to note as well. Immigrant speakers' affiliations provide information about the kind of often ethnically based social environments that sustained them. For instance, Socialist meetings were held at Caribbean immigrant Martin Luther Campbell's Tailor Shop, and the first meeting place of the African Blood Brotherhood was at the brownstone lodge building owned by the American West Indian Benevolent Association at 149 West 136th Street. Ethelred Brown had also held the first meetings of his Harlem Community church in the rooms of the 136th Street association. In 1917 Jamaican W. A. Domingo was a founder of the Jamaican Benevolent Association, which had its own headquarters. Several Virgin Island associations, including Hendrickson's AWILAS, were part of the social network in which activists operated. In addition correspondence files of other Caribbean benevolent associations show a connection between their officers, particularly female officers, and progressive community causes supported by stepladder speakers. There was also a clear connection between stepladder speakers, Harlem Caribbean organizations, and the anticolonial movements which expanded in the Caribbean after 1930.

In Harlem stepladder speakers' legacy lay in a number of key areas. They introduced an alternative politics, whether in more structured movements like those of the Socialists, Communists, or nationalist UNIA or simply by giving voice to the basic concerns of the community. Speakers like Hubert Harrison challenged Eurocentric history and provided ordinary Harlemites with the first information they had ever heard about the African past. Street speakers most effectively introduced protest tactics, the boycott, demonstration, and the protest rally tactics taken up by twentieth-century African American social movements. The concept of protracted agitation—"bughousing" the power structure and "respectable Negroes"—helped alter strategies of conventional politicians and perhaps made them more responsive to community concerns. By the 1940s the methods of the street speakers were being utilized by candidates for electoral office, who harangued crowds from 125th Street and Seventh Avenue. Perhaps the tactics employed by Harlem's first congressman, Adam Clayton Powell, Jr., best illustrate the "leavening" of traditional politics. WPA researcher

Sadie Hall wrote that Powell "moved the soapbox into the church" or, more accurately, moved the church into the street.[87] In 1938 Powell started a column in the *Amsterdam News* entitled "Soapbox," thus helping to legitimize the "tell it like it is" approach for those Harlemites who may earlier have dismissed the practice as a tool of the rabble-rouser. Stepladder speakers influenced growing numbers of community activists. By the mid-1920s Tyrell Wilson saw that he could do little for his race through the Seventh-day Adventist Church structure and, disillusioned by his unsuccessful search for a decent job, joined the Socialist brigade in Harlem. He recalled being greatly impressed by Socialist A. Philip Randolph and Communist Richard B. Moore. By 1929 Wilson was a "full-fledged activist for the poor generally and the blacks particularly."[88]

Historians have rarely treated the street corner in black communities as an institutionalized location for the proliferation of political ideas, although sociologists and anthropologists have focused on it as a particularly vital locality for a study of grass roots urban culture. Indeed the oral nature of the often unrecorded street meetings and the transient and unidentified audiences make it difficult to document or define the street corner meeting as a historical institution. But by 1930 Harlem street corners became the sites of regular meetings with identifiable speakers and locations. Moreover, sidewalk locations became the sites of two merging traditions carried by black immigrants and southern migrants whose most effective organizing technique was their direct contact with their audiences. This kind of organizing did not require a pulpit, newspaper, or meeting hall, though all of these forums came to be tools of the most successful street speakers. Only inclement weather or the Harlem police stood between the speaker and his or her audience.[89] Caribbean speakers gained an acceptance from native-born audiences and the audiences shaped their politics as well. But in the shaping of the stepladder tradition, birthplace was not an irrelevant issue; critics stereotyped many speakers as "foreign rabble-rousers." And particularly during Marcus Garvey's most controversial Harlem period, even the radicals themselves failed to rise above ethnic divisions.

7

Marcus Garvey
"Negro Subject of Great Britain"

IN OCTOBER 1919 U.S. Attorney General A. Mitchell Palmer's young aggressive assistant, future FBI head J. Edgar Hoover, received an agent's report from the Panama Canal, Washington Office, relative to the activities of one Marcus Garvey. Hoover forwarded the report to the office of the Postmaster General along with an accompanying memo and newspaper clipping. He noted that Garvey was a "West Indian negro . . . particularly active among the radical elements in New York City in agitating the negro movement." He added,

> Unfortunately, however, he has not as yet violated any federal law whereby he could be proceeded against on the grounds of being an undesirable alien, from the point of view of deportation. It occurs to me, however, from the attached clipping that there might be some proceeding against him for fraud in connection with his Black Star Line propaganda and for this reason I am transmitting the communication to you for your appropriate attention.[1]

Hoover's early memo set in motion the circumstances leading to Garvey's later conviction on mail fraud charges in 1923 and his eventual deportation in 1927.

The conflicting issues of race and ethnicity surfaced nowhere as clearly as in reactions to Marcus Garvey's contentious leadership. By 1921 Garvey, who never became a U.S. citizen, headed the Harlem-based movement which became "the major political force among blacks in the postwar world."[2] Over the course of the government's pursuit of a case against him, some of Garvey's American-born critics claimed his unfair persecution on racial grounds while ignoring or even supporting discrimination based on national origins. It comes as no surprise that the *Age* editor Fred R. Moore favored his exclusion from the United States in 1921 and opposed any support for his reentry. But Garvey's leadership also provoked reactions and opposition among Harlem's radicals and intellectuals who led a "Garvey Must Go" campaign to remove the Jamaican from his political base in America. Garvey's own shifting political strategies, including his meeting with the Ku Klux Klan, fueled this campaign aimed at his eventual deportation. These reactions must also be understood in the context of coordinated efforts by federal and local governments to exploit the UNIA leader's foreign status. Taken as a whole, official strategies linked with those shaped by controversies within the broader African American community itself provide a telling commentary on a previously unexplored American nativism.

Like many other Caribbean immigrants, Garvey settled in Harlem upon his arrival in 1916. He lodged with a Jamaican family and found work as a printer.[3] He had come to the United States to raise funds for his Universal Negro Improvement Association, which he founded in Jamaica in 1914. In a 1917 *Champion Magazine* article, he described his mission to the country as a lecture tour in which he hoped to gain financial support for an industrial and educational institute on the order of Tuskegee Institute in Alabama.[4] He traveled to thirty-eight major American cities before turning his energies to establishing a permanent organization based in Harlem.

In this early period Garvey's activities were not unusual. Other intellectuals, particularly educators in the Pan-African diaspora, sought financial support and co-operation in the United States for projects of race uplift in their homelands. Earlier Garvey corresponded briefly with Booker T. Washington and intended to visit him, but Washington died in 1915 prior to the young Jamaican's arrival. While still in the posture of a visitor, there was little in Garvey's public statements that would make him objectionable to the American-born black leadership. In the *Champion* article, "The West Indies in the Mirror of Truth," he praised black Americans for progress made since their emancipation from slavery, particularly in the area of commercial enterprises and self-help. He lauded the leadership capabilities of individuals such as journalists John E. Bruce and Ida Wells Barnett. He was critical of black immigrants who with "vain bluff" claimed that conditions were better in their Caribbean homelands. He called for commercial cooperation between African Americans and African Caribbeans, asserting that African Americans' greater access to capital and material goods was an important model for blacks in the Caribbean.[5]

When the UNIA leader decided to remain in the United States and launch his movement from Harlem, he gained many followers among American black leaders, including prominent church men and women, heads of fraternal and benevolent societies, journalists, a range of intellectuals, and, of course, working people. The UNIA was incorporated under the laws of the State of New York in 1918, and Garvey appeared nightly on the stepladder before hundreds of discontented Harlemites, his militant discourse sharpened by the open-air forums. The popular gatherings were monitored by government informants. J. Edgar Hoover acknowledged, "He is an exceptionally fine orator, creating much excitement among the negroes. . . ."[6]

Equally exciting was Garvey's *Negro World*, which began publication in 1918 with a worldwide distribution in the United States, the Caribbean, Latin America, and Africa. The newspaper was launched with some financial backing from multi-millionaire cosmetics entrepreneur Madame C. J. Walker, who also donated funds for the purchase of Liberty Hall.[7] Walker herself had far-ranging ties to African American women in small towns and cities in the United States and the Caribbean through her training programs and community-service oriented Walker Clubs. Although this point needs further research, there is evidence that some of her agents were also active in local UNIA chapters and possibly served as local agents for the *Negro World.*[8]

By the fall of 1918, before Liberty Hall became his headquarters, Garvey's widely publicized meetings moved inside to the Palace Casino. At one of these meetings, in November 1918, delegates were nominated to represent the organization at the Post–World War I Paris Peace Conference. They were expected to call on the Allied Powers to give up German control of African colonial lands (1,026,220 square miles) and return them to black—possibly American black—control. A. Philip Randolph and antilynching campaigner Ida B. Wells Barnett were among those chosen to attend.[9] This initial alliance with Randolph would later dissolve, but it demonstrated Garvey's early appeal to political radicals as well as to older race men and women such as Wells Barnett. According to Garvey, his first challenge came from Harlem's aspiring black politicians, who wanted to use the organization as a base to launch their own political agendas.[10]

Significant challenges to the spread of the movement were swept aside by 1919. To any casual observer the UNIA was much broader than the "West Indian" movement some Garvey critics would soon assert it to be. The UNIA's geographic diversity alone attests to this fact. There were large and strong divisions in the major cities—New York, Boston, Chicago, Philadelphia, and Detroit—but there were also chapters in the deep South—Mississippi and Alabama—in North Carolina and Georgia, and in small cities in California, such as Bakersville, Santa Monica, and Wasco.

In Harlem, where Caribbean immigrants were most numerous, Garvey still drew hardshell southern Baptists, including a large female contingent, into the local division. When the UNIA moved its regular meetings into Liberty Hall, the former site of the heavily southern-migrant Metropolitan Baptist Church, Garvey continued to make important allies with members of the native African American community, especially with key Harlem clergymen who regularly spoke from the Liberty Hall platform. His plans for black economic nationalism—black self-reliance and independence—had historic significance in the African American community and the black church.[11] These plans culminated in the launching of new black-owned businesses in Harlem and in the Black Star Steamship line in 1919. On the local-community level in Harlem and elsewhere, the UNIA functioned to provide organized benevolence, mutual improvement, and uplift.[12]

The organization also attracted important personalities of the African American "Talented Tenth," who either joined or in other ways supported the organization. Among these were key African American women, some of whom had international connections. American-born elocutionist and actress Henrietta Vinton Davis (1860–1941) became the international organizer for the UNIA in 1919. She had been well known as a dramatist in the United States since the nineteenth century. In 1912 and 1913 she toured Jamaica, where she established permanent ties both in the theater and in the community. She managed Kingston's Convent Garden Theatre and organized a branch of the Loyal Knights and Ladies of Malachite, a black American benevolent society. Previously in Costa Rica in 1913, she received a donation of land from a Jamaican woman to build a school for girls in Jamaica. During her performances, Davis conducted fund-raising efforts for this project until she became associated with the UNIA. Wherever Davis traveled in the Caribbean as UNIA organizer, people came out to hear her, and she used her influence to set up UNIA divisions.[13]

Garvey also gained the support of influential AME missionary Emily Christmas Kinch, who was one of the strongest supporters of a literal return to Africa. Kinch spoke at Liberty Hall on the topic "Back to Africa" in June 1920 and expressed her strong endorsement of the UNIA. Kinch had been an AME missionary in Sierra Leone and Monrovia, Liberia, where she founded the Eliza Turner Memorial School in 1909. For a number of years she was the organizational secretary of the 8,000-member AME Woman's Parent Mite Missionary Society, responsible for supporting missions in Sierra Leone. She later became the first woman to be elected permanent chair of the lay electoral college of the AME Church.[14]

As one of the most successful black publications of the period, the *Negro World* also attracted other African American Talented Tenth. By 1921 it was self-supporting and one of Harlem's largest employers of black workers. In addition the newspaper contributed over a thousand dollars a month to the UNIA's general treasury. William Ferris and John E. Bruce, former associates of Du Bois at the launching of the Niagara Movement in 1905, and T. Thomas Fortune worked for the paper. Ferris, a respected writer, became its literary editor during the Harlem Renaissance. Fortune had been founder and former editor of the New York *Age*. He left this paper in 1909 and worked for various other publications before joining the *Negro World* as editor in 1923. He remained with the paper until his death in 1928. Veteran journalist, Pan-Africanist, and bibliophile John Edward Bruce, or "Bruce Grit" as he was known by African American readers, began a regular column in the *Negro World* in May 1920 and also continued writing for the paper until his death in 1924. In addition to these veteran race men, younger New Negro writers, such as Zora Neale Hurston, had some of their early work published in the paper.[15]

Despite his influence and his intricate associations within the American black community, Garvey's nationality and lack of status as a U.S. citizen continued to be used as a rallying point at the center of the rhetoric against him. A representative article appeared in Robert Abbott's Chicago *Defender* in September of 1919. It gleefully reported a government investigation of Garvey's Black Star Steamship Corporation:

> Things moved swiftly in the case of Marcus Garvey last week. The foreigner, who since coming to America has made himself a rabid agitator, found himself pretty well entangled in the grip of the law. It is significant that the loud mouth bellower for race rights in this country, who himself is not even a citizen of the United States, did not employ counsel of his own race to defend him. . . . [16]

In a misleading editorial statement, the paper added, "His organization too, is composed mostly of foreigners, and certainly does not represent one iota of the American

Race men." As in Harlem such attacks were often motivated by rivalries over constituencies within the black community. Despite Abbott's assertions to the contrary, the UNIA had already attracted thousands of black Americans, and the *Negro World* was widely read in Chicago, posing direct competition to the editor's Chicago *Defender*.

In addition the UNIA's activities were widely broadcast in the white press. The public appeal of UNIA activities, the splendid parades, and the monthlong August conventions beginning in 1920 were all covered in New York's major dailies. The now-famous Madison Square Garden opening convention, attracting thousands from Harlem, towns and cities around the United States, the Caribbean, Central and South America, and even Africa clearly stunned and worried some African American leaders.

At first W. E. B. Du Bois simply ignored UNIA activities in the NAACP's *Crisis*, including the launching of the Black Star Line in 1919. Without mentioning the organization by name or the name of its president, a *Crisis* article entitled "The Rise of the West Indian" referred to the UNIA immediately after its monthlong 1920 August convention.[17] Du Bois continued to describe the UNIA as a "West Indian" movement when clearly Garvey had garnered a strong base of support, not only among the black American-born masses, but among its elite as well.

Meanwhile Garvey's activities continued to be under government surveillance. Some of the earliest correspondence in U.S. Justice Department files reveals the UNIA leader had been followed by local New York City police, federal agents, and informants early in his Harlem career. A 1918 FBI report pointed out: "there is a man by the name of *Garvey* (colored) who preaches [on the stepladder] every night against the white people, generally from 134th to 137th Street Lenox Avenue. . . . There are several men who speak in this district. . . . It might be a good idea to run down [investigate] these negro speakers. . . ."[18] The first informant's letters quickly point to Garvey's alien status. Informants also inadvertently reveal clues for historians about the movement's activities and followers.

One anonymous New York City letter addressed to the U.S. Justice Department began, "As an American citizen, I beg to direct your attention to the activities of Marcus Garvey, a Negro Subject of Great Britain, who is carrying on a serious and intemperate agitation among Southern Negroes as well as those of Africa and the West Indies." Although the writer did not call for Garvey's deportation, he or she did provide a detailed description of Garvey's movement to that point, including an estimated 6,000 members in New York City and 25,000 subscribers to the *Negro World*. The writer also criticized the government for "hounding Hindu nationalists" while allowing the UNIA to use the United States as a base for "revolutionary propaganda." Garvey's followers, in the writer's view, were "deluded foreign Negroes" and "ignorant American Negroes" and if Garvey was "not checked now his movement [would] gain momentum." Finally the writer enumerated alleged violations under which the UNIA leader might be vulnerable.[19]

Justice Department officials turned this letter over to the Department of Labor, where immigration and naturalization matters were handled at that time. That department's assistant secretary, Louis Post, informed Attorney General A. Mitchell Palmer that the matter would be given "proper consideration" to determine whether Garvey was "subject to the immigration law."[20] That kind of suspicion of foreigners reflected the atmosphere of the era of "100 percent Americanism," culminating in the federal government's crackdown on all radicals, black or white, and on all ethnic backgrounds during the Palmer Raids in the summer of 1919. Unnaturalized immigrant radicals were subject to deportation. Agents reported UNIA activities in detail and followed Garvey wherever he traveled.

Surveillance activities reveal how U.S. officials searched for a loophole on the basis of which Garvey could either be deported or imprisoned. In this regard authorities carefully coordinated efforts between the several departmental divisions under which Garvey might be prosecuted. "In the event your Department determines that there is no action it can take looking to the deportation of Garvey," another assistant attorney general wrote to the Secretary of Labor in 1919, "it is suggested that you refer all papers to the Post Master General in order that an investigation may be conducted for the purpose of determining whether Garvey has been guilty of using the mail in furtherance of a scheme to defraud."[21] Garvey's later conviction was ultimately based on a single mail-fraud charge, and he was imprisoned in 1925 and deported in 1927.[22]

Meanwhile, officials even considered using the Mann Act (White Slave Act) passed by Congress in 1910 to prevent the interstate transportation of women for immoral purposes. Apparently the basis for charging Garvey under this law was his travels with his secretary, Amy Jacques, whom he was later to marry.[23] Garvey and Amy Ashwood married in 1919 and after only one year were separated. According to her biographer, Ashwood brought Amy Jacques into the movement in 1919 as her own and later Garvey's secretary. As Ashwood's relationship with Garvey deteriorated, Jacques and the UNIA leader became romantically involved. But when Garvey began his 1921 tour of the Caribbean and Central America with Jacques, Ashwood and Garvey were not divorced. Garvey was not charged under the Mann Act, and he continued to travel with Jacques in the United States until their marriage in 1922. However, at the time of his overseas tour, Walter Smith, an informant, sent a July 1921 telegram to the Secretary of State, Charles Evans Hughes, to suggest Garvey's susceptibility under the Mann Act. He observed that while still married to Amy Ashwood, "he left here in company of Amy Jacques, an unmarried woman negress residing at 133 West 129th New York where her people still live." Smith added that Garvey was a dangerous agitator "preaching force of arms against whites everywhere." In Smith's opinion Garvey was entirely unfit to represent "American loyal negroes."[24]

But Garvey, having firmly established the UNIA in Harlem, set out on his spring 1921 tour of Panama, Costa Rica, Cuba, Jamaica, British Honduras, and Guatemala.

His travels continued to attract U.S. agents and local police, who attended UNIA meetings and submitted detailed reports to the State Department. One report submitted by the U.S. Minister at Panama specified the locations of speaking engagements, arrival and departure dates, and other information. The State Department's instructions to the American consul at Jamaica were to "refuse him a visa" in light of the activities of Garvey in "political and race agitation."[25] Anticipating this obstruction, the UNIA leader had himself hired as a member of the crew of the *Kanawha*, a vessel belonging to his own Black Star Line.

Having been outwitted in this episode, an American official in Kingston wrote to the State Department to inquire if it were legal to refuse a bill of health to the steamer on which Garvey was a member of the crew. "There seems no authority of law for refusing to grant a bill of health except for failure to comply with the health requirements," was the official reply. Adding that such a refusal could hardly be warranted by the "objectional character of a member of the crew or his political views," the memo suggested that the consul at Kingston "refuse to visa the crew list" and to inform the master of the vessel that all of the alien members of the crew would be kept on the ship if it arrived at a port of the United States without a visaed crew list.[26]

Due to a miscommunication, however, an uninformed member of the consular staff at Kingston inadvertently granted Garvey a visa. But authorities briefly delayed his reentry when he arrived in New Orleans on July 13, 1921. By this time the UNIA leader had been indicted on mail-fraud charges. As suggested by Garvey historians, the UNIA leader was probably allowed reentry to assure his virtually prearranged conviction on such charges.[27]

Garvey was of course aware that as an alien claiming leadership in the United States, he would be vulnerable to a variety of charges, and in September 1921 he filed a declaration of intention to become a U.S. citizen.[28] But by the time he would have met the residency requirement for citizenship, the UNIA leader had already been convicted of a crime, which made him ineligible. The campaign against him climaxed just before he could legally have obtained protection against the threat of deportation by becoming an American citizen.[29]

Curiously, it was during his absence from Harlem and his near aborted attempt to reenter the United States that Garvey's shifting political strategies began to take shape. Though the fiery rhetoric of the street corners surfaced frequently in his speeches, his underlying political approach appears to have shifted to one of accommodation. And though he was aware of the government's role in attempting to restrict his movements, imprison, and deport him, he carefully avoided openly blaming authorities, publicly castigating enemies "[who are] members of my race" instead.[30]

A further indication of Garvey's accommodationist shift was his deliberate avoidance of anticolonial labor strikes during his 1921 tour. Back at Liberty Hall his political retreat was noted by an agent who observed that "Garvey is now more patriotic and is now preaching nothing but loyalty to the flag."[31] Furthermore, even before his ill-fated visit with the KKK, he appeared to distance himself and the UNIA from integration. Robert Hill explains:

> Prior to his reentry crisis in 1921, Garvey had not found it necessary to resort to the argument of racial purity or to attack 'social equality.' Garvey's decision to seek a resolution of his conflict with the American state brought about the change. His belief at the time that his political opponents conspired to use the state against him prompted him to challenge their influence by provoking the issue of social equality while promoting his commitment to the ideal of racial purity. This shift was made all the easier by the fact that it came after Garvey's protracted absence from America. His loss of critical contact with the pulse of the movement's rank and file probably led him to overestimate the importance of his political critics and, correspondingly, the readiness of the American state to enter into meaningful dialogue with him.[32]

Fueling Garvey's suspicion was the fact that W. E. B. Du Bois's and other black journalists' coverage of UNIA activities became more openly critical. Du Bois published the results of his "investigation" of the Black Star Line in the December 1921 and January 1922 issues of the *Crisis*. His comments were generally critical of the business policies of the corporation. Meanwhile Garvey began a series of articles in the *Negro World* highly critical of Du Bois's Pan-African Congresses (held between 1919 and 1927) and what he considered the "race mixing" policies of the *Crisis* editor and others.

In observations following these early articles, however, Du Bois's reviews became more nativist in tone, especially after Garvey's unexpected and startling 1922 meeting with the KKK. The articles attempted to discredit and ridicule Garvey as a leader in the United States while also disparaging his nationality and the nationalities of his followers. An often-quoted example is Du Bois's 1923 article in *Century Magazine*, directed mainly at white readers. Describing the UNIA president as a "little fat, black man, ugly, but with intelligent eyes," Du Bois told readers that Garvey was seeking "to oppose white supremacy and the white ideal by a crude and equally brutal black supremacy." Garvey's movement, he wrote, did not represent the thinking of "intelligent American Negroes," for the moving nucleus were black Jamaican peasants, "mostly poor, ignorant and unlettered":

> When the rank and file of ignorant West Indian Negroes were going wild over Garvey, the American Negroes sat cool and calm, and were neither betrayed into wild and unjust attacks upon Garvey nor into uncritical acceptance.[33]

Despite this and other efforts to distance "American Negroes" from the Garvey movement, members of the white press sometimes confused the UNIA with the NAACP as well as with the Du Bois-inspired series of Pan-African Congresses.[34] In March 1922 the Urban League's director of research, Charles S. Johnson, wrote James Weldon Johnson, the NAACP executive secretary, to alert him to references in the press which "linked Mr. Garvey with a name so similar to the National Association of Colored People that it would be extremely difficult for a person who did not know to detect the difference." Garvey, Charles Johnson noted, had been described as the head of the "National Association for the Advancement of the Welfare of the Colored People." James Weldon Johnson replied that the NAACP had received "a great many complaints" and that the error had been due to Associated Press releases in newspapers "all over the country." The AP had printed a correction, and several major newspapers had done the same, but the New York *Tribune* "has not yet been courteous enough to comply with our request for correction."[35]

The NAACP also received additional correspondence from both black and white people inquiring about the Garvey movement. James Weldon Johnson himself had written in the *Age* that the "Back to Africa" concept, largely identified with Garvey, had no credence among "American Negroes." To one inquiry Johnson replied that the NAACP had never officially endorsed or disapproved of Marcus Garvey's UNIA. For clarification he then referred the writer to the New York *Age,* the *Messenger,* and the *Crusader,* publications which were among Garvey's severest critics.[36]

Confusion distinguishing the programs of the UNIA from those of the NAACP continued to surface during the Paris peace negotiations after World War I, when Du Bois took his Pan-African Congresses to Europe. Because of the international nature of Pan-Africanism, Garvey's black American critics found it difficult to discredit him in this arena on the basis of his foreign status. European and American officials were suspicious of plans for Pan-African Congresses anyway since they viewed these moves as similar in aim to Garvey's UNIA. The congresses, held in European capitals in 1919, 1921, and 1923, were frequently mistaken for the Garvey movement.[37] In fact Du Bois's congresses and Garvey's UNIA appealed to the same small group of black colonial elites in Africa and the Caribbean. But to clarify matters to the white press before leaving for the second Pan-African Congress, held in Brussels in August 1921, Du Bois sent out a news release which read in part:

> The Pan-African Congress is not a scheme of migration either to Africa or elsewhere. It is not a project of veiled or open war or conquest. It is not based on revolution or race hatred. It seeks knowledge and action through reason and law. It believes in the equality of men and races but it seeks to realize this through education and opportunity and periodic conference.[38]

In spite of this explanation, the French publication *Le Journal* printed a short announcement of the Brussels Pan-African Congress and included a photograph of Garvey with the caption "Un enemi des blancs." The article revealed little about the objectives of the Pan-African Congress, while describing Garvey's *Negro World* and the Black Star Line.[39] In truth, postwar Pan-Africanists were frequently UNIA sympathizers if not active members. In 1921 Du Bois had to seek out UNIA supporters to help push the congresses. For example, he invited the well-known Garveyite John E. Bruce to attend the second European Congress. Bruce refused, publicizing his reasons in his *Negro World* column.[40]

The last congress, held in Harlem alternately at St. Mark's Methodist Episcopal Church and St. James Presbyterian Church in 1927, was arranged by an organization of black Harlem women who were members of the Circle for Peace and Foreign Relations. They also asked Du Bois to direct these meetings. The idea to hold the congress in New York was apparently theirs, too, and they raised the necessary funds to do so because financial support for the sessions had been abandoned by the NAACP after 1921. A reported five thousand people attended, in sharp contrast to the previous conferences where the delegate count never numbered over fifty or sixty. The relationship of the congress to the Garvey movement inevitably came up. According to one account, on the last day of the conference an unidentified delegate proposed a resolution asking clemency for Garvey, who was then serving a five-year sentence in Atlanta Federal Penitentiary. Despite the favorable response from the audience, this version goes, Du Bois maneuvered the resolution into a committee session from which it never returned.[41]

Despite the difficulties Garvey's critics faced in attacking his international program, at home his nationality continued to be the most common weapon against him. The white press as well as the black American press rarely failed to associate Garvey's legal difficulties with his birthplace and foreign status. These press accounts understandably provoked protests from the Caribbean community. A typical article in the New York *World* following Garvey's conviction and in the midst of the "Garvey Must Go Campaign" prompted a letter to the editor from Ethelred Brown. Brown objected to language such as "American Negroes in Harlem were elated yesterday over Garvey's conviction . . ." and "Federal authorities say nine-tenths of Garvey's army are West Indian Negroes who have not been naturalized. . . ." Brown, himself a Garvey critic, felt the article distorted the real issues:

> What impressed me was the clear intention of the writer in putting these two paragraphs one after the other. He intended to convey that only American Negroes are on the side of justice and therefore approve the conviction, and that the majority of West Indians were and are in sympathy with the aims and methods of Garvey. Nothing is further from the truth. West Indians were in the forefront of those who opposed both the aims and methods of the fallen man . . . [but] the end is too tragic for spiteful glee or fiendish satisfaction.[42]

In Harlem the ethnic bias inherent in the slogan and the intent of the "Garvey Must Go" campaign helped drive a wedge between between key Caribbean and American black Garvey critics. Announcing the plan "to drive Garvey and Garveyism . . . from the American soil," *Messenger* editors soon resorted to ethnic slurs and name-calling. A July 1922 article referred to Garvey's claim that the United States was a white man's country: "This fool talk emanates from a blustering West Indian demagogue who preys upon ignorant, unsuspecting poor West Indian working men and women who believe Garvey is some sort of Moses." Adding that they were acquainted with many "splendid . . . intelligent" Caribbean people, the editors nevertheless called upon all ministers, editors, and lecturers to "gird up their courage . . .

and drive the menace of Garveyism out of this country."[43] But such disparagement, culminating in a January 1923 *Messenger* article entitled "A Supreme Negro Jamaican Jackass," led former allies to denounce the editors for nativism and jingoistic ethnic bias. Contributing editor, Jamaican W. A. Domingo responded in a *Messenger* article:

> Emphasizing nationality unfavorably can have only one result, whether it is desired or not, namely, extend public hostility from an individual to his group. . . . Need I point that the policy you are now pursuing will logically culminate in dissension within the race, and if sufficiently disseminated, make the life of West Indians among American Negroes as unsafe or unpleasant as is the life of American Negroes among their white countrymen?[44]

The ensuing exchange between Domingo and coeditor Chandler Owen is a striking illustration of the race vs. ethnicity issue. In reply, Owen failed to admit any bias in his statements, defended his emphasis on nationality as merely descriptive, and questioned whether Domingo was more concerned about "nationality—the great island of Jamaica—than the entire Negro race: Is Jamaica a more sensitive and tender darling than the Negro?"[45]

In the next issues the *Messenger* not only printed ethnic slurs, but the editors denied intraracial ethnic identities or sensitivities had any significant import. This was a curious position for a radical/Socialist publication to take since many Socialists—black and white—were foreign born. In April 1922 the magazine had taken a different stance when the editors had taken issue with Roscoe Conking Bruce,[46] whom they accused of unfairly attacking Garvey on the basis of nationality in an issue of the Chicago *Defender*. Claiming to be tired of ethnic intolerance, the editors asserted that criticism of Garvey based on this kind of narrow-mindedness was "a little barrack behind which mental impotency hides when it cannot answer logic."[47] But by August the *Messenger* altered its approach and set up the Friends of Negro Freedom, an anti-Garvey umbrella organization which held weekly Sunday meetings in Harlem. Randolph now communicated directly with NAACP officials, exchanging information and suggestions about strategy in the "Garvey Must Go" campaign.[48]

The NAACP's field secretaries, William Pickens and Robert Bagnall, described as "fearless, devoted and incorruptible public servants in the cause of Negro Freedom," were billed as speakers in a flier announcing the Sunday meetings: "Should Garvey, who is not a citizen, advise Negroes in the United States to surrender their citizenship rights?" According to a Baltimore *Afro-American* article reporting on an August gathering, the crowds attending were quite spirited and a number of Garveyites were present and in a bellicose mood. Only prompt interference by the police prevented serious violence. Pickens reportedly told the Caribbean immigrants in the audience, some of whom had been disruptive during his address, that "the best hope of the West Indian in the United States is to ally himself with the better element of Negroes in the United States and forget where he came from."[49]

At another meeting outside of Harlem, the Baltimore *Afro-American* commented, "Garveyite West Indians in Canada recently attempted to intimidate William Pickens, but misjudged their man." Pickens was reported to have said, "We criticize even the President of the United States, the head citizen among us in our country—and no West Indian alien can consider himself immune."[50] In partial response to these remarks, the *Negro World* black American columnist Robert Poston announced that Pickens was to "hereby be placed in the ranks with all other enemies of the race."[51]

The Harlem-based weekly newspapers agreed that Garvey's actions in meeting Klan leaders only underscored his unfamiliarity with the American race problem. "There has been nothing done by one of their race since emancipation that has angered and alarmed Negro citizens more deeply than the recent effort of Marcus Garvey, an alien and native of Jamaica, B. W. I., to form an alliance with the Ku Klux Klan," wrote alderman George W. Harris in his New York *News*. Referring to the UNIA leader as an "interloper," Harris accused him of "damnably misrepresenting colored Americans and 75 percent of the foreign-born." On the defensive, Garvey answered in the next issue of the *Negro World* that he never intended to make an alliance with the Klan but met with the wizard for the "sole purpose of getting first hand information about the Klan's attitude towards the race I represent."[52]

Still Garvey's apparent naiveté in this matter is hard to grasp. The Klan ("Knights of the Invisible Empire") had millions of dues-paying members in the 1920s. And its anti-black, anti-foreign, anti-internationalist, anti-Catholic, anti-Jewish, anti-Communist, anti-evolutionist, anti-bootlegger, and anti-birth control positions were widely understood. Basically it was only pro–white Anglo Saxon and pro-Protestant. As a black man, a foreigner, and an internationalist, Garvey might have made life easier for himself by taking the Klan at face value. In this instance his inclination for action was unfortunate, if a rationally explained reading about an organization whose terrorism and name evoked such an intensity of emotion in the African American community.

In a further attempt to explain Garvey's actions, the *Negro World* reported that the UNIA's southern divisions had complained that Klansmen were harassing its members, accosting them on the streets, and coming to their homes demanding information about the UNIA. Garvey's intentions, the paper explained, were to assure the safety of the southern divisions by making clear his separatist politics. His success in this regard appears to have had little impact on the Klan, but white supremacists continued to express interest in blacks leaving the United States for Africa. And Garvey maintained contacts with some white supremacists after his return to Jamaica.[53]

After the Klan meeting, Garvey's difficulties increased as he also began to face internal problems within the UNIA. There were apparent Caribbean immigrant and native-black schisms, though the *Negro World* rarely reported any hint of intraracial ethnic strife within the organization. The split between the prominent clergyman Rev. James Eason, "the leader of American Negroes," and Garvey during the August

1922 convention was the most public breach within the organization and probably the most damaging to solidarity between Caribbean and native-black American members.[54] This dispute ended with Eason's ouster from the organization and his unfortunate murder in New Orleans by a Caribbean-born Garveyite. Evidence never directly linked Garvey himself to the tragedy. After the Klan meeting, the organization was plagued with many other internal problems and near constant discord between other prominent UNIA leaders.

However, the tone of Garvey's critics began to soften after his imprisonment in early 1925. Still, not a few of his detractors hoped that when released from jail Garvey would be deported. Fred R. Moore of the *Age* editorialized that such a move would be a "wise combination of mercy and justice." Elsewhere there had always been an undercurrent of genuine feeling, even among those detached from the movement, that Garvey was being unfairly punished because of his race and politics. After his arrest and detention without bail in the summer of 1923, the Richmond *Planet* remarked that a charge of mail fraud did not warrant such severe treatment. In August an Associated Negro Press article released in black newspapers throughout the country editorialized that "the denial of bail of Garvey in [this] circumstance is far more dangerous than all the crimes ever charged against Marcus Garvey."[55]

In Harlem conviction and imprisonment only slightly dampened the enthusiasm of Garvey's rank and file followers. In a review of the movement, sociologist E. Franklin Frazier observed that not only Garvey, but other "foreign Negroes have successfully converted hardshelled Baptists to the movement in spite of the opposition of their ministers." On August 5, 1925, when he had served six months of a five-year sentence in Atlanta Federal Penitentiary, the *Amsterdam News*, no friend of the UNIA leader, reported, "It was literally Garvey's Day in Harlem." At the opening of the annual convention, thousands of men, women, and children crowded the sidewalks to view the UNIA parade, now a tradition in the community. During the convention the following year, support for the incarcerated Garvey was even more impressive.[56] The New York *Herald Tribune* described the scene this way:

> From every window on the route and from hot roof tops hung thousands of Negroes cheering the name of Marcus Aurelius Garvey. . . . On the sidewalks ten deep stood 100,000 more waving and shouting and applauding as the procession opening the first day of the local convention of the U.N.I.A. went blaring by. But Marcus Garvey himself, dreamer of dreams for the future of the Negro race, was not present. He is in the Federal penitentiary in Atlanta, serving a term of five years for fraudulent use of the mails, but his grip on the Negroes of Harlem, whose new and conscious pride of race he was foremost in instilling, apparently had been weakened none at all by his absence.[57]

In the summer and fall of 1927, a series of articles appearing nationwide in the black press called for Garvey's release from prison. In September, as Garvey's health suffered from an asthmatic condition, Kelly Miller, a Garvey critic, called upon blacks to "join in one united petition for the pardon of Marcus Garvey. . . . [T]he government that pardoned Debs, the unreconciled radical, on the ground of health certainly could not with moral consistency insist on keeping Garvey in prison for purpose of breaking his health." Terming Garvey a "political prisoner," the African American *Birmingham Recorder* further noted "there are much worse criminals out of prison than Garvey."[58] Similar statements appeared throughout the country in the *Chicago Whip, Atlanta Independent, Norfolk Journal and Guide*, and other papers.

In such a national atmosphere, the UNIA leader's critics in New York found it difficult to continue assault upon him. In the August 3 issue of the *Amsterdam News*, William Pickens wrote, "Why keep Marcus Garvey in prison? No purpose of any sort is to be served by his continued incarceration; therefore there is no real justice in holding him." Pickens noted that even Garvey's worst enemies, "if they are honest," would admit that the UNIA leader was not a crook.[59]

These sentiments, even among Garvey's critics, together with lengthy petitions to President Coolidge calling for clemency, caused federal authorities considerable concern. Advising the president in November 1927 that the black population now regarded Garvey as a martyr, Attorney General John Sargent urged commutation at once to be followed by immediate deportation. In his opinion, holding Garvey any longer would only create more sentiment in his favor.[60] Indeed by the end of 1927 all but Garvey's most embittered foes were pressured by mounting opinion to at least favor his equal treatment under the law. Concern among blacks as a group appears to have been founded on racial solidarity rather than an awareness of discrimination against Garvey based on his nationality and foreign status. For while some in the press believed his imprisonment was unfair, his deportation was not widely protested by the press.

From the beginning of Caribbean immigrants' visibility in Harlem, some individuals—few more blunt than Fred R. Moore—felt that this group should aid blacks in the American race struggle without threatening native-born dominance in the leadership of the struggle. As for the NAACP position, Du Bois wrote in the *Crisis* that he hoped Garvey could renew his movement—but in Jamaica:

> We have no enmity towards Marcus Garvey. He has a great and worthy dream. We wish him well. He is free; he has a following. He still has a chance to carry on his work in his own country among his own people and to achieve some of his goals. Let him do it. We will be the first to applaud any success he may have.[61]

Ethnicity as an element of community in Harlem failed to be adequately articulated by radicals or more moderate black leaders. Even the Pan-African Congresses, while promoting international linkages within the worldwide black community, failed to address problems among immigrant and native leaders at home. Perhaps the span of years leading in the early part of the twentieth century to the Great Depression of the 1930s was not sufficient in length to provide an arena in which these political differences could be addressed. If only limited though crucial cooperation could be achieved between black leaders in a competitive political arena in America, where repression on the basis of race and national origin ensured Marcus Garvey's expulsion, could black immigrants and natives find more common ground in other fields?

8

Ethnic and Race Enterprise

THE LINK BETWEEN black business development and race progress was almost universally promoted among disparate interest groups and individuals in Harlem during its formative years and after. The conservative *Age*—mouthpiece of the National Negro Business League, the radical press, some key street corner speakers, and the black clergy—believed Harlem's greatest shortcoming was its lack of a strong entrepreneurial base. Between 1900 and 1930 almost any individual of African descent engaged in a business, however small, could expect to be lauded in the black press as a racial hero. "It is hardly possible to place too great stress on the deep significance of business ventures among American Negroes," wrote W. E. B. Du Bois in his 1899 study *The Negro in Business*. Booker T. Washington expressed a similar view in his 1907 publication of the same title.[1] The *Age* advised in 1924 that "Harlem can be helped to progress along the lines of normal social development by a greater number of Negroes engaging in business."[2] The *Negro World*, emphasizing the role of racial and economic solidarity, told readers in 1925, "Every Negro must be brought to realize that every dollar returned to the race is another step up." It editorialized, "the next time a little struggling Negro business in your neighborhood closes its doors, ask yourself how much you have contributed to that failure."[3]

These views may have been a reflection of an era's nationwide ideology that supported the expansion of business along the lines of "the business of America is business." But even some Socialists and Communists felt the expansion of black-owned businesses was a fundamental goal in community life. The columns of Cyril Briggs's *Crusader* regularly highlighted Harlem race businesses.[4] Opinions in Harlem reflected those popular in black communities all over the country. "To the Negro community a business is more than a mere enterprise to make profit for the owner," concluded St. Clair Drake and Horace Cayton in their pioneering Chicago study.[5] A successful black business served as a model of the race's capabilities in a field in which African Americans had been systematically denied opportunity. The Washington, D.C., *Tribune* editorialized in 1926: "The business interest of the group does not belong entirely to the individuals who operate them. They are to a greater extent the property and responsibility of all of us and the posterity of each of us."[6]

Caribbean immigrants' involvement in business enterprises was one of the most conspicuous aspects of their settlement and interaction with the Harlem community.

Most black immigrants' entrepreneurial backgrounds were rooted in experience quite different from the historical realities of the African American minority in America. In the post-Reconstruction American South, a white majority dominated the merchant class, allowing blacks very few opportunities to compete in markets within their own communities. Successful black competitors sometimes faced lynch mobs,[7] though important African American business communities did develop in key southern cities, particularly in nonretail enterprises. In general the Caribbean immigrant entrepreneurs' historical experience had not been shaped by this level of competition in their homelands. Starting a business could be a realistic goal for those who had capital and experience.

In a 1911 study of black business enterprise in Manhattan, sociologist George Edmund Haynes concluded that the social stimuli of the environment and preparation were important factors distinguishing immigrant and native-born entrepreneurs. Of the 330 businesses surveyed, Haynes found that 65, or 19.7 percent, were Caribbean owned. This number was about 10.3 percent greater than the Caribbean immigrant proportion in New York's African American population. "This condition," wrote Haynes, "can hardly be explained on the ground that West Indian Negroes reach New York with more capital, nor is it because West Indians secure employment that is better paid, for they, like the native-born Negroes, are confined to domestic and personal service." In Haynes's opinion, it was due both to the better general education of the average black immigrant and to "initiative developed in an atmosphere freer than that which the southern Negro comes."[8]

Taking Haynes's early study into account, other observations can be made about entrepreneurship throughout the period. While the average black immigrant probably possessed better educational skills than the average southern migrant, and was more accustomed to business as an occupation in his or her homeland, he or she also sometimes brought the experience of a skilled trade which could be turned into a small business. In addition, importing and exporting provided opportunities based on the specialized needs of a growing Caribbean community in New York.[9]

These historical conditions and others partially explain the marked presence of the "West Indian business" in Harlem. But black ethnic entrepreneurship in Harlem must be framed in the larger context of the control of Harlem's businesses by white, often ethnic, entrepreneurs. In 1925 columnist Edgar M. Grey described the black consumer market as "the Negro Slavery in Harlem." In an informal survey of white businesses, he attempted to demonstrate the extent of exploitation. He found that in

> 321 delicatessens, the average daily sales [was] $60, which amounts to $115,560 weekly. Negroes were employed as help in four of these with an average salary of $18 per week, which aggregates the fine sum of $72 in the pockets of Negroes. In these there were employed 642 clerks (not Negroes), who received as salary a total of $25,680 per week. These clerks belong to a union, which does not permit Negroes to become members.[10]

In contrast to black consumers, "the attitude of the white purchasing public has had a tremendous effect on Negro business, because it has failed to forget color in its business dealings. In many lines of business white people will not patronize Negroes at all. . . ."[11] In such an environment the Caribbean-born merchants were important symbols, and their penetration of some business fields represented racial breakthroughs.

But who were Harlem's black-immigrant business people? And how did they interact with the Harlem community? Immigrant and native-born entrepreneurs in Haynes's survey were not new arrivals; most had lived in the city more than ten years and worked in often related occupations before entering business. The typical establishment was a small retail enterprise with floor space of less than a thousand square feet. In 1907, 87 of 128 businesses surveyed had gross receipts of $2,999 or less, and 4 had receipts of $15,000. Haynes felt this was a "creditable showing" for all black business people, indicating that the small amount of capital invested was handled with "considerable energy and ability."[12] Like most community leaders of the day, immigrant entrepreneurs were generally churchgoers, closely allied to preachers and congregations, members of benevolent and fraternal societies, and naturalized citizens. These associations were among their closest ties to the pulse of a broad immigrant and native consumer group. It is difficult to arrive at a reliable business count and even more difficult to identify Caribbean ownership from newspaper accounts. But in one of the rare instances in which the New York *Age* identified the ethnicity of a successful black entrepreneur, a front-page article noted in 1929 that A. A. Austin, president of the Antillian Holding Company, headed the largest business in the country "owned and managed by foreign-born Negroes." Austin's property holdings in Harlem were estimated at two million dollars. In October of that year, Austin and other Caribbean entrepreneurs hosted a dinner in honor of the National Negro Business League president R. R. Moton, Booker T. Washington's successor at Tuskegee. An alliance with Moton, the most influential spokesman for black business development in the country, was an important political move on the part of Harlem's Caribbean businesspeople. Moton made it clear to those present and to the press that he supported cooperation between immigrant and natives. He made peace the theme of his talk.[13]

It is clear from the emphasis of this dinner that ethnic tensions in other aspects of Harlem life extended to the entrepreneurial affairs as well. Native-black consumers did not always view the Caribbean-immigrant entrepreneur favorably. At times the latter's apparent aggressiveness in business matters evoked stereotypical characterizations and unfavorable comparisons to Jewish merchants. But in one view, the immigrants' economic involvement in the community presented no challenge to native blacks' supposed hegemony in politics. As a group, Harlem's immigrant businesspeople were a largely untried political force. Well-known conservative journalist George Schuyler criticized the immigrants for "extremism" and "flights of fancy" in politics but applauded their business pursuits.[14] The editor of the

Age publicized Marcus Garvey's community-based business projects without mentioning the UNIA leader's affiliation with them.[15]

Due to differences in earlier opportunities and work experience, Caribbean and native blacks' enterprises sometimes overlapped but were more often concentrated in divergent fields. Unable to find jobs in the skilled trades, immigrant men launched out as entrepreneurs in their trades. But most of the barbers, hairdressers, painters, dressmakers, mechanics of all kinds, plumbers, butchers, and bakers were natives. They were of about equal numbers with Caribbean-born carpenters and tailors. But black immigrants were more often shoemakers, cigar makers, milliners, jewelers, and importers and exporters. Native-born men were more visible as undertakers, poolroom operators, restauranteurs, and caterers.[16] Caribbean immigrants could be found in all of these enterprises however. New York State censuses suggest that though their numbers increased, black entrepreneurs—immigrant and native born— as an occupation category did not gain proportionately between 1905 and 1925. Throughout the period persons engaged in entrepreneurial pursuits hovered between one and two percentage points of the working population. A sampling of the largest population grouping taken to date counts the figures at 2 percent for native black and 1 percent for Caribbean immigrants. In rank order of participants, these included retail storekeepers, ice and coal dealers, restaurateurs and caterers, undertakers, poolroom operators, pharmacists, and peddlers.[17]

Those engaged in the jewelry business usually learned their skill in their homelands. Failing to find a job in New York's jewelry district, these immigrants with small capital, perhaps earned from a menial job, opened shop in Harlem. Other trades and their unions were almost impossible to enter. "Printers no matter how adept at their trade are driven to their only refuge, operating their own shops," wrote a WPA researcher.[18] A few who did find jobs and were admitted to white unions worked for "colored" wages while saving enough money to go into business for themselves.[19] But the entrepreneurial possibilities for black Caribbeans were enhanced by the demand for island products and foods:

> Thomas & Thomas, Inc., located at 368 West 135 Street, do a considerable exporting and importing business in addition to conducting a tourist agency and automobile express service to railroad stations and steamship piers.
>
> S. P. Thomas of the firm and resident buyer for Grenada, told the *Age* representative that the firm's importing consisted in buying West Indian products wholesale and selling them in the United States. Imports from the West Indies consist largely of cocoa, nutmeg, nuts of many varieties, cinnamon and sarsaparilla bark.[20]

If they could not so easily blend their concerns in other areas, the dietary tastes of the community's diverse people were more comfortably merged. A small group of immigrants was engaged in the transport and distribution of tropical fruits and vegetables. And Harlemites knew Socialist W. A. Domingo as a successful Jamaican businessman engaged in this trade. By the mid-1930s he had the longest record of service in his field.[21] Because blacks often found wholesale marketing of any kind closed to them, Domingo's contribution was important. By distributing his products to black retailers, he expanded race enterprise. His independent income allowed him to pursue his political views more freely.

But in the main, residents' hard-earned dollars were pocketed by merchants who lived elsewhere. The pattern was not accidental. Central Harlem had a relatively small commercial sector as one of the more gentile white sections of Manhattan. As blacks moved in by the thousands, the white merchant class expanded to capture a growing and increasingly profitable consumer market. And according to the New York *Age*, white ethnic merchants made a special effort to keep blacks out of business. Businesses conducted by members of the race had "a hard struggle to keep going." On certain streets merchants and landlords combined efforts to prevent black entrepreneurs from operating at all. A white owner on Seventh Avenue "positively refused" to rent an empty commercial building to blacks, noted the *Age*.[22]

In 1921 the more desirable blocks on Lenox Avenue, so important to Harlem's commercial life, were almost entirely closed to blacks.[23] By mid-decade columnist Edgar M. Grey observed that "the landlords see to it that the stores are put out of the reach of Negro finance, either by 'family leases' or by advertising vacancies only in Jewish and foreign language newspapers."[24] In an editorial entitled "Advice to 125th Street Merchants," the *Age* criticized the narrow outlook of one group of organized merchants:

> Although the Harlem Board of Commerce is made up of Jews and other groups which have been forced to quaff from the cup of race prejudice, at no time had the organization maintained a friendly attitude towards the Negroes of the community. The board's efforts have been more definitely confined to retarding the Negroes' progress than in giving them a helping hand. Keeping the Negro in a prescribed area has been one of the chief aims.

The Harlem Board of Commerce and other similar neighborhood protective associations, while effective in blocking black advance in real estate and commerce, were not supported in their efforts by all uptown Jews and others. The Anglo-Jewish paper the *American Hebrew* condemned the practice while the *Yiddishes Tabgeblatt* supported what it regarded as the self-help efforts of Payton's Afro-American Realty. Jewish small-shop owners did not reap enormous profits from their usually modestly capitalized family businesses and many remained as residents, while most of white Harlem left the neighborhood in a steady stream during the 1920s. The biggest profits were made by outsiders in real estate, the larger grocery markets, and department stores. Speakeasies, pawn shops, and theaters, among the most profitable enterprises, almost never employed black Harlemites. Cabaret owners employed black entertainers, but black patrons were excluded from Harlem's most successful nightclubs.[25]

In such a competitive field the Caribbean-born businesspeople often associated themselves with the concept of the "race enterprise." Real estate agent William Roach told fellow black business people to exercise their "racial and ethical duty" and follow the "Golden Rule" in their dealings with the community. "[T]here is nothing so noble in one's life," he added, "as consciousness that they have rendered their bit to the development of their race."[26] Other businesspeople publicly expressed similar responsibility to race and community. Of course not all were sincere, nor did they uniformly live up to these standards, but because of the precarious and limited opportunities of the marketplace one's abuses could lead to loss of clientele, friends, and livelihood.

Harlem newspapers provide the best record of such enterprise. And the New York *Age*, especially, continued to give its columns to periodic surveys of black business and provided an informal index of black entrepreneurship. In 1921 the paper concluded on the basis of its own survey that in Harlem the race was making progress despite the resistance of white merchants on Lenox Avenue. The *Age* regarded the expansion of the race enterprise as a social as well as an economic development. All "respectable" business people of color, whether from the British-held Caribbean, Cuba, or Puerto Rico, were likely to be included in the survey. While the nativity of Cuban and Puerto Rican business people was usually specified, the paper apparently assumed that English-speaking black immigrants were "race" entrepreneurs. In the case of the Spanish-speaking merchants from the Caribbean, the *Age* made a special effort to define these businesses as race enterprises.[27]

In its various surveys the *Age* took special notice of blacks in business fields in which only whites had formerly operated. A 1921 headline read, "Lenox Avenue's Perfumery Company Only One of Kind in U.S." This business, the Verbena Perfumery Company, was owned by Bernard Augustine, an immigrant and chemist. Augustine had worked for years at a downtown French perfume company. With savings from his earnings, he opened a small shop in Harlem, where he manufactured his own line of powders, perfumes, and toilet articles. His company sold perfumes in wholesale lots to many of the large, white retail stores of the city and distributed to black barbershops and beauty salons in Harlem. In addition the company conducted a large export business in Puerto Rico, Cuba, the Panama Canal Zone, the Dominican Republic, Haiti, and the Virgin Islands.[28]

Mixed with the satisfaction that blacks were breaking into areas formerly dominated by whites was a concern for demonstrating the race's capabilities as craftspeople. Skills in the crafts not only could lead to more secure and higher-paying, wage-stabilized jobs, but could permit skilled workers to start their own businesses. Yet most craft unions of the time barred blacks altogether by constitution, ritual, or simply by agreement of the membership. Race prejudice, a desire for job security and job monopoly, and wage control were among the reasons for this. Apprenticeship ranks were therefore cut off or restricted because they led to skilled training in the craft.[29]

Facing discrimination in New York's garment industry and gaining no outlet there for their creative talents, a few immigrant and native women opened businesses in Harlem. Some shopkeepers who had formerly worked in downtown dress or millinery stores attracted white customers who had previously shopped there. W. A. Domingo noted in Alain Locke's 1925 *New Negro* that "on Seventh Avenue [in Harlem] a West Indian woman conducted a millinery shop that would be a credit to Fifth Avenue." Odessa Warren Grey opened her business in her apartment before moving to Seventh Avenue. The *Age* pointed out that "the store had one of the largest stocks of any millinery store in Harlem, and has trained several girls as milliners, who are now employed in the shop."[30]

The millinery trade was not limited to immigrants, but as the case of southern migrant Frank Yancy shows, natives encountered great difficulty in learning the technical side of the industry. Working in a hat factory was the best way to learn the craft of hat making. But Yancy found that in his native Georgia as well as in New York no such work was available to blacks. He finally paid three thousand dollars to an old Connecticut hatter to teach him the trade by day while he worked other jobs at night. To learn the chemical process, he was compelled to offer his labor free. He finally entered the business in 1921 only after "mountains of obstacles and discouragement." Referring to Yancy's enterprise in 1930, the *Amsterdam News* informed its readers, "Harlem boasts a single factory where men and women's hats are made under the ownership of a Negro."[31]

Similar welcomes greeted the opening of Caribbean-owned businesses. When Jamaican Arthur Q. Hart launched his five-and-ten department store in 1920, the New York *Age* observed, "He is the first Negro to bring the Woolworth idea to Harlem." In 1922 Hart moved his store to the ground floor of the new black-owned Renaissance Theater Building at 138th Street. The store's opening nearly matched the enthusiasm stirred by Garvey's Black Star Line. "Thousands of people thronged the auspicious space all day and were charmed and delighted by the splendid display of useful things which have made the name of Hart a household word in Harlem. . . . At last Harlem has a real store owned and controlled and managed by colored people that commands respect and admiration." The store hired twenty native and Caribbean black women as clerks. The *Amsterdam News* editorialized that Hart and Company, Inc., which covered a quarter of a block, was a matter of "historic importance to us all, as it should mark a new era of our business development in Harlem." The Hart store was in the end unable to counter competition from the Woolworth chain.[32]

Community excitement over the opening of the Renaissance Theater Building that housed Hart's Department Store was typical of the community's enthusiasm for race enterprise. William Roach's Caribbean-owned Sarco Realty completed construction on the building in 1922 at a cost of $175,000. The theater seated 950 people and its adjacent building provided space for six stores leased to black proprietors.[33]

But despite gains in individual self-esteem, many business achievements, though important, did not translate into economic gains for the community. By the mid-1920s optimism about expansion of black-owned enterprises turned to more realistic appraisal of an economic situation over which residents struggled to gain control. Caribbean editor R. T. Brown of the *Negro World* told readers in 1929 that self-reliance was needed more than ever: "There are those of us who feel a smug complacency, as we strut about the streets of Harlem and feel the presence of these piles of brick and stone and mortar as they flank our walk, and we think Harlem is a Negro section, a colored township."[34] But most property, Brown pointed out, was still owned by those outside the community.

Indeed the Renaissance Theatre met with hard times by 1926. In that year, because of heavy indebtedness, financial backers took over the property and leased it back to the Renaissance Theatre Corporation. By 1933 the last vestige of black management was gone and the last two black cashiers were fired.[35]

While the failure of the Renaissance Theatre project could be traced to the strains of the depression, the cashiers' dismissals and the replacement of black by white management was interpreted as outside encroachment. Harlem readers might have gleaned even more sinister motives from a front page *Age* article in 1930 in which Nelson Mona Roach, spouse of William Roach and an officer of the corporation, was reported to have been arrested for passing a bad check in the amount of $154. Despite her community stature, she was sentenced to a term of one to three years on Welfare Island. In a letter to the *Age*, Mona Roach maintained that certain Park Row lawyers had told her that if she exposed their plans to take over the company she would find herself in the insane asylum or jail and "[I] wouldn't know how I got there." For the other company officers, the takeover was an even greater personal tragedy. One of them, treasurer and Montserratan Joseph Sweeney, committed suicide following the foreclosure.[36]

The fact that not a single bank in Harlem was owned by blacks until 1948 was a major problem faced by race enterprises. Community leaders of every description made several attempts to set up such an enterprise in the 1920s but were never granted a charter. Many businesses, including those of black immigrants, suffered from inadequate capitalization. Often initial investments had to be made from savings of hard-earned dollars since black entrepreneurs were generally not considered good business risks by New York bankers.[37]

Black businessman Charles H. Anderson (no relation to the Republican politician) of Jacksonville, Florida, attempted to start a bank in Harlem in 1921. He acquired a building at the corner of Lenox and 135th Street, opposite the New York Chelsea Bank. But according to press accounts, white bankers who feared the loss of black depositors prevented Anderson from obtaining a charter. In an attempt to placate disgruntled depositors, the Chelsea Bank hired two black tellers.[38]

The Dunbar National Bank, established in 1928 by John D. Rockefeller, Jr. as part of the Dunbar Apartments, was billed as a community enterprise, but from its first day Harlem's business people found that their interest would not be served. "The desire on the part of prominent and capable Negro businessmen of Harlem to have serving the community a bank with a white and colored board of directors has not been realized . . . ," reported the *Amsterdam News*. Adding insult to injury, a Rockefeller representative said, "The Dunbar Bank is an experiment and we must move slowly in deciding upon our policies, and until we see the response of the representative Negro businessmen of Harlem to this effort to be of assistance to them, we have to delay consideration of appointing any of them as directors of the institution."[39]

Harlem businessmen were also told that 50 percent of the available stock would be offered for sale to blacks. When the bank opened, however, Rockefeller held 75 percent and refused to sell the remaining 25 percent until he was "sure the bank would succeed." Scores of people opened accounts on the first day of business and a reported five thousand people visited the bank. The New York *Age* called it a significant event in the "commercial development of Harlem."[40] Rockefeller sold no stock and in 1938 withdrew his support when even well-to-do black depositors could no longer maintain accounts. Finally in 1948 the black-controlled Carver Federal Loan and Savings Association was founded as the inspiration of former Garveyite Dr. Joseph D. Gibson of Barbados and Charles Petioni of Trinidad.[41] Before leaving for the United States in 1918, Petioni formed a Penny Savings Bank and had gained some experience in this area.

The absence of credit from orthodox financial institutions in New York encouraged middle- and upper-class Caribbeans to adopt the practice of rotating credit. It is not possible to determine its extent among black enterprises in Harlem, but Amy Jacques-Garvey noted that in general the system known as "partners" was fairly widespread in the 1920s and 1930s, though the depression lessened its usage.[42] Louise Burnham, a hairdresser and native of Barbados, ran a rotating credit association "for years" after 1930, according to an account of her daughter-in-law, Dorothy Burnham. She bought the family home on "Strivers Row" from money she saved.[43] Amy Jacques-Garvey noted that women were active in running the "partners," raising initial capital for family members to launch small businesses. Shopkeepers then operated bigger pools to finance the operation of existing businesses.

To be sure, black enterprises could not and did not emancipate Harlem. It could not do so whatever the contribution of immigrants or the social consciousness of the black business community. Nor did success in business or property ownership much alleviate the race problem for individuals so engaged. In Harlem white owners never relinquished their hold on property or on the community's retail market. Yet, the expansion of black business during the 1920s by Caribbean-born entrepreneurs did have significant implications for the group's entry into the Afro-American community. Almost immediately, they became significant members of the black middle class in Harlem, winning and sharing positions of influence.

In 1929, with the help of the National Negro Business League, more than a hundred of Harlem's black-owned businesses were organized into the Colored Merchants Association (CMA) with immigrant Harold C. Francis, owner of the West

Indian Bakery, as its first president. Representing more than one-fourth of Harlem's businesses, its primary purpose was to "buy merchandise cooperatively" and sell it at a price more competitive with whites and to extend credit to members. A native member of the CMA stores, James A. Jackson offered a three-month modern-management training course for grocers, which enrolled more than 138 individuals.[44]

A. A. Austin's Antillian Realty Corporation was also affiliated with the CMA.[45] Austin later had one of the best financial records during the depression, although the company nearly folded in 1938. Through business, individual Caribbean-born Harlemites and natives gained considerable access to power through the traditional channels in Harlem. The business sector's influence grew steadily throughout the period and was enhanced by experiences gained trying to find practical solutions to pressing economic problems. But it lagged behind developments in the political and social spheres, where organizational efforts proved to be so important to the community's sense of progress and development. In business the individual entrepreneur, rather than organizations such as the CMA, were the norm. Still it was largely via their economic entrenchment that certain immigrants gained a notable presence in politics later. The community as a whole did not reap a lasting economic benefit from business accomplishments. The depression was too overwhelming a force for such new business energies to overcome. Yet Harlemites in theory remained supportive of the concept of the "race enterprise."

The cooperative organizational developments may suggest Harlem's potential as an economically independent community. The most stimulating influences along these lines had been achieved through the black church and, despite its ultimate difficulties, the UNIA. The tremendous fund-raising capacity of this organization had demonstrated that an ideology together with an organization could accomplish goals which the individual African—American or Caribbean—entrepreneur could not achieve alone.

9

The Underground Entrepreneur

"THE CASUAL STROLLER along Harlem thoroughfares can hear without conscious efforts at eavesdropping, comment from almost every group of two or more which he might pass concerning some phase of the 'Numbers playing game,'" observed the New York *Age* in 1924.[1] This illegal lottery was the largest employer in Harlem and for a while the largest business controlled by blacks anywhere. Moreover, many small businesses would not have survived had they not been connected with numbers. "In every street either a candy store, barber shop, beauty parlor or tavern is a collection headquarters called a 'drop,'" observed writer Roi Ottley.[2]

When the African American community moved uptown, numbers became virtually an industry, and by the 1920s immigrant names such as Cuban Alexander Pompez, Panama Francis, Stephanie St. Claire, and Casper Holstein were heard most often. They had native associates, but immigrant names stand out in the field. Numbers was played widely in the Caribbean and Latin America throughout much of the nineteenth century and in the United States in the last quarter of the same century. In general, at first Caribbean immigrants were able to organize numbers operations faster than native blacks in New York because of past experience at accumulating capital for such purposes. But in other urban centers, such as Chicago, black Americans originated and dominated the numbers operations.

Until the mid-1920s, numbers was played openly in Harlem with little concern about interference from the police; the latter played regularly themselves.[3] The New York *Sun* reported that during this period, activity "flourished so openly that anyone, even a perfect stranger had only to ask where he might lay a bet, to be swamped with offers from runners."[4] Ministers seldom denounced the game from their pulpits because they sometimes played.[5] Indeed, the head of a numbers operation, a banker, was likely to be an active member of the church and a generous contributor to the Sunday collection plate.[6]

With a few notable exceptions, few scholars have given any significant consideration to this pervasive community activity still common in black urban settings.[7] In most studies of Harlem, numbers is mentioned only in passing or not at all. Many Harlem contemporaries shared the opinion that black numbers operators played influential, even positive, roles in the community. The appeal of numbers in Harlem as elsewhere was rooted in the scarcity of money, work, and opportunity. "The reasons for the Negroes playing and banking the numbers was [purely] economic," wrote columnist Edgar M. Grey. "Harlem plays the numbers because Harlem wants and needs money."[8] Still, this reality did not mean that an economy dependent on numbers was a preferred way of structuring or building community life.

The form of lottery known as "policy" was not new to New Yorkers. However, the game was declared illegal by state law in 1901 and virtually stamped out with the arrest of Al Adams, one of its most powerful bankers. Still, enthusiasm remained. Policy was revitalized when thousands of English-speaking black immigrants came to New York after 1914 from Cuba and Central America, where lotteries were popular and legal. According to Claude McKay, these new arrivals played numbers in Cuban and Puerto Rican barbershops in Manhattan's east nineties. The Hispanic version was called *bolita* or *paquerita*. Immigrants from the British-held Caribbean called it numbers or policy and helped popularize the game in Harlem.[9]

A numbers operation consisted of a banker, a group of collectors or runners who took bets from customers, and perhaps several controllers who gathered the money and turned it in to the "bank." Others were employed at the bank as clerks and accountants plying adding machines and typewriters. A legal staff was also necessary, for even in the early days the police were compelled to make a certain number of arrests to "keep their records up." A bail bondsman came in handy in case a collector was arrested. The banker paid all fines imposed on his employees. He also arranged all necessary political alignments so that neither the police nor crusading reformers could effectively interfere with the smooth running of the business.[10] A successful Harlem banker would have made special campaign contributions to key political candidates, to black and white political bosses, and to police and court officials. Even after these expenses the banker might pocket $2,000 to $6,000 a week.

A banker employed ten to fifty people in his or her operation. At the height of black control during the 1920s, there were approximately 30 to 50 banks in Harlem, and this count did not include the smaller operations.[11] No precise figure of persons is possible, but estimates range from 1,000 to 2,000 in the 1920s. It was at this level that numbers began to affect the community directly. As perhaps the largest supplier of jobs, some numbers bankers held respected community positions and exercised considerable influence. But they had to be shrewd manipulators of the social, economic, and political scene to accomplish this. In Chicago near the end of—and in spite of—the depression, one numbers syndicate was paying a weekly payroll of $25,000 according to Drake and Cayton.[12] Before its takeover by white gangsters in the 1930s, the operation in Harlem—where the individual banker rather than a syndicate prevailed—a bank could still net several thousand dollars a week after expenses. This was the case even after large wins or "hits" by players. Normally, "hits" averaged around 40 percent of a bank's gross take. More successful operations took in even more money on a daily basis.

The large sum of money many bankers made and invested in Harlem property and other businesses helped raise their own as well as the community's expectations about economic progress. A banker's success depended upon his or her good reputation and sense of responsibility. Caribbean immigrant numbers bankers collaborated effectively with other bases of power, such as the press and Harlem business people. Residents expected bankers to deal fairly with players and to give back some of their profit to Harlem or to a worthy race cause. A banker's investments took many forms. No one knew how many legitimate community businesses were set up by numbers money, but it was substantial. Legitimate businessmen, candy stores, and mom-and-pop operations also sometimes rented space to numbers bankers to help cover expenses.

Newspapers seldom mentioned bankers by name in their coverage of the numbers operation. Even articles favorable to numbers rarely revealed names. Edgar Grey informed New York *News* readers that "one of the numbers bankers made it possible for five colored students to be sent to the Hampton Normal and Industrial Institute, and is now supporting those five young men in that school."[13] But, to be sure, the majority of residents did not get back the millions of dollars—in pennies, nickels, and dimes—they put into the lottery, and some were hopelessly lured by the dream of making a big hit. "What excites people about the policy game are the gaudy returns," noted Roi Ottley. "One cent played on a number brings five dollars but the chances of winning are [very slight]. Yet not a day passes in the Negro neighborhood, but somebody wins, and naturally shows his winnings to the neighbors."[14]

Anyone could play the lottery with bets as low as one cent. The odds made winning difficult, but regular players usually "hit" from time to time. The basic rule of the lottery was very simple: The player took a chance that he or she could pick the set of three digits between 000 and 999 that would match the set appearing in an agreed upon tabulation at a race track, clearinghouse, or elsewhere. Though bets were taken from anyone, the runner often had a close relationship with his regular customers. They were usually friends, family members, fellow laborers, or students. The success of the system was based on self-enforced honesty, for the people a runner dealt with were usually the people he or she saw and lived with every day. Collectors were well known to residents. According to the New York *Times* in November 1925, a crowd of 1,500 Harlemites gathered on Lenox Avenue in front of Edward Piper's cigar store when police arrested him for collecting policy slips. Only the officers' drawn pistols prevented the crowd from rescuing Piper.[15]

Numbers playing was not limited to the working classes. The New York *Age* reported that "men and women from all walks of life are addicted to it. . . . They are not always of the lower social strata." Successful business people were known to place large bets.[16] White New Yorkers also played the Harlem numbers. In 1926 an *Evening Graphic* reporter claimed, "I know one apartment house in West End Avenue where most of the white tenants are betting . . . and paying their dues to a colored collector."[17]

The careers of some of Harlem's Caribbean bankers provide important insights into numbers as a social phenomenon and the manner in which these immigrants interacted with the community. Because Harlem newspapers did not focus extensive publicity on the numbers during the 1920s, most information about individual bankers became available only after the era of black control ended during the 1930s. Investigation of illegal lotteries by federal judge Samuel Seabury in 1931 was the center of considerable publicity. But the 1938 trial of celebrated Tammany boss Jimmy Hines, accused of selling protection to the notorious "Dutch" Schultz gang, brought out some interesting revelations about Harlem numbers. With Hines's "protection," Schultz allegedly beat and bloodied a dozen black policy bankers in his effort to control the game.

Newspaper accounts of their "persecution" by the law or white gangsters reflect a general conviction that the black bankers of whatever ethnic origin were regarded as race heroes in Harlem. In his 1938 coverage of the trial, Jamaican Wendell Malliet, a reporter for the *Amsterdam News*, was convinced that "had the white gangsters not 'muscled in' on the policy game as it was then being operated by the pioneers . . . it would no doubt have continued an illegal but not an immoral and racketeering enterprise. . . . But when . . . Dutch Schultz and his henchmen . . . [moved in] every conceivable method known to be used by gangsters was brought into the policy game." In the same issue the *News* editorialized that "Negroes originated numbers playing. . . . It is ironical but true that Negroes build things only to have them taken away and successfully exploited by the white man."[18]

When Schultz and government investigators moved in, some successful black operators closed down completely, went into legitimate business, or left the country. Choosing the last alternative was Panama Francis, so called because he wore only Panama hats and because he had lived and worked in Panama, where he learned the policy game. In the twenties Francis lived at 132 West 128th Street, where rumors held he kept his money in nail kegs and suitcases in a cellar guarded by three Belgian police dogs.[19] Panama Francis was known as one of the most fearless bankers in the business because he accepted large plays of one, two, and three dollars when most numbers barons preferred the smaller nickel and dime games. The larger bets could break a banker if a number hit, but Francis always paid off. According to the *Amsterdam News*, Francis fled to his native Grenada in 1932 with a reported $1,000,000 to escape arrest for income tax evasion. In an article entitled "Panama Francis Is Set for Life," the paper reveled in the fact that he had made good his escape. In Grenada he reportedly bought the Western Union Building for $250,000 and leased it back to the company for ninety-nine years. "The income from the Western Union alone, some of the policy king's friends declare, is enough to keep him on easy street for the rest of his life." Francis also reportedly loaned the government of Grenada $500,000, on which he collected 4 percent interest.[20]

Cuban-born Alexander Pompez was another successful banker but was forced, at gunpoint, to submit to Schultz's ring. Said Pompez, "I was ordered to visit the home of 'Dixie' Davis in West End Avenue in 1932. The Dutchman came after I got there. He took me in a small room and placed a gun on the table." Pompez was allowed to continue in business but was forced to pay Schultz a percentage of his bank. Pompez, "Big Joe" Ison, and a number of other barons maintained banks in Harlem's fashionable black bourgeoisie section, known as "Sugar Hill," on Edgecomb and St. Nicholas Avenues.[21]

Pompez was nationally known in black political and fraternal circles. Most sports-minded African Americans knew him as an influential member of the Negro National League (NNL), organized in 1920, and as the owner of the famous New York–based Cuban Stars baseball team, which he purchased with his numbers earnings. Sports, particularly baseball and boxing, were an important cross-cultural link between immigrant and native men. Many black players went down to the Caribbean to play baseball in the off-season. In Harlem, as in other places around the country, the Cuban Stars and the New York Black Yankees drew thousands whenever they played. This was the era of the "Negro Leagues," when black teams were compelled to remain separate from the national white professional leagues. Pompez, a passionate baseball fan and former player, spent large sums of money earned from numbers to "make professional baseball among Negroes a success" in the 1920s.[22]

Other numbers bankers joined him in this endeavor, most notably "Gus" Greenlee, a native of North Carolina, the "policy king" of Pittsburgh, whose team, the Pittsburgh Crawfords, with players like pitcher Leroy "Satchel" Paige and slugger Josh Gibson, dominated the colored leagues in the 1930s. As fans flocked to see their teams, both Pompez and Greenlee responded to community leaders and fans and purchased or built sports facilities for team and community use. Pompez purchased Dyckman Oval, one of the largest sports arenas in New York, and Greenlee built his own stadium at a cost of $100,000 so that—as he told the public—the black community in Pittsburgh could have a facility close by.[23]

When Schultz fell victim to gangland bullets in 1935, Pompez re-emerged as a major Harlem banker. Having earned a reputation as a "good, square guy," the *Amsterdam News* reported, he gained the backing of many numbers runners and controllers. But he was soon forced to flee to Mexico as government agents moved in to stamp out the game. In 1938 he returned under indictment and testified for the prosecution in the Jimmy Hines affair.[24]

Like Pompez, banker Wilfred Brunder was compelled to flee to his native Bermuda during the Seabury investigations. The New York *Times* reported that Brunder deposited $1,750,000 in banks over a six-year period. When federal agents cooled their search, Brunder returned, divested himself of his interest in numbers, and went into Harlem real estate.[25]

Another banker who made large sums of money during the twenties was Puerto Rican Jose Enrique Miro, better known by his Anglicized name, Henry Miro. He came to the United States in 1916 but only went into the policy business ten years later. In four years Miro reportedly deposited $1,251,000 in his bank account. In 1930 he was "as large an operator as any in the city." In New York City he set up millinery shops where black women were employed. He was believed to have collected a million dollars a year until prosecuted by federal authorities in 1931.[26]

Most policy bankers were closely involved with building up a wide variety of businesses and influencing public opinion about business through their philanthropy. Their assets would not be matched, and during the 1920s established and emerging leaders in Harlem never launched any organized assault upon them. This was collaboration, but most regarded it as necessary.

Perhaps more spectacular than that of any of the black male policy bankers was the career of Madame Stephanie St. Clair. The details of her biography are sketchy, but she was believed to have been born in France, probably of French Caribbean immigrant parents. She was known in Harlem during the 1920s and early 1930s as the "Numbers Queen." It is not clear how she got her start in policy, but according to the *Amsterdam News* she began her operation in 1923 at the age of 24.[27] She lived at 409 Edgecomb Avenue in the heart of fashionable "Sugar Hill" and gained notoriety—and the admiration of Harlemites—by exposing connections between the New York police and numbers and by successfully defying Dutch Schultz when few other bankers could or would.

During 1928 and 1929, amidst increasing reports of brutality against Harlem citizens, the police began systematic raids on community policy operations. Their vigilance, however, was selective within a pattern of graft, where some individuals caught with policy slips paid the police or went to jail. In the fall of 1929, St. Clair, in a surprise move, began a public campaign against the practice of search without warrants and other police harassments.[28] In space she purchased in the *Amsterdam News*, she wrote a series of weekly articles accompanied by a large photograph of herself. Such an open admission of her connection to numbers was daring and quite unusual. She reprinted letters she had written to Mayor James Walker and Governor Franklin Roosevelt protesting the actions of Harlem police. In one letter to the mayor, she claimed that both black and white detectives framed individuals. "Sometimes the detectives find policy slips in their search, but if you pay them from $500 to $2,000, you are sure to come back home. If you pay them nothing, you are sure to get a sentence from 60 to 90 days in the workhouse."[29]

St. Clair's exposé led to the suspension of several police officers, and she warned in her October 9 message that "many more . . . will be in the same predicament if they do not stop framing colored people." Black policemen would meet the same fate as white, she warned.[30] However, St. Clair herself was arrested in January of 1930 for "possession of policy slips." Though she claimed that the arresting officers framed her, she was later sentenced to eight months and twenty days in jail, but when released in December, she returned as fiery as ever. As the *Amsterdam News* reported, "Mme. Stephanie St. Clair, 31, militant enemy of the Harlem police, stepped from prison walls on Welfare Island last Wednesday and threw a bombshell in the investigation of the 'policy' racket, police and Magistrate Courts on Monday when she declared she paid $6,600 to a lieutenant and plain clothes officers of the

Sixth Division, only to be framed and sent to the Work House."[31] St. Clair's story, according to the *Amsterdam News*, was borne out in part by canceled checks.

Though she may have been motivated as much by revenge as by a desire to stamp out injustice, the attention that she directed to police corruption and brutality only gained her more support among community residents. She was also the organizer of the French Legal Aid Society in Harlem. A naturalized citizen herself, she urged her fellow immigrants to qualify and become registered voters to stamp out corruption.[32]

Her crusade coincided with other community movements against police harassment and brutality by stepladder speakers and establishment spokesmen. Crowded and poor housing, rising unemployment and sickness, a lack of recreational facilities, and double and triple school-day sessions had serious social consequences. As the depression drew near, street gangs and petty crime increased. Police stepped up their arrests of black males, women, and children. In 1919 black children accounted for only 4.2 percent of the cases in New York's Children's Court. By 1930 this ratio had risen to 11.7 percent and by 1938 to 25 percent, all while the numbers of white children arraigned were declining by nearly 40 percent. Police arrests of black males and females increased at an even faster rate. In the late 1920s and early 1930s, the number of black women arrested soared to nearly 50 percent of all arrested women in New York City. Too frequently—in 80 percent of all cases—these women were erroneously charged with prostitution. The Harlem community was enraged. St. Clair's campaign against the police was a shrewd political maneuver.[33] She also formed an alliance with and in 1936 married the popular, flamboyant jobs campaign leader Sufi Abdul Hamid, though the union was short-lived.

By the time Dutch Schultz moved in on numbers, St. Clair was already a folk hero. She openly defied the "Dutchman" and, when warned about the gangster's capacity for violence, reportedly declared, "I am not afraid of Dutch Schultz or any other man living. He'll never touch me!"[34] Instead, St. Clair organized the small black numbers bankers ignored by the racketeers and operated outside Schultz's influence. She also waged a private war against white shopkeepers who worked with the gangster's henchmen. These were usually cigar, candy, and newspaper stand proprietors whose businesses served as fronts for Schultz's collectors. "She entered their stores one after the other and single handedly smashed plate glass cases, snatched and destroyed policy slips and ordered the 'small timers' to get out of Harlem."[35] According to the *Amsterdam News*, when government officials finally attempted to arrest Schultz, she supplied information for the raid. In her crusade against the white bankers, she reported they were writing slips for minors and she furnished evidence against them and communicated with representatives of the Children's Aide Society.[36] In 1935 when Schultz lay dying in a Newark hospital, he reportedly received a telegram which read, "So you Sow—So shall Ye Reap, signed Madame, Queen of Policy." Even after her reign as the "Numbers Queen" ended, Mme. St. Clair remained a colorful figure. During her brief marriage to Sufi Abdul Hamid, the two were a dashing couple. Sufi, a black American, was now an imposing personality spearheading noisy protests in Harlem. Dressed in long green robe and turban, he was the most exciting community leader since Marcus Garvey. After considerable pressure, his organization, the Negro Clerical and Industrial Alliance, succeeded in gaining work for blacks in Harlem's shopping districts. Sufi's marriage to St. Clair did not seem at all incompatible with a community action campaign, although personal incompatibilities had by 1938 doomed the union.[37]

While St. Clair appears to have doggedly clung to her place in the numbers racket by sheer defiance and clever manipulation of public opinion, the banker with the most intricate connections to Harlem's black establishment was Casper Holstein. His preeminence in fraternal circles and crusade for Virgin Island citizenship were known and respected. Born in Christiansted, St. Croix, in 1876, Holstein came to New York with his mother in 1894. He graduated from high school in Brooklyn but could only find work as a bellhop in a New York hotel. After serving four years in the United States Navy, he found employment with a Wall Street broker from whom he learned financial investment. Since Holstein preferred to keep a low profile in his numbers operation, it is not clear how or when he became involved in the game. But WPA researcher Sadie Hall reported that at the peak of Holstein's operation he took in five thousand dollars a day. From his profits, he purchased three of the "finest apartment houses in Harlem, a fleet of expensive motor cars, a home on Long Island, and several thousand acres in Virginia."[38]

But Holstein, a millionaire by the mid-1920s, gave away much of his money. For this he was admired by the masses and "the best people of the community." He reportedly circulated with the "cream" of Harlem society. But unlike Harlem's "upper crust," Holstein gave five hundred baskets of food and gifts at Christmas to needy residents and was known to have contributed to a number of charities, including Catholic and Jewish.[39] He also gave to Marcus Garvey's UNIA; wrote a regular column in the *Negro World*; and in 1927, when Liberty Hall was sold at an auction, Holstein paid $36,000 for the facility and took over its mortgage in order to "keep the structure in black hands." The New York *Age*, without reference to Holstein's numbers connections, regarded this action as a community service.[40]

Hubert Harrison described Holstein as the only black patron of the arts in New York.[41] He sponsored the annual Urban League's *Opportunity* magazine writer's contest, contributing $1,000 to contest winners in the Casper Holstein Award.[42] Native-born poet Langston Hughes, recalling that his work had been snubbed by segments of polite black society, noted that Holstein "was a great help to poor poets." The literary contests, he wrote, "were held with funds given by . . . a wealthy West Indian numbers banker who did good things with his money, such as educating boys and girls at colleges in the South, building decent houses in Harlem, and backing literary contests to encourage colored writers."[43] Holstein also reportedly contributed money toward the publication of Alain Locke's *The New Negro*, a leading anthology of the Harlem Renaissance. In 1928, he contributed the first gift of $1,000 in a

$100,000 Fisk University fund-raising drive. He also gave sums to Howard University and other African American schools. According to a Virgin Islands Department of Education biography, he paid for the education of students who attended Harvard, Columbia, New York University, Howard, Hampton, and other institutions at undergraduate, graduate, and professional levels. "Numbered among them were future college presidents, deans, professors, attorneys, medical doctors and heads of government departments."[44] In addition, Holstein generously contributed to the education of young people in the Caribbean.

In Harlem, Holstein was a friend to the working class from his homeland. "Here in New York," wrote Eric Walrond, "among Virgin Islanders he is looked upon as some sort of messiah."[45] He gave money to pay their house rents, medical and grocery bills, funeral expenses, and countless other costs.[46] His financial support to Virgin Islanders at home was considerable. After a disastrous hurricane in 1924, he established a hurricane relief fund of $100,000. When another storm struck in 1928, he chartered a steamship to deliver lumber and other building materials and sent tradesmen from New York to help residents rebuild their homes. Holstein also purchased an estate in St. Croix, imported purebred cattle from the United States, and established a dairy farm from which free milk was distributed to needy children.[47]

Holstein's apparent unselfish generosity to numerous worthy causes generally served to protect his reputation, though many in Harlem knew he acquired his wealth through the illegal numbers operation. In most early newspaper references to him—1920 to 1927—he is referred to only as a "wealthy Harlem businessman." However, on August 3, 1927, the *Amsterdam News* reported: "An apartment said to be owned by Casper Holstein, philanthropist and erstwhile disciple of Marcus Garvey, at No. 507 Lenox Avenue, near 135th Street, was raided Friday afternoon by police sent out to round up 'numbers bankers.'" In the issue of the following week, editor William Kelley defended the paper's decision to print the story. "[We] do not permit friendships to interfere with what we consider news." It is not clear why Kelley printed Holstein's name in connection with a numbers raid when the paper had not previously done so. "Unlike one of our contemporaries [the *Age*], we do not now, nor have we ever waged a campaign against 'policy' or numbers playing in Harlem, despite the fact that we believe this form of gambling to be extremely demoralizing upon the community."[48]

But some in Harlem were of course annoyed by Holstein, though wary of his money and influence. Among these were a few older, established intellectual and professional leaders who perhaps scorned his folk celebrity and lack of family background and standing. Still, they were not loud in their disapproval. A lack of economic and educational opportunities for blacks had encouraged if not determined lopsided community development at all levels of its social, economic, and political life.

In any case, by August 17, Holstein served the general manager of the *Amsterdam News* with a libel complaint alleging that his "credit, reputation, and general standing" in the community had been damaged by the paper to the extent of $100,000.[49] Apparently the suit was later dropped and settled out of court. Meanwhile, a number of articles favorable to Holstein appeared in the *Age*. Just before the Elks National Convention in New York, he helped complete preparations costing $20,000, reported the paper. The *Age* also gave him credit for using his diplomacy to avert a split in the organization.[50] In December, the Harlem Elk Monarch Lodge No. 45 banquet honored Holstein and two other distinguished members. Mayor James Walker and Aldermanic President Joseph K. McKee sent telegrams in recognition of the occasion.[51]

In truth, Holstein's "standing in the community" was unaffected by the *Amsterdam News* report. He continued to meet socially with key political figures. Alderman Fred R. Moore, owner of the *Age*, and Mrs. Moore were the special guests of an annual Ladies Night Dinner sponsored by Holstein's Turf Club, Inc. in February 1928. Moore made a brief address complimenting the club and its founder for the "splendid charitable work it had done in the community."[52] Neither the *Age* nor the *Amsterdam News* focused on Holstein's Caribbean background, unless in reference to his connection with the well-known Virgin Islands Congressional Council.

The influential position Holstein attained in the Harlem community was not, however, protection enough from mobsters hoping to hone in on the Harlem rackets. In September 1928, gangsters abducted him from the street in front of his apartment building. He was reportedly blindfolded, driven away, and held for $50,000 ransom. Harlem residents were alarmed during Holstein's two-day absence and feared he would not return alive. "He is Harlem's favored hero," the New York *Times* reported, "because of his wealth, his sporting proclivities and his philanthropies among the people of his race." "All Harlem Is Stirred with Excitement when Fraternal Leader and Philanthropist Falls Victim to Ruthless Bandit Group," read an *Age* headline.[53]

Though relieved, residents were puzzled when the numbers banker returned as suddenly as he had disappeared and refused to assist police in the capture of the perpetrators. Because of Holstein's closed-lipped stance, some Harlem residents suspected the kidnapping had been a hoax. But cigarette burns, bruises, and evidence that Holstein had paid up to $30,000 quickly convinced skeptics.[54] And increasing violence against other black bankers by white mobsters made Holstein's kidnapping look like a general invasion of the black numbers industry. One former Harlem resident recalled that Holstein, the most successful black operator, was reportedly ordered to "get out" of the numbers business.[55]

When the Schultz gang took over in 1931, Holstein retired completely and devoted his time to lodge politics, legitimate business, and the Virgin Islands Congressional Council. As with a few other leading numbers bankers, Holstein's focus not only on business but on social and political issues tied him even closer to the native-born and immigrant Harlem community. His concentration on securing equal political rights for black Virgin Islanders eventually drained his financial resources. But his support of the movement for a civil government was believed to be a key factor in the removal of U.S. naval rule in 1931.[56] The governor of the new civil administration, a white southerner, was unpopular and a mass movement of home people and New York Virgin Islanders led by Holstein resulted in his removal in 1935. But as his resources dwindled, Holstein found he had few friends among white establishment politicians. His legitimate businesses began to fold during the Great Depression and, having no "protection" downtown, he was constantly followed by police. In 1937 he was finally indicted as a numbers banker, though he had reportedly quit the business years before. He was convicted and remained in prison for nearly a year. By 1938 Holstein was a poor man.[57]

But in what ways did control of the numbers by Holstein and other Caribbean immigrants during the 1920s make Harlem different from other settings? A look at Chicago's south side, where the game was controlled by natives, shows that, as in Harlem, numbers flourished disproportionately to other economic pursuits because blacks were denied full participation in the economic life of their city. And political bosses allowed the illegal operation and more serious criminal activity to operate in exchange for payoffs. Attitudes toward policy kings were similar in both communities. Attacks on them by police or gangsters were considered attacks on the race, and this was to some extent true, since white racketeers operating in black communities were seldom pursued with the same rigor as black operators.

In Chicago and Harlem, policy kings emerged as race leaders, though never as either community's central spokespersons. Occasionally, as in Holstein's case, race leadership became a primary undertaking. During the depression, Drake and Cayton note in *Black Metropolis*, policy kings in Chicago emerged in the roles of "race leaders, patrons of charity, and pioneers in the establishment of legitimate business."[58] Those who made such investments usually retained such properties when their numbers operations were usurped by white racketeers.

The *Amsterdam News*, while not consistent in its position on the social good of policy, was adamant on one point: If played at all, the numbers should always remain black controlled. When the Seabury investigation cracked down on white racketeers in the early 1930s, the paper reported the proceedings with satisfaction: "The feeling is one of getting even now. Harlemites remember that the policy game was organized by Negroes from Cuba, Puerto Rico and the West Indies; that it afforded a good living for many thousand people. . . ."[59]

The white invasion of numbers banking elicited similar reports in the New York *Age*, which, unlike the *Amsterdam News*, vowed—somewhat inconsistently—to "never cease" its effort to curb "the wild and reckless abandon" with which Harlem had taken up policy.[60] As part of an earlier 1924 series on the game, the *Age* named two rival Jewish businessmen, Moe Immerman, owner of Connie's Inn, and Hyman Kassells, as the chief competitors of black and Hispanic operators. But the pair were having "no easy job of it." Harlemites still patronized the race bankers.[61]

In this connection, the *Age*'s perspective on foreign-born operators proves interesting. One of these bankers, Cuban-born Marcellina, was a pioneer in the numbers business in Harlem. His Spanish-speaking customers, along with "hundreds of American Negroes," enabled him to "live in luxury," the *Age* reported. Marcellina, who had "come to New York a short while ago," had invested his profits in "valuable real estate." He owned several brownstones on 139th Street in Strivers Row, reported the *Age*, and was remodeling one structure into a "veritable palace for his own occupancy."[62]

The *Age* more readily named Hispanic bankers in its pages, although its survey noted that the "insidious evil" had penetrated all ranks of Harlem citizenry and all its nationalities. While the names of one or two English-speaking Caribbean bankers appeared, and the paper noted this group's participation in the numbers operation, they were not singled out. Casper Holstein's name never appeared in the *Age*'s anti-numbers campaign. While noting that women were prominent in the operation, the *Age* did not mention Stephanie St. Clair, though she boldly admitted being head of a bank. When the name of Joe Tanner, a prominent businessman and Florida native, did appear in connection with numbers, the *Age* received a letter of protest from a reader. According to the reader, Joe Tanner was not engaged in the numbers business, had been a New York resident for 23 years, a member with "high degrees of Masonry," and a supporter of many charitable institutions of the city.[63] Whether Joe Tanner was actually a numbers operator could not be ascertained, but his distinguished memberships were the norm for bankers rather than the exception. The black press seldom exposed bankers with such important community connections.

On the other hand, white operators, especially Jews, were attacked freely. The *Age* claimed that cabaret owner Connie Immerman, brother of Moe Immerman, attempted to move into numbers operation by offering runners and collectors 100 to 200 percent more than their black employers. "One woman, who acknowledged that she had been made such an offer, declares that she indignantly refused the proposition."[64] Moe Immerman, described by the *Age* as "formerly one of the most notorious Jewish bootleggers operating in Harlem," allegedly obtained the cooperation of the police in his effort to take over the numbers operation from black bankers.[65]

The *Age*, as the severest critic of the numbers in Harlem, demonstrated ambivalence in its treatment of individual immigrant and native operators. The names of some but not other bankers were mentioned. The reason for this can be partially explained. The key bankers, like Casper Holstein, wielded power in almost every sector of Harlem life. Holstein was an associate of *Age* editor Fred R. Moore and possibly a contributor to his campaign for the city's Aldermanic Board, to which Moore was elected. Other critics of the numbers operation could seldom be thorough or entirely credible in the crusade against the practice. A special meeting of the Harlem branch of the New York Urban League called to consider the "evil of numbers" was a case in point. In defense of numbers, Edgar M. Grey correctly charged that the Urban League itself had benefited from the black-controlled game in Harlem. Without naming Holstein, he referred to his donations to the annual essay contest sponsored by *Opportunity*, the League's official journal.[66] It is noteworthy that, as an immigrant, Casper Holstein's nativity received less attention as a numbers banker than it did when he tried to run for president of one of African America's most powerful fraternal orders.

Numbers in Harlem was distinguished by the participation of Caribbean immigrants as bankers and collectors, activities which flowed from a cultural pattern of their native homes. Immigrant politicians' early connections to Tammany through the United Colored Democracy should not be discounted either. The ability to buy or influence officials was key in starting and maintaining a place in the racket. But the function of immigrant numbers people vis à vis the Harlem community closely resembled that of others so engaged in urban areas where black ethnicity was not a major factor.

Ultimately the successful numbers banker walked a narrow path. Harlem leaders' ongoing discussion of community included him or her but never assumed that a numbers banker would remain an element in its future. A banker's behavior did not necessarily win him or her respect—if sought—or the community's protection if too far outside its mores and expectations of what was owed in return. Although numbers was played mostly by poor people, the economic weakness of the black middle class was clearly demonstrated by its involvement with the game. "There was a West Indian lad earning his way through college as a numbers runner . . ." began one of Wallace Thurman's lively sketches of Harlem life. When a banker left him with a batch of unpaid winning slips, his "fellow students," who should have been winners, manhandled him. They then revealed his occupation to police, and he was chased "upstairs, across roofs, through a skylight, and down more stairs by a pair of energetic plain-clothes men from headquarters."[67]

The black press's constant reference to the real property owned by numbers bankers as a means of enhancing race self-esteem is a further example of middle-class marginality. Numbers bankers were often the only people in the community with enough money to wield clout with the white power structure. In this manner, Harlem's black middle class probably received greater advantage from numbers than the masses, who, except for various job assignments, were in most cases merely the players.

10

Harlem Writers
and Intraracial Ethnicity

THIS CHAPTER EXAMINES intraracial ethnicity in the context of one of the more lasting products of Harlem's emergence as a black community—its literary arts movement and press. The complex relationships between black immigrants and native African Americans is often reflected in their writings—autobiography, fiction, and many periodicals and journals. Many of the resources for this study have been drawn from these materials. Caribbean Harlemites were especially active contributors to the black press and to a number of left-leaning white publications. While they wrote primarily to a race audience, immigrants clearly though perhaps less publicly mediated between racial and ethnic identities. One recent scholar has noted, "In many aspects of their private lives the first cohort of West Indian migrants retained a strong sense of ethnic pride which they passed on to their children."[1] And while some native blacks denied ethnicity a place in Harlem's public arena—particularly politics—others clearly understood its dynamics in everyday life.

Though its study is beyond the scope of this book, much of the literature of the Harlem Renaissance drew upon commonplace themes of migration, adjustment, interaction, and conflict among different groups whose lives intersected in the city. A few examples from the work of Claude McKay, Eric Walrond, Rudolph Fisher, and Wallace Thurman help illustrate ways writers tried to redefine race in the context of a multiethnic black community. In another sphere explored in this chapter, Caribbean writers helped institutionalize various forms of propaganda and protest through their editorials and newspaper columns. Most of New York's race papers, like the black urban press elsewhere, were sustained by the growing urban masses of the black migration. The press in turn wielded considerable influence in Harlem between 1900 and 1930 and especially after 1917, when many new journals were launched. James Weldon Johnson observed in his *Black Manhattan* (1930) that it "shook up the Negroes of New York and the country and affected some changes that have not been lost."[2] Certain immigrant writers provided ordinary readers with a more anticolonial/imperialist and international outlook in the weekly newspapers, while others brought intraracial class and colorism issues into the public arena.

Claude McKay, who lived on three continents and twice as many countries during his most productive period, probably grappled with the topic of cultural pluralism and his own feelings of alienation as much as any writer of the period. In *Home to Harlem* (1928) and *A Long Way from Home* (1937), he demonstrates that one of the major cultural preoccupations of black immigrants centered around race and race consciousness and national/ethnic identity. Coming from majority-black societies, some immigrants initially questioned race as a framework for social organization or identity. In a Pennsylvania railroad-barrack scene in *Home to Harlem*, one of McKay's central characters, Ray, a native of Haiti and an aspiring writer, questions solidarity with his fellow railroad porters on the basis of their common racial background:

> These men claimed kinship with him. They were black like him. Man and nature had put them in the same race. He ought to love them . . . if he had a shred of social morality in him. . . . They were all chain-linked together and he was counted as one link. Yet he loathed every soul in that great barrack-room . . . Race . . . Why should he have and love a race?[3]

Indeed the ambitions of black immigrants who came to America seeking opportunity only to be relegated to the misfortunes of a despised race were terribly frustrated. In some minds this treatment created what W. A. Domingo described as "an artificial" identity and a closing of ranks for protection against "outsiders." Others developed a "deep feeling of resentment" when the "color line," legal or customary, was drawn.[4] For *Home to Harlem* character Ray, resentment was directed at native African Americans:

> He remembered when little Hayti was floundering uncontrolled, how proud he was to be the son of a free nation. He used to feel condescendingly sorry for those poor African natives; superior to ten million of suppressed Yankee 'coons.' Now he was just one of them and he hated them for being one of them. . . .
>   But he was not entirely of them, he reflected. He possessed another language and literature that they knew not of.[5]

Perhaps Ray's pride was in an independent Haiti. But several years after he left New York, British Guiana native Eric Walrond believed Caribbean immigrants' similar pride in England and things British were deeply rooted in the colonized mind. Of the British Caribbean elites he wrote:

> We took on as much of English civilization as lay in our power. In one island, Barbados [*sic*]—a British colony since 1605—the native drifted so far away from the African ideal as to be considered even more English than the English themselves! Our love of England and our wholehearted acceptance of English life and customs, at the expense of everything African, blinded us to many things. It has even made us seem a trifle absurd and ridiculous in the eyes of our neighbours. But the absurdity of our position—an ostrich-like one—was not revealed to us until we began to travel.[6]

In New York, Walrond relates, the Caribbean immigrant "with his Scottish, Irish or Devonshire accent, was to the native Black, who has retained a measure of his

African folk culture, uproarishly funny." The black immigrant, Walrond continued, was joked at on street corners, burlesqued on the stage, and discriminated against in business and social life. "His pride in his British heritage and lack of racial consciousness were contemptuously put down to 'airs.'" The tensions Walrond described appear to have been rooted in class as well as ethnic/cultural differences.[7]

McKay's fictional immigrant, however, has a variety of experiences with African Americans. In another section of *Home to Harlem*, Ray eventually comes to terms with his fellow workers on the basis of genuine friendship, and because of this he realizes his identity had been redefined *for* him by his fellow blacks as well as by white Americans. He describes an encounter during his first days in Harlem:

> It was the winter of 1916 when I first came to New York to hunt for a job. I was broke. I was afraid I would have to pawn my clothes, and it was dreadfully cold. I didn't even know the right way to go about looking for a job. I was always timid about that. For five weeks, I had not paid my rent. I was worried and Ma Lawton, my landlady, was also worried. She had her bills to meet. She was a good-hearted old woman from South Carolina.[8]

Ma Lawton helped Ray find a job in an eating establishment where he got free food and tips. Ray's experience was probably drawn partially from McKay's own life. Though he was himself of Jamaican middle-class stock, his early social contacts in New York were among working-class people of Brooklyn and Harlem. In 1914 his marriage to a Jamaican sweetheart lasted just six months, and he had an equally unsuccessful career as a restauranteur in a tough section of Brooklyn's Myrtle Avenue, according to biographer Wayne Cooper. He soon went on the road as a railroad dining-car waiter—like fictional character Ray—while he pursued his interest in writing. McKay enjoyed the bohemian lifestyle of the cabarets and saloons of Harlem. "The cabarets of Harlem in those days enthralled me more than any theater downtown. They were so intimate." He roomed on 131st with a black southern migrant landlord with whom he became friends. He wrote of this landlord in his autobiography, *A Long Way from Home* (1937): "When he was a young man in the South, he 'sassed' a white man. And for that he was struck. He struck back, and barely escaped with his life. He was a kind landlord and pleasant mixer." McKay also described his relationship with a southern migrant woman—a girlfriend of sorts: "There is always an unfamiliar something between people of different countries and nationalities, however intimate they may become. And that something between me and Manda helped rather than hindered our relationship. It made her accept little eccentricities on my part."[9]

In *A Long Way from Home*, McKay conveys his perception that the violence of white racism bound him to his fellow railroad workers in profound ways. During the Red Summer of 1919, when a series of race riots plagued American cities where black migrants had settled, McKay stayed close to fellow workers on stopovers in Washington, D.C., and Pittsburgh. They traveled in groups to their boarding houses, some of them carrying guns for protection. "If We Must Die," McKay's most famous poem, was an outgrowth of the "intense emotional experience" through which he lived with thousands of other blacks. The first time he read his poem to his fellow workers, "one who was a believer in the Marcus Garvey Movement suggested that I should go to Liberty Hall, the headquarters of the organization, and read the poem."[10] McKay did not do so, but he did write for the *Negro World* for a brief period in 1920.

If McKay's autobiographical and fictional writings are suggestive about intimate cross-cultural interactions, at least two black American writers depicted other forms of ethnic interaction as part of everyday life in Harlem. Two characters in Rudolph Fisher's short story "City of Refuge," published in Locke's *New Negro* (1925), illustrate how easily conflicts between unsuspecting southern migrants and Caribbean immigrants could be nourished. King Solomon Gillis, a rather stereotyped and gullible southern migrant, becomes the near victim of a petty swindle by an equally stereotyped Jamaican immigrant who, within minutes of the North Carolina native's arrival, makes a phony demand of Gillis for payment for apples accidentally knocked into the street. Gillis had harmlessly spilled the apples as he passed Tony Gabriellis's Harlem market en route to his lodgings. Gillis is saved from the scam by a more experienced and even more dishonest North Carolina homeboy, Mouse Uggam, who advises Gillis to take the bill to the Jamaican's employer. When Gillis does so, the employer, Tony Gabriellis, fires the Jamaican on the spot and hires Gillis in his place. Grateful to Mouse for saving him from a swindle, Gillis agrees to sell "French Medicine" for him out of Gabriellis's store. The gullible Gillis does not realize he is dealing illegal drugs and is arrested within weeks of his arrival in Harlem.

Though ethnic dynamics is not the central theme of "City of Refuge," Fisher presented scenarios that evoked common situations or viewpoints. The black immigrant character is depicted as a comical figure willing to do anything to make a few bucks. The Jamaican and the North Carolinian contest for a subsistence-level job from a white man who is himself an immigrant. The southern migrant is instructed early on to despise the Jamaican. This point is illustrated in a dialogue between Mouse and Gillis, who is at first reluctant to install himself in the Jamaican's job:

> "What make you keep callin him monkey-chaser?" [asks Gillis].
> "West Indian. That's another thing. Anytime you can knife a monk, do it. They's too damn many of 'em here. They're an achin' pain."[11]

Though competition for jobs among the laboring masses of immigrants and natives is harder for the historian to document in this period, Fisher's identification of economic competition as a major source of conflict is substantiated by Reid. In *The Negro Immigrant* an unidentified informant recounted: "Ugly epithets were hurled at me by native-born Negroes at employment agencies and places of employment; landladies tried to 'play me for a sucker' because they thought I was ignorant of living standards. I was handicapped, too, by the fact that most native-born Negroes hold that all foreigners are rich. . . ."[12] Although this immigrant said he cultivated a sense of humor and threw aside customs and traditions imported from home as a survival strategy, other immigrants did not assimilate so easily or develop close friend-ships with native African Americans.

In his *Blacker the Berry* (1929) the black American writer Wallace Thurman ex-plores colorism as depicted in the experiences of dark-complexioned Emma Lou Morgan, a native of Idaho and a new arrival in Harlem. But in one sketch about the difficulty Emma Lou has making intimate friendships in the city because of her color, Thurman also suggests why it may have been even more difficult for immi-grants and natives to develop cross-cultural friendships:

> Emma Lou was very lonesome. She still knew no one save John, two or three of the Negro actors . . . and a West Indian woman who lived in the same apart-ment with her. The West Indian woman was employed as a stenographer in the office of a Harlem political sheet. She was shy and retiring, and not much given to making friends with American Negroes. So many of them had snubbed and pained her when she was newly emigrant from her home in Barbados, that she lumped them all together, just as they seemed to do her people. She would not take under consideration that Emma Lou was new to Harlem, and not even aware of the prejudice American-born Harlemites nursed for foreign-born ones. She remembered too vividly how, on ringing the bell of a house where there had been a vacancy sign in the window, a little girl had come to the door, and, in answer to a voice in the back asking, "Who is it, Cora?" had replied, "Monkey chaser wants to see the room you got to rent." Jasmine Griffith was wary of all contact with American Negroes, for that had been only one of the many embittering incidents she had experienced.
>
> Emma Lou liked Jasmine, but was conscious of the fact that she could never penetrate her stolid reserve. They often talked to one another when they met in the hallway, and sometimes they stopped in one another's rooms, but there was never any talk of going places together, never any informal revela-tions or intimacies.[13]

Here even a child has learned to refer to the immigrant by a common epithet and to tip off the landlady about the identity of a potential tenant. The sketch is also sug-gestive about women's relationships, though Thurman himself does not elaborate on this particular theme.

While there were exceptions, socializing among women, perhaps even more so than men, developed not only with others from the same region, but with persons from the same island community in the Caribbean. Similar patterns with somewhat less frequency are suggested by the living and lodging arrangements of southern mi-grants. It is not surprising that Jasmine Griffith may not have developed a close friendship with Emma Lou Morgan, though they lodged in the same house. Paule Marshall suggests that primary relationships were reinforced by social and cultural factors:

> [T]he women looked to each other for their social life—and with the women in *Brown Girl, Brownstones* as well as with my mother and her friends in real life, this consisted mainly of sitting around the kitchen table after their return from

work each day and talking. Endlessly talking. Much of the talk had to do with
home—meaning Barbados; the places, people, and events there as they remembered them. It was clearly an effort on their part to retain their cultural identity
amidst the perplexing newness of America. Perhaps sensing the disregard in
which they were held by the society, their triple invisibility as it were, they felt
the need more strongly than other immigrant groups to hold onto the memories
that defined them.[14]

Thus ethnic identity was clearly important to the first black immigrant generation. In addition new identities appear to have been constructed in response to the
American experience within and outside the intraracial community. The Harlem
writers discussed here almost incidentally help us reach this conclusion. Their main
themes were not devoted to the black immigrant experience.

Black immigrants, however, made unique contributions to the "New Negro" literary Renaissance in poetry, drama, musical theater, and fiction. George Reginald
Margetson, a native of St. Kitts, immigrated to the United States in 1897 at age
twenty. He authored several books, among them *Of England and the West Indies*
(1906), *Ethiopia's Flight* (1907), and *Songs of Life* (1910), before his best-known
works, *The Fledgling Bard* and the *Poetry Society*, appeared in 1916. The latter
writings serve as a kind of poetic discourse on contemporary racial issues, while the
earlier works were clearly inspired by Margetson's status as a colonial exile.
      Playwright Eulalie Spence was born a short boat ride from Margetson in Nevis
in 1894 and grew up in Harlem. She arrived at Ellis Island with her parents and
seven sisters when she was eight years old. The family moved to the Payton block on
131st Street. Little of her biography is known, but she received her B.S. from New
York University in 1937 and an M.A. in speech from Columbia University two years
later. Thereafter she worked as a teacher of drama in the Eastern District High
School. Spence's plays all focus on the lives of ordinary Harlemites, working people,
numbers runners and players, hustlers, and churchgoers. Although greatly neglected
in the literature of the Harlem Renaissance, Spence was one of the more prolific
playwrights of the era, writing eight one-act plays and one full-length production
during the period between 1926 and 1933. Her female characters are independent,
willful, and challenging individuals with their own tastes and aspirations. One recent
scholar, Elizabeth Brown-Guillory, has described her as "a daring and vociferous
woman playwright who might one day be credited with initiating feminism in plays
by black women."[15]
      Spence's plays, while not containing obvious Caribbean immigrant themes, are
nonetheless an important reflection of folk life in Harlem during the 1920s. The
female-run Harlem boardinghouse in *Undertow* (1929), the numbers runners and
players in *The Hunch* (1927), and male and female relationships in *The Episode*
(1928) provide valuable insights to the times. Spence was also active in community
theater, producing and directing her own plays and those of others. She was one of

the founders of the Dunbar Garden Players in the late 1920s and the Krigwa Players, founded by W. E. B. Du Bois and housed in the basement of the 135th Street Branch of the New York Public Library. Despite her contributions to African American and women's theater, with the exception of a small remuneration she received from Paramount for her screenplay *The Whipping* (1933), Spence never received money from her writing. After completing her education she earned her living as a public school teacher and dramatic society coach.[16]

Another little-recognized creative artist was Amy Ashwood Garvey, who, like Amy Jacques, is better remembered for her marriage to Marcus Garvey. According to her biographer, Lionel M. Yard, Ashwood had an abiding interest in the musical theater as well as in politics. After her arrival in New York in 1918, Ashwood's relationship and marriage to Garvey quickly disintegrated. Ashwood left New York for London and traveled to Paris, Brussels, Berlin, Rome, West Africa, and Canada before returning to Jamaica and to New York in 1924. Yard does not explain how she acquired funding for her travels and artistic ventures—perhaps some came from income from her father's businesses in Panama and Jamaica.

But in New York Ashwood met and collaborated with the well-known Caribbean-born theatrical performer, Sam Manning, who introduced Caribbean comedy and calypso to Harlem audiences. Ashwood first collaborated with Manning on the musical comedy "Hey, Hey," performed at the Lafayette in the fall of 1926. The play's plot focused on two dissatisfied husbands who divorce their wives and are determined to find their true soul mates in Africa. After much adventure and searching, the men locate two women who have the necessary qualifications, only to discover they are their ex-wives, who have preceded them to Africa.

The play was performed in Caribbean English and dancers performed to a calypso beat. Harlem newspapers heralded the play as a satire of Marcus Garvey. According to Yard the play had an "enchanting ethnic dynamism that captured the imagination and provided the audience with a theme to which they could culturally relate."[17] A second comedy, "Brown Sugar," also performed by Caribbean actors, opened at the Lafayette Theater in the summer of 1927 and later traveled to Panama and various Caribbean islands. As a writer and producer of these two plays, Ashwood successfully integrated Caribbean themes into Harlem's popular theater. Accompanied by Manning, she left New York for London in 1929, where they opened a nightclub and restaurant, the Florence Mills, named for the famous Harlem actress. The restaurant became a gathering place for Africans and Pan-Africanist intellectuals such as Kwame Nkrumah, George Padmore, and C. L. R. James.[18]

Two of Harlem's best-known immigrant writers, McKay and Walrond, were connected to creative production as well as the local New York press. But McKay, more so than Walrond, publicly expressed his alienation from the native black establishment. His first intellectual contacts were with members of New York's white literary left. And his first American work was published in the avant-garde journal the *Seven Arts* in 1917 with the support of Joel Spingard, a white literary critic and, at that time an official of the NAACP.[19] His sonnet "If We Must Die" appeared in Max's Eastman's *Liberator*, where McKay got his first important literary job as an associate editor. However, in 1921 his friend Harrison remained dissatisfied with the Jamaican poet's reception by the black American media and said so in the *Negro World*:

> If McKay had waited until one of our "race" publications had given [him] recognition to his genius he would have starved first. Yet his famous poem of new Negro manhood, entitled "If We must Die," has been quoted in Congress and recited by many of our readers and elocutionists.[20]

Actually, as the first black poet of the period to receive significant recognition, McKay firmly established his place in the Harlem Renaissance by 1922, when he left the black metropolis for Europe. He remained there until 1934, sending back his poetry and fiction to New York publishers and building a voluminous correspondence with black American and Caribbean intellectuals.

While McKay became a kind of double exile—from Harlem and his native Jamaica—British Guianan Eric Walrond remained in Harlem for most of the 1920s before he left permanently for London in 1928 or 1929. Walrond came to New York in 1918 after having lived in Panama during the Canal's construction days, when he worked as a stenographer and as a reporter for the *Panama Star and Herald*. Though he applied many times for work as a stenographer in New York, he could not find a job. In a 1922 article for the *New Republic* entitled "On Being Black," he described these encounters: "I walk in and offer my services. I am black, foreign looking and a curio. My name is taken. I shall be sent for, certainly, in case of need. 'Oh, don't mention it sir. . . . Glad you came in. . . . Good morning.' I am smiled out. I never hear from them again."[21] While studying creative writing at City College and Columbia University in 1919 and 1920, Walrond was employed as an associate editor of the black weekly *The Brooklyn and Long Island Informer*. He later worked as an associate editor of the *Negro World*.

Walrond introduced *Negro World* readers to the work of native and immigrant writers through his weekly book reviews. He described a work of NAACP executive director James Weldon Johnson called a *Book of Negro Poetry* (1922) as "a volume every lover of the beautiful in poetry ought to possess, and Mr. Johnson has done a great racial work."[22] McKay's *Harlem Shadows* (1922) was "a wondrous collection and indispensable to any representative collection of Negro poetry." William Pickens's *Vengeance of the Gods* (1922) was "a tragic disappointment."[23] Walrond's review column appeared at the peak of the *Negro World*'s circulation, and he continued to write for the paper until 1924, when a dispute of uncertain origin caused him to cut all ties with the UNIA for the rest of his stay in Harlem.[24]

After an interval of a year, Walrond joined the staff of the Urban League's *Opportunity* as business manager. At this time, *Opportunity* was the most influential black-establishment journal catering to young writers. Walrond's skills as a manager helped keep this publication financially solvent.[25] It was during this period with *Opportunity* that the wealthy Virgin Islander and numbers banker Casper Holstein offered financial support for the journal's writers contest. Walrond also influenced the selection of material for editor Charles S. Johnson's important November 1926 Caribbean issue. Included were the works of Harlem's Caribbean writers and journalists as well as a listing of prominent African Caribbean–based men and women.

At other times during Walrond's affiliation, *Opportunity* published the work of black writers in the diaspora such as René Maran (Martinique), who in turn introduced the Harlem literary movement to other colonials such as Aime Cesaire (Martinique), Leon Damas (French Guiana), and Leopold Senghor (Senegal).[26] The U.S. occupation of Haiti between 1915 and 1934, widely protested in Harlem, also sparked interest in the Haitian Renaissance of the 1920s and 1930s. Writers like Walrond, Langston Hughes, and McKay inspired and were inspired by Haitian Jacques Roumain and others. Harlem's internationalism also captured writers of the Hispanic Caribbean, such as Cuban Nicolas Guillen.

Walrond's promotion of *Opportunity*'s literary influence is an example of shifting relationships within the Harlem community. He moved comfortably among Harlem's "older Negro intellectuals" when necessary, a feat not so easy for McKay and others. His move from the UNIA's *Negro World* to the Urban League's *Opportunity* did not signal an ideological change. Instead, Walrond helped shift *Opportunity* toward inclusion of more global black perspectives, especially on developments, literary and otherwise, in the colonial territories. In the meantime he afforded Harlem's younger writers with a representative on a black mainstream journal. Moreover, the support of Walrond's contact, Casper Holstein, whom he had met while associate editor of the *Negro World*, offered the young writers some financial reward for their work.[27]

And for himself, after Walrond cleared some initial hurdles, he was never in dire financial straits. By 1927 he had left *Opportunity* to devote more time to his own work. His *Tropic Death*, a collection of stories about Caribbean workers and peasants from Barbados to Panama, had appeared in 1926 and sold fairly well in bookstores. Historian J. A. Rogers found Walrond's description of the tropical environment "accurate and vivid."[28] The young Langston Hughes, author of a volume of proletarian poetry, *Weary Blues* (1926), felt Walrond had captured the real and intimate side of Caribbean life without "both eyes on what the white public will think."[29]

Actually Walrond had attempted with *Tropic Death* what novelist Jean Toomer had done with *Cane* (1922). While Toomer had focused on the experience of Georgia peasants, Walrond focused on the harsh realities of poor people in his native Caribbean. The stories, written in the dialect of the working poor, were like McKay's *Home to Harlem*, distinctly anti-assimilationist. In recognition of his work Walrond received a Guggenheim Fellowship in 1928, left Harlem for the Caribbean and finally London in 1932. Whatever literary assessment one makes of the stories themselves, they helped bring the Caribbean experience into the literature of Harlem.[30]

As is evident in Walrond's career, the most accessible mediums to black writers were African American newspapers and journals, which could provide employment and in many cases the only jobs in journalism available to a small group of well-educated immigrants before 1930. McKay's early affiliations with white publications were an exception. Langston Hughes capsulized conditions for most African American writers. "It is very hard for a Negro to become a professional writer. Magazine offices, daily newspapers, publishers offices are tightly closed to us in America."[31] On the other hand, black-owned newspapers and journals provided immigrants with significant access to large numbers of African American readers. "The Negro seems to have newly discovered his fourth estate," wrote Virginia African American Professor Robert Kerlin in 1919, "to have realized the extraordinary power of his press." In the same year the Associated Negro Press reported that the average African American home received two or more race periodicals.[32] Harrison, McKay, Walrond, Cyril Valentine Briggs, Edgar M. Grey, Hodge Kirnon, J. A. Rogers, Vere Johns, Wendell Malliet, R. L. Dougherty, and others wrote regularly on one or more of Harlem's publications or had syndicated columns in major black newspapers. One major immigrant woman journalist, Amy Jacques-Garvey, made important contributions to journalism and helped internationalize black feminist ideas through the *Negro World*.

As one might expect, Caribbean-born writers directed a few journals and pamphlets toward an immigrant-community readership. The *West Indian Review*, edited by Wendell Malliet, is an example. Such periodicals were not institutionalized in this period as they would be in the second large wave of Caribbean immigration in the 1960s and 1970s.[33] The early twentieth-century immigrant journalists wrote primarily to a race audience, though they also recorded many aspects of Caribbean life and culture. The most distinctive features of their work were the launching of their own, usually radical, journals and their writings on New Negro topics like colorism, self-defense, black history and culture, and important community issues. The *Negro World*, first edited by W. A. Domingo, and Cyril Briggs's *Crusader* both appeared in August of 1918. Domingo began his own weekly newspaper, the *Emancipator*, after resigning as the *Negro World*'s first editor in July of 1919 over stated opposition to Garvey's authoritarian methods and unorthodox business practices. Hodge Kirnon, an early protégé of Hubert Harrison's, began his own publication, the *Promoter*, in 1920 while continuing to write for the *Negro World*.[34]

Harrison's *Voice* set the tone and served as the forerunner of subsequent radical Harlem publications after the summer of 1917. Launched on July 4, 1917, Harrison called the journal "a newspaper for the New Negro." According to Montserratan journalist Hodge Kirnon, the paper "really crystallized the radicalism of the Negro in New York and environs."[35] One approach was a willingness to publicly criticize "old guard leaders" and to discuss unpopular intraracial issues. An important article, entitled "Descent of Du Bois," challenged the *Crisis* editor's famous "Closed Ranks" editorial calling on African Americans to forget "their special grievances."[36] The *Voice* ceased publication after a few years, but Harrison's articles later appeared in traditional black publications such as the Pittsburgh *Courier*, the New York *News*, and the Urban League's *Opportunity*.

Harrison and other Caribbean journalists regularly wrote on intraracial problems. In the *Voice* he entitled the color issue "A Tender Point," one "seldom touched upon by Negro Americans who characteristically avoid any public presentation of a thing about which they will talk interminably in private."[37] Indeed, color divisions appeared to be alive and well among the African American elite as well as between themselves and the masses. Immigrant columnist Edgar M. Grey cited an embarrassing example in his New York *News* column, entitled "Dr. Pickens Is Too Black." According to Grey, New York's black Republican nomination committee refused to consider Yale-educated William Pickens as a candidate for the United States Congress because his skin was too dark. Grey, also dark complexioned, was incensed by such a display of racial impotency: "If it comes to the place where, these white men's children think that they are going to deprive black men and women of representation, when they are qualified, because of the blackness of their skins, let us speak right out here and now, and say that it is going to be a most bitter and vicious war."[38] Grey included in his attack the Harlem branch of the Urban League and Harlem's YWCA, which he claimed hired only light-complexioned women in their offices.

Grey was a journalist of considerable experience, talent, and influence. He was born in Sierra Leone, West Africa, in 1890, probably of Caribbean parents. But he was raised and received his secondary education in Antigua. In 1906 he worked as an interpreter for the United States government in Puerto Rico and later as an English secretary to the president of the Dominican Republic. He immigrated to the United States in 1911, after attending Aberdeen University in Scotland between 1909 and 1911. Like a number of other educated Caribbean immigrants, he found a job as a postal clerk. He later worked as a bookkeeper for the Daily Lunch Corporation. Grey enlisted in the U.S. Army in 1918 and became a naturalized citizen that same year. After being discharged from the army, he organized the Foreign-born Citizens Political Alliance. In May 1919 Marcus Garvey employed Grey as general secretary and business manager of the *Negro World*. But the relationship was short-lived. In August Grey was expelled from the organization. He became a professional chiropractor in 1921, was reemployed by the post office, and resumed his career in race journalism in 1925, working first as an associate editor at the New York *News* and then contributing editor of the *Amsterdam News* (1926–1928).[39]

Although he had dropped these affiliations by the mid-1920s, Grey was at one time associated with Hubert Harrison's Liberty League and the African Blood Brotherhood. He also had some contacts with old-line political groups such as the United Colored Democracy. Now without organizational affiliation and probably financially stable, he wrote controversial, sometimes acrimonious articles against the black establishment and white "slumming" uptown.[40] Grey was not always fair-minded. While he frequently criticized native blacks for their biases against

Caribbean immigrants, he charged "the Spanish Menace" with being "in large degree" responsible for the immoral conditions in Harlem. This article, which appeared in 1928, provoked a wave of protest letters to Harlem newspapers. Grey did not appear as a columnist for the *Amsterdam News* after this year and went to work for the short-lived *American and West Indian News* in 1929.[41]

If Grey wrote himself out of a job on a mainstream journal, other immigrants had a much longer tenure. Cyril Briggs was one of the first black immigrants to get a job on a major Harlem weekly. Briggs, who had begun his career as an assistant reporter for the *St. Kitts Daily Express* and the *St. Christopher Advertiser*, joined the New York *Amsterdam News* just after it opened as a small independent paper in 1909. After a three-year period with this paper, he resigned to become editor of the *Colored American Review*, an organ of Harlem's black business community. The first issue of the *Review*, while supporting "colored business," also preached "manhood rights and race pride." Briggs's association with this publication did not last long, and he returned to the *Amsterdam News*, where his reporting covered Harlem's theatrical and dramatic scene. He eventually became editor and remained with the paper until 1918.

Under Briggs's editorship, the *Amsterdam News* took stronger and stronger positions against the involvement of blacks in the First World War, the treatment of black soldiers, and President Woodrow Wilson's mandated proposals for Germany's colonies in Africa. With Briggs's editorial agenda, the paper earned the reputation from a government censor as "the worst of the colored newspapers." Briggs left the paper nine months after he began publishing the *Crusader*.[42]

Support for the *Crusader* magazine reflected a broader strata of radical politics as well as backing for Briggs in the Caribbean and native black communities. This can probably be explained in Briggs's history of support of black business in the *Amsterdam News*. Financial support came initially from Caribbean merchant Anthony Crawford and later from Harlem journalists and publishers. Briggs's ties to the sporting and theatrical worlds aided the dissemination of the magazine among a wide constituency. Also, Briggs's association with the Hamitic League of the World, an Afrocentric organization headed by Nebraska native George Wells Parker, helped to push the magazine in even wider venues. But as Briggs shifted his politics to encompass the working class and socialism, ties with Parker's organization disappeared.

The *Crusader*'s emphasis on self-defense in the face of white violence was an issue which appealed directly to the concerns of all blacks. As editor, Briggs often focused on the Ku Klux Klan, before and after Garvey's ill-fated meeting with the Klan in 1922. Klansmen, he wrote, were a menace to blacks and also to Catholics, immigrants, radicals—and to progress. They had spread their racial influence in the fertile ground of the North, including parts of New York, and had a membership of bigots and patriots, societal failures, and "citizens who historically had enjoyed power and prestige, the prerogatives of the nation's senior partners."[43] The rise of the urban Klan and other violence against blacks in the 1920s slowly moved the black masses away from an established leadership's claim that blacks' "fight is on the brain and soul of America," using legal and constitutional means. Briggs's ideas on self-defense effectively captured the mood of many African Americans.

By 1929—the Great Depression at hand—Briggs, whose *Crusader* folded in 1922, edited the weekly Communist newspaper the *Harlem Liberator*. Declaring itself the voice of the laboring masses, the *Liberator* attacked white and black landlords who raised rents and evicted tenants. Eviction, made highly visible by the belongings of tenants piled upon sidewalks, became a strong community issue. In a conscious attempt to fan the flames of discontent, the *Liberator* announced Tenants League Meetings and urged residents to come out and join the struggle against unscrupulous landlords. Accounts of mothers with young children being kicked out of their apartments in a wintry Harlem filled the front pages.[44] In the next few years the *Liberator* continued to focus upon community issues, including lynchings and deportations.

Pressing community matters were only one of the topics New Negro writers turned to in tandem with their audiences. Equally important was the search for a past that complemented the undertakings of the present. The recovery of pride and racial self-esteem through exploration of the black experience was an important undertaking of Jamaican immigrant J. A. Rogers, whose articles on black history appeared in every major black newspaper in the country from 1920 into the 1950s. Rogers came to American in 1906 to study art in Chicago while he worked as a Pullman porter. He was shocked to find that in the United States he was subjected to so many racial indignities. In Jamaica he had been among the privileged, light-complexioned upper strata. When some of his half-siblings migrated to the States, they passed into the white community. But in America Rogers was told all blacks had never accomplished anything in "all of history."[45] He devoted his life's work to refuting this.

The first of his many books, *From Superman to Man*, appeared in 1917 and set out to demolish the theory of black inferiority through a fictionalized conversation between a Pullman porter and a southern Senator. The porter, a Harvard graduate, successfully attacked, through his store of historical facts, the legislator's mythical conception of blacks. *From Superman to Man*, which Rogers published himself, ran through four editions. At one dollar, it sold ten thousand copies in its first year and appeared as a serial in many black newspapers in later years. The *Negro World* described it as "the greatest book on the Negro we have ever read." By 1920 Rogers had moved to Harlem and gained a kind of fame as the "people's historian."[46]

But this self-taught, meticulous note-taker and researcher was not well received by Harlem's university-trained establishment scholars. In 1922 Hubert Harrison felt that Rogers had not achieved the recognition he deserved for *From Superman to Man*:

> During the period from 1917 to the present this book has made its way to success without one word of encouragement from or praise from any one of the

more prominent Negro writers or editors except Mr. Ferris and myself, although free copies had been sent to Dr. Du Bois, Kelly Miller, Benjamin Brawley, Monroe Trotter, Professor Scarborough, Braithwaite, and many others including the National Association for the Advancement of Colored People. Almost the only colored people who helped to spread its fame were the lesser known humble classes, who still pilgrimage to 513 Lenox Avenue [135th Street Library] in quest of it.[47]

In his newspaper columns Rogers presented interesting, little-known facts about the African past of his readers. During the 1920s, his column began appearing in the Chicago *Defender*, Baltimore *Afro-American*, Norfolk *Journal and Guide*, Philadelphia *Tribune*, and Pittsburgh *Courier*. His work appeared simultaneously in the *Messenger*, the *Negro World*, and the *Amsterdam News*.

Here Rogers appealed to African American readers' thirst for information about themselves absent in their formal educations. Street people often came into the 135th Street Library to read Rogers's pamphlets; they still do today. His *One Hundred Facts about the Negro*, first published in 1934, went through eighteen editions in eight years. It was the "bible" of Afro-centric minded Harlem stepladder speakers in the 1930s and was widely used by other lecturers throughout the country.[48]

It is not clear why the university-trained scholars Harrison mentioned did not review Rogers's work. They probably regarded as eccentric Rogers's practice of tracking down the racial pedigree of famous people and digging up evidence to "prove" racial equality.

Arthur Schomburg took a middle position, allowing that race reconstruction was "legitimately compatible with scientific method" because of widespread "disparagement and omissions," but felt "history cannot be properly written with either bias or counterbias."[49]

However Rogers tackled theories of race inferiority, he tried to promote an enhanced self-esteem. Amy Jacques-Garvey demonstrated the range of women's interests in her *Negro World* "Our Women and What They Think," which she edited between 1924 and 1927. Unlike similar columns appearing in other periodicals, including radical ones like the *Crusader*, her topics were predominantly political. She avoided the common fare of women's pages and their focus on society news. Much in the style of the street corner orators, she prodded readers to economic and political autonomy.[50] If she supported her husband's strategy of accommodation after 1922, she did not reveal this in her columns. A typical admonition appeared in 1927: "It is folly to expect the white race will voluntarily change its cruel attitude toward the darker races. Any appeal to their conscience or religious protestations is a waste of time." Instead:

> The duty of the oppressed, therefore, is to know the mind of the oppressor, and pay him back in his own coin. The Negro cannot afford to demonstrate the "brotherhood of man" on earth until he has extricated himself from slavery and oppression.[51]

There were other characteristics of Amy Jacques-Garvey's women's page which distinguished it from most other women's pages in white or black journals. She devoted considerable space to the status and struggles of women under colonial rule in places such as India, China, and Africa. She applauded women who broke away from restrictive cultural traditions, noting Indian women's participation in politics, Egyptian women's discarding the veil, and political schools for women opening in Sun Yat Sen's China. Not surprisingly, the status of Soviet women received considerable attention in her columns, too, as members of the colonial Third World and African Americans assessed the workability of the Bolshevik model.[52] Articles about women emerging in nontraditional roles, whether in the Third World or Europe, were readily reprinted with Jacques-Garvey's own personalized headline: "Woman Marches On." A 1926 article about the first woman to swim the English Channel received a prominent location on her page, as did "Where Is Woman's Place? Question Being Satisfactorily Answered by Flapper and Grandmother Alike."[53] Her own ideas fit well within the context of the late nineteenth- and early twentieth-century African American women's movement. She subscribed to the feminism of her era, which held that women possessed an inherent humanizing quality they could better use to the advantage of their group and society.[54] From time to time Jacques-Garvey and other leading women in the UNIA addressed the issue of sexism within the organization. Women in the UNIA, like in many African American organizations, functioned in auxiliaries such as the Black Cross Nurses and other units. The national organization and local branches elected "lady presidents," who exercised limited power. The sentiment held by men that women should play a supporting rather than a central role became a full-blown issue by the time of the 1922 convention. UNIA women openly objected to notions of following rather than working alongside men in the organization. Madame M. L. T. De Mena, the assistant international organizer, criticized the discrimination against women for leadership positions. And in a 1926 column Jacques-Garvey set out the women's position:

> We serve notice on our men that Negro women will demand equal opportunity to fill any position in the Universal Negro Improvement Association or anywhere else without discrimination because of sex. We are very sorry if it hurts your old-fashioned tyrannical feelings, and we not only make the demand but we intend to enforce it.[55]

As one of the few Harlem women with access to a public voice, Jacques-Garvey deserves fuller attention from feminists and Garvey scholars. A survey of her weekly page, which appeared between 1924 and 1927, reflects thinking quite independent of Marcus Garvey.

Caribbean immigrant men and women had significant involvement in creating and shaping Harlem's media during its formative years, whether as editors, columnists, business managers, or creative writers. Several key Harlem writers—immigrant and native-born—integrated into their fiction the commonplace yet complex experiences in an intraracial African community. Though a discussion of it was not publicly encouraged, ethnicity pervaded the private lives of Caribbean men and women.

By the end of the 1920s and into the early years of the depression, immigrants were permanently installed in influential positions on local newspapers such as the *Amsterdam News*. Immigrant writers such as Briggs, Grey, and Walrond established media positions both inside and outside the native black establishment. While writing primarily on race concerns, their prominence in Harlem's media make it impossible to ignore the role of diversity in shaping the politics of the era. Functioning outside the black American mainstream leadership, such as that of the NAACP, Urban League, or the black Republican club, key immigrants helped devise and institutionalize a social class—not just a race analysis of the "Negro Problem." As columnists or editors they perceptibly changed the papers for which they worked. These publications no longer functioned simply as tools of local black political machines, liaisons to white influence, or newsletters of the black bourgeoisie. This independence was most effectively accomplished in their own journals, though many of these were short-lived. In addition, immigrants such as Amy Jacques-Garvey helped internationalize readers' perspectives and connect Harlem's interests to those of the Caribbean and the rest of the Third World. Understanding this is important to appreciate the full range of their interaction with the native-born black population as well as the unique contributions they made in the formation of the black metropolis.

11

Conclusion
Blood Relations in the Black Metropolis

THE SOCIAL SIGNIFICANCE of foreign-born blacks in Harlem—nearly 25 percent of the community's population in 1930—has been almost completely ignored in African American history and migration studies of the early twentieth century. Yet as a contemporary put it, "almost every important development originating in Harlem" involved the participation of black immigrants.[1] The present study has shown that, in addition to other forces shaping its configuration as a community, including gender, Harlem developed on the basis of ethnic and not simply racial dynamics. The basic contours of a multiethnic African American Harlem were formed during the years between 1900 and 1930.

Foreign-born blacks were present in older downtown Manhattan African American communities in numbers large enough before 1900 for distinct patterns of social life to appear there. But it was the steady increase in migration streams from the South and the Caribbean after 1900 which expanded the black community, created new institutions, and made distinctly ethnic-based affiliations possible.

Immigration to New York increased via expansion of international shipping and other transportation between the United States and the Caribbean region, especially the Panama Canal after 1904, when the Americans took over its construction. While this immigration favored individuals from the more advantaged circumstances, many could not afford the passage without help from extended family and other social networks. In New York these networks continued to function in locating lodging, jobs, marriage partners, and eventually in promoting political interest groups. At first the immigration furnished the elevator operators, janitors, hall-boys and porters, household workers, and washerwomen of upper Manhattan and finishers in garment factories downtown. But by the end of the 1920s, immigrant men also won their way in limited numbers in New York's black community as businessmen, lawyers, doctors, and journalists.[2]

Caribbean women played major roles in facilitating the immigration of female and male relatives and forming social networks between their homelands and New York City. Networks such as those formed by Barbadian immigrant Aletha Dowridge Challenor and her relatives and friends illustrate both the strength and strains of bonds maintained between the city and home. In addition, a steady stream of cultural and political ideas as well as items of clothing and money traveled over these networks. "From what I can hear Barbados is getting quite gay," an Aletha Dowridge friend writes in 1910, at the start of the Jazz Age. "Some of the New York spirit seems to have been diffused over there. I don't know, perhaps it left in the people's trunks as they go from here."[3] Many immigrants were able to sustain aspects of their Caribbean identities through links with "home" while they also contributed to the complexity of an expanded African American community.

Between 1900 and 1930, Caribbean immigrants in Manhattan established residential patterns quite similar to those of the native African American population. They joined with the first African Americans who settled in Harlem, renting apartments and bringing in lodgers to help pay the rent. Unlike other European and other immigrant groups who formed distinct residential patterns in collections of city blocks or neighborhoods, black immigrants, including those from the Anglophone and Francophone regions, did not form an ethnic enclave in this period as they would in the 1960s and 1970s.[4] Enforced patterns of segregated housing compelled their settlement with African Americans, but the black community's opportunities and historic ties to the Caribbean were also important magnets. Once in Harlem the Caribbean newcomers lodged, married, and conducted their primary social relationships mainly, though not exclusively, with other black immigrants.[5] This did not mean, however, that all newcomers remained isolated. Their activities overlapped, paralleled, and frequently converged with those of southern migrants and the larger African American community.

In 1915 one of the most ethnically heterogeneous—but not untypical—blocks in New York was located on Harlem's 131st Street between Lenox and Fifth Avenues. Philip and Maggie Payton's purchase of a brownstone at No. 13 in 1903 initiated a transformation of this block from mostly second-generation northern Europeans to a far more diverse block comprising newcomers of African descent from the southern states, almost every country of the Caribbean region, Central America, Puerto Rico, Cuba, the Cape Verde Islands, Bermuda, the Bahamas, China, and Europe. An examination of New York State manuscript census information collected from the residents in 1905, 1915, and 1925 provides a useful profile.

It is evident from oral interviews, biographies, and other qualitative information that the Payton block's multiple-dwelling construction—brownstones, apartment houses, and railroad flats—attracted a mix of social classes. Despite their education, family background, or ethnicity, however, almost all of the residents were confined by their race to service occupations.[6] While occupations of native and immigrant blacks were remarkably similar to one another in 1915 and 1925, this category was in sharp contrast to occupations of white residents in 1905. Unskilled and service categories were the smallest job categories reported by residents. Most of the latter worked in "low white collar" jobs as clerks, salesmen, and saleswomen.

The fact that black immigrants were more similar than different from native black workers is important in understanding both groups' comparative relationship to white immigrant workers. The work of social scientists and immigration scholars is helpful here. Most scholars agree that white ethnic concentrations in "industrial beachheads" aided their mobility and rise from poverty. Coethnics were able to assist newer immigrants in finding work. In New York, for instance, Jews and Italians recruited their fellows into the garment industry, Italian men into construction, and so on. Personal sponsorship of kin and friends provided employers with a "reservoir of untapped labor" from the homeland. In contrast black workers—immigrants and natives—were dispersed in a wide variety of low-paying, service occupations as the list of over twenty male job categories on the Payton block shows (see Table II-5). Although black workers used social networks to find jobs, openings were likely to dry up sooner in most companies where only a few "colored jobs" were available. Men were forced to "go from workplace to workplace in search of openings."[7] Low pay and lack of collective bargaining power plagued service workers. With the exception of railroad portering, black men were unable to establish niches in any major industry. The structural characteristics of the African American job market, where opportunities were so limited, slowed their rise from poverty and undoubtedly heightened competition between immigrant and native black job seekers.

Black women's concentration in the domestic service field—over 90 percent—probably enabled them to take greater advantage of the personal sponsorship method of job recruitment. It is clear that the networks formed by Caribbean women strengthened a sense of obligation and responsibility to immediate and extended kin. Similar patterns have been observed among southern migrant women domestic workers. Caribbean women and southern migrant women were more similar to one another than they were to the white female newcomer. Black women from both groups were required to work outside the home to enable a household to survive.[8]

A few differences in black immigrant and native men's occupations are noted. Immigrant men had a higher proportion of representation in the skilled trades. This was due in large degree to the historical background of the Caribbean immigrants from the more advantaged classes, who were apprenticed in a trade after grammar school. In his larger survey of Harlem occupations in 1925, Gutman found that 22 percent of Caribbean immigrants, as compared to 11 percent of native blacks, worked in skilled trades. This fact has significance for the rise and importance of a Caribbean middle class in New York after 1930. While most skilled immigrants—printers, carpenters, cabinet makers, jewelry makers, and other craftsmen—could not find jobs in their trades because of discrimination, they could find work or start a business in the black community.

In general immigrants were more likely to find a market for their educations, talents, and skills in uptown Harlem than in downtown Manhattan. Social-class advantages—possessing education, a skill, and sometimes a light complexion—privileged individuals within the African American community. Also, many immigrants who had attained professional status by 1930 arrived with the above criteria or were able to advance by building upon social-class advantages. In addition, middle-class immigrants utilized the practical advantages as well as the politics of naturalized citizenship. In general they were seasoned and African-Americanized, but most never relinquished ties to their immigrant communities. On the other hand, immigrant women of the same social class and, in some cases, educational background as men found fewer opportunities in the public arena of the African American community.

The color issue may have exacerbated this for both women and men. The subject is mentioned so frequently by dark-skinned Caribbean immigrants and others as a factor in social relations that it appears certain it also heightened ethnic strife. Many dark-skinned "talented tenth" who had left their homelands, in part to escape the restrictions of the color-class system, now faced a similar system within the African American community.[9] It is important to keep in mind that the black professional class, including Caribbean and native born, totaled less than 2 percent of Harlem's population. Competition for space in this marginalized, segregated milieu only intensified conflicts.

But all immigrant-native relations must be understood in the larger context of black urban community formation in the early part of this century. Like African American migrants the Caribbean immigrants established institutions which helped knit the fabric of a new community. Voluntary associations, including churches, benevolent societies, lodges, and fraternal organizations, served to sustain Caribbean immigrants' identification with the homeland, but they also served as links between the immigrant communities and the larger African American society. Ethnic interactions within the black church provide a good example of this. At first the historic African American denominations attracted young, ambitious, educated Caribbean men to leadership positions such as in the AME Church. Without an ethnic base large enough among Caribbean immigrants, the route to influence lay within the native African American church. Men such as Bishop William Derrick, who at one time served as head of the AME overseas mission for the Caribbean, connected these communities to African Americans in the United States. As migration increased and immigrants established new denominations (Moravian, Wesleyan, Anglican/Episcopalian, Catholic) in Harlem, leadership positions could be more effectively supported by the Caribbean community in New York. The Caribbean churches also served as vehicles through which immigrant individuals and groups could cooperate with and advance themselves within the African American community. These were not merely insular institutions.

Similarly, while home associations served to help newest arrivals adjust to the city, they were even more successful as vehicles through which more established residents could attain social and sometimes political clout inside and outside the Caribbean community. These benevolent associations also bought property in Harlem, rented space to an array of Caribbean and native organizations, purchased organizational membership in the NAACP, and in general participated in the larger life of the community. Organizers and leaders such as Charles Petioni (Trinidad), W. A. Domingo (Jamaica), Helena Benta, and William Roach (Montserrat) were well-known in Harlem and beyond. The Virgin Islands women organizers of the American West

Indian Ladies Aid Society were not devoted solely to performing social service to their group, but were participants in larger community social movements, such as strikes of the Harlem Tenants Association and the Virgin Islands political action movement. The home associations' strict rules and regulations, adherence to parliamentary procedures, and meticulous financial record-keeping served as training grounds for young people and as models of middle-class standards. Although true benevolence was an important aspect of the associations' activities—sick and death benefits were the only life and health insurance available to most black people—their larger social and political impact were important in the life of the community.

Fraternal organizations and lodges, historically significant within native African American communities, became important vehicles of social respectability within the American Caribbean community as well. Marcus Garvey's UNIA, basically a fraternal organization, drew upon the roots of this tradition in both groups. Immigrants in New York established branches of lodges unique to the Caribbean region, such as the Lebanon Foresters, but also formed predominantly immigrant chapters of the Elks or Masons. Almost no one in Harlem who aspired to middle-class status, respectability, or leadership failed to join a major lodge or fraternal organization. Immigrant numbers banker Casper Holstein, for example, broadened his constituency and influence through his leadership of the powerful Monarch Lodge.

Another kind of institution established by Caribbean Harlemites was the protective association organized to assist Caribbean immigrants with problems connected with their status as foreigners in New York. Protective associations served as liaisons between the black foreigner and local consulates in New York and provided advice on employment and naturalization. There were a series of associations set up over the years. Some, such as R. L. T. Richardson's Americanization school, were oriented toward naturalization. As part of her civic responsibilities, numbers banker Stephanie St. Claire set up the French Legal Aid Society to assist mainly in naturalization. Both Samuel Duncan and Edgar Grey were at one time founders of similar associations, but the stability of these organizations contrasts with that of the benevolents. After 1930, when many native black members became inactive, the local branch of the UNIA functioned like a protective association, facilitating naturalization and providing legal advice.

Their colonial status inspired considerable institutional effort by Caribbeans in Harlem. A small collection of intellectuals from diverse places in the Caribbean united on the basis of their common drive for independence and around specific political events in their homelands. Charles Petioni set up the Caribbean Union in 1930, and this effort inspired other independence-minded organizations, such as the Jamaica Progressive League, set up by W. A. Domingo and others. Before 1930 anticolonial sentiment brought together a loosely organized group of compatriots who associated in their street meetings, study groups, and forums. These groups both inspired and were inspired by labor and anticolonial unrest in their homelands. The connections would solidify even more after 1930. Events in Harlem, such as demonstrations against the 1935 Italian invasion of Ethiopia, increasingly became centered in Caribbean immigrants' anticolonial politics.

But a local politics claimed the attention of the black mainstream, and by 1930 Caribbean immigrants were well represented in the more moderate councils of the African American community. It is not surprising that the traditional political party activities were at the center of some of the most acrimonious exchanges between immigrant and natives. All African Americans operated from an extremely disadvantaged position as they tried to gain control of Harlem's assembly districts, controlled by white leaders until well into the 1930s. Both immigrants and natives jockeyed for position in the limited space Republican and Democratic bosses allowed blacks to operate in. The system of doling out a prescribed number of city or federal jobs to blacks in Harlem's white-controlled assembly districts could only encourage infighting. Competition was keen, and sides often formed along ethnic lines.

Caribbean Americans' first footholds in politics began in the Democratic party. While many native blacks remained loyal to the party of Lincoln, at the turn of the century black immigrants were among the first to join and become leaders of the United Colored Democracy, a segregated African American political club tied to Tammany. Over the years, while some immigrants remained with the club, it became increasingly unpopular among all Harlemites for its accommodationist strategies. Others, especially the influential Caribbean professional class, sought and obtained leadership positions in the regular, predominantly white Democratic political clubs. By 1930 key black immigrants were in positions to obtain nominations and support from the regular party structure. The UCD eventually faded into obsolescence.

In gaining the early advantage, Caribbean Americans forged ahead in Democratic politics in New York, but in the process became embroiled in bitter fights with native African American rivals. Political jobs, which became more professional and better paying, were still at stake. African Americans felt white Democratic leaders looked over them in favor of Caribbean immigrants, and when in power the immigrants looked out for their own.[10] Indeed professionals may have been more successful than the working class in taking advantage of niches gained through politics. The expansion of the Caribbean middle-class after 1930 was abetted by their progress in the early days of the Democratic political machine. The ability to employ coethnics, Charles Tilly notes, "fostered capital accumulation within an ethnic group, and thus facilitated investment in the occupational and investment chances of the next generation."[11] But Caribbean immigrant politicians, though often accused by their rivals of ethnic bias, appealed to and were supported by a predominantly native African American electorate. For instance, Harlemites elected Jamaican James Watson in 1930 as one of Harlem's first two African American municipal judges. In general, the mass-based community supported Caribbean leaders. This probably led W. A. Domingo, among others, to conclude that although educated Harlemites were "loudest in publicly decrying the [ethnic] hostilities," anti-Caribbean American feelings were "strongest" among members of that class. Domingo believed hostilities were based on "professional jealousy and competition for leadership."[12]

Although the public arena of traditional party politics was probably the most hotly contested field in the community, the street corner provided the space for outsiders to compete on their talents alone. Immigrants could test out and even merge their own politics with the populist concerns of the community. Not all speakers were immigrants, but here individuals could battle for their ideas and win the attention of Harlem's masses. Around 1917 Hubert Harrison set the standards of educational and political lectures, open to any one with enough time to listen. Porters, domestics, and elevator operators could get free lessons in biology, history, and philosophy. The street corner meetings, as much an outgrowth of the mass-based urban community as the speakers' talents, helped install lasting changes in the content and direction of political discourse. Here the old uplift strategies were debated and exchanged for the politics of the "New Negro." Harlem street audiences considered iconoclastic ideas and rejected or altered deeply rooted beliefs. Once tried and tested on the stepladder, a variety of ideas and positions could be more easily accepted elsewhere.

Community discontents were increasingly expressed in the form of protests held at well-known stepladder locations. Labor demonstrations, rent strikes and the jobs campaigns were some of the immediate outcomes of the stepladder forums. As protests became more contentious in the late 1920s and at the start of the depression, Harlem's alarmed establishment and the police tried to stop the meetings. Immigrants' ethnic backgrounds as much as their ideas and methods then became targets of critics.

The difficulty some Harlemites had with incorporating a cultural-pluralist perspective into a basically assimilationist politics was evident in the Marcus Garvey controversy. This should not be surprising in an era of "100 percent" Americanism. Native African American critics' focus on Garvey's foreignness reflected their confidence that he could be more effectively discredited on the basis of nativist rhetoric than on a serious evaluation of his ideas and methods. The UNIA leader's most antagonistic critics, members of the African American leadership class, aimed their rhetoric at white public opinion perhaps as much as at the native African American community. For them Garvey clearly was not a "representative Negro." Members of the black press frequently repeated assertions that Garvey did not "represent American Negroes," that the organization was comprised of "ignorant West Indians," and that Garvey himself was an alien. African American leaders feared the possible subversion of a fledgling integrationist movement through Garvey's spectacular programs and tremendous public appeal. In their opposition, most native-born critics realized that an integrationist critique aimed at the white establishment could never be effective in a largely segregationist society. Most critics chose nativist rhetoric and propaganda as the most practical tools in the campaign to discredit the UNIA leader and ensure their own hegemony. But the general onslaught on Garvey's nationality rather than his politics provoked schisms within the larger African American/Caribbean community.

The Garvey controversy is particularly revealing about an African American elite-led nativist propaganda. But it cannot be considered an index to all native-immigrant interactions. With the exception of *Age* editor and one-time alderman Fred R. Moore's steady and often hostile campaign against unnaturalized black immigrants, the African American press conveys ambiguity about black immigrants. For example, labels such as "alien" and "foreigner" were seldom used in reference to immigrant Harlemites. In most accounts if a descriptive label is used at all, writers refer to black immigrants by their nationalities or as "West Indians." Press accounts are often selective in identifying birthplace. For instance, journalistic accounts about his work rarely emphasized the birthplace of Harlem's "representative" poet Claude McKay. Nor was his noncitizen status ever an issue among his critics.[13] Similarly, "success stories," particularly about entrepreneurial activities, often deemphasized nativity in favor of race pride. In these situations membership in the racial community required neither American citizenship nor cultural conformity. In other situations lack of tolerance for the diverse customs of the immigrants became a source of tensions.[14] In still other areas relative to economic advance, it is important to keep in mind that native African Americans' attitudes about black and other immigrants were more complex than a simple nativism. Their ambivalence about all immigration was rooted in their antagonism toward a social system wherein native African Americans were continually displaced by each new wave of immigrant workers.[15] Black immigrants' economic competition, deliberately enhanced by a segregated occupational structure, was a familiar reminder with a new racial twist.

In the beginning and largely on the basis of racial solidarity, many African Americans supported black immigration. Educated Caribbean newcomers filled needed African American professional positions. But as more and more newcomers poured into Harlem in search of jobs, and as the middle class competed for mass-based clients and constituents, Caribbean immigrants were "hated and abused by their fellow Harlemites." While the Harlemites competed for jobs, W. E. B. Du Bois admitted to being uninformed about the effects of the Immigration Act of 1924. Perhaps the "Ethiopia of the Isles" would not "stretch out hands of helpfulness" after all. Indeed, when immigrants constructed new identities distinguishing themselves from native African Americans, the potential for conflict rose. It was clear that the concept of racial solidarity would not be so easily incorporated into the daily relations of immigrants and natives.

Yet Caribbean immigrants could not be truthfully classified as "outsiders." Despite conflicts, their activities formed an integral part of Harlem's identity as a racial community. Immigrants' high visibility in business enterprise was an important aspect of their cultural integration into the African American community. However, the word *domination*, used by some scholars to describe their functioning in this area, is misleading. In proportion to their numbers in the population, immigrant participation in business was only slightly higher than that of native African Americans if we rely upon George Edmund Hayes's 1911 study and census reports for 1915 and 1925. A slightly higher figure might also be noted if we could document the lively but unreported enterprises many Harlem residents engaged in. Before 1930, in actual numbers native African Americans were more numerous than Caribbean American businesspeople. But both the politics of uplift and of the New Negro coalesced around the expansion of business in Harlem. To put their concerns in perspective, this example from the Payton block is illustrative: In 1915 only six individuals on the block reported operating a business—three immigrants and three native-born—in contrast to the predominantly white block in 1905 when seventy-one individuals, including Philip Payton, reported entrepreneurial occupations. The word *domination* is more appropriately applied to the control of the marketplace by first- and second-generation Europeans. A clear conclusion of the present study is that both Caribbean immigrants and African Americans faced extreme disadvantages in operating businesses in Harlem's rapidly expanding consumer market, real estate, lending institutions, and eventually the numbers operation.

Keeping these points in mind, certain historical distinctions between black immigrant and native-born entrepreneurs are important. Immigrants frequently engaged in businesses which were an outgrowth of a skilled trade for which they could not find employment in New York. They also developed entrepreneurial niches in import-export and other areas that catered to a black immigrant population. Finally, Caribbean immigrants, unlike native-born African Americans, historically had not faced virulent competition from a hostile white majority and, based on their experiences in their homelands, they, like other immigrants, saw small business as a realistic way to make a living. Still, in Harlem black immigrants faced racial discrimination not experienced by other immigrant groups.

It is difficult to document the kinds of informal enterprises immigrants and natives engaged in. But in the numbers operation Harlem sustained a lively underground economy in which immigrants were major figures. An examination of their activities and the reaction of community people to them has provided another way to understand the interaction of race and ethnicity. Harlem's black numbers operators, whether immigrant or native, were often regarded as race men and women. A number of factors were necessary for a banker's inclusion. He or she was expected to be "fair" to employees and to the community. Bankers seeking community respectability had to contribute substantially to community projects: financing the construction of a baseball stadium, contributing prize money to literary contests, and so on. Race bankers were also members of key community institutions, including churches, and in general their behavior was subject to community sanctions. For these reasons, even those who opposed numbers playing supported black bankers when white gangsters moved in to take over numbers in Harlem. These gangsters were also associated with other forms of vice, including prostitution, hooch joints, and bootlegging. While black immigrant bankers such as Casper Holstein attempted to neutralize opposition from all quarters by donating to Jewish and Catholic charities as well as to African American/Caribbean ones, Dutch Schultz, using muscle to enforce his takeover, was accountable to no one.

The ethnic backgrounds of key foreign-born black numbers bankers were never targeted by Harlem newspapers in the way that Marcus Garvey's nationality was, although the backgrounds of some Hispanic bankers and Anglophone Caribbean bankers were identified in the press. There are several reasons for this. Although some bankers, such as Holstein, became race leaders, they never really threatened native African American hegemony. (In the one instance in which Holstein attempted to become head of the national Elks organization, his nativity did factor into his defeat.) In addition Harlem bankers' financial largesse was so widespread it was politically unwise to launch nativist crusades against them. Race bankers, like most entrepreneurs were often naturalized citizens. Finally, some bankers, such as Stephanie St. Claire, became folk heroes and Harlem subscribers did not want to read unfair and disparaging stories about them.

It was an irony of Harlem life that the most widespread business controlled by blacks before 1930 was based on a game of chance. But other developments of the emerging community are perhaps more encouraging to examine. One of the most important aspects of their encounter with African Americans was Caribbean immigrants' participation in Harlem's historic Renaissance in literature and in the development of an independent press. Harlem's many newspapers and periodicals provide significant evidence about the public aspects of an intraracial ethnic community, while it is more difficult to document the private interactions and feelings of immigrants and natives.

Although a fuller analysis of its ethnic themes awaits another study, the literature of the period is suggestive here. Claude McKay, in one of the few autobiographies written by an immigrant, illuminates—at least in his own case—the alienation of the black stranger, especially from the black middle class. Perhaps reflecting Socialist influence, McKay's autobiographical narrative conveys that he found the native African American working class much more tolerant of ethnic diversity than the middle class. In his nonfiction McKay explained the class-based nature of ethnic conflict in this way: "The natives call the West Indians 'monkeychasers' and the West Indians call them 'coons' and they fight or laugh over it. But they work together, play together, marry one another and share equally the joys and sorrows of the group."[16] Though McKay probably exaggerated the extent of class solidarity between ordinary Harlemites, immigrant men probably had more opportunities for the social exchanges he describes than women, who were more isolated from other African Americans in domestic work, in household and lodging arrangements, and through marriage.

The journalistic writings of immigrants and natives provide some of the best insights into their more public ideas. Writers often focused upon Harlem's diversity and not always the conflicts that it produced. Harrison observed people "exchanging cultural gifts with increasing facility" toward the end of the 1920s.[17] An important and permanent development was the internationalization of political discourse inspired by Harlem's global black community. W. A. Domingo noticed in 1925 "a world-wide re-action of the darker races to their common as well as local grievances, . . . [and] extension of race organizations beyond American boundaries."[18] Immigrants wrote primarily to a racial community but expanded political discourse in other ways. Amy Jacques-Garvey's regular *Negro World* column presented new feminist topics from around the world, and immigrant Socialists and other radicals emphasized class contradictions as well as racial problems.

The first significant urban contact between multiple cultures of the African dias-pora was unparalleled in immigrant-native American experience. Africans in the Western Hemisphere, separated for centuries by slavery and brought together for the first time by migration and systematically denied equal opportunities, perhaps faced even greater challenges in creating community. Community formation con-nected but did not necessarily merge multiple historical and cultural traditions. Blood relations—immigrants and natives of African descent—struggled to define the nature of their bonds to one another. In countless ways their historic encounter produced an interchange of ideas, people, and institutions that made Harlem, black metropolis, the center of the African world.

Appendix

BETWEEN 1905 AND 1925 the block on 131st Street between Fifth and Lenox Avenues, comprised of brownstones, apartment houses, and "railroad" flats, provides a unique opportunity to examine a cross section of Harlem households as well as the transformation of the block from predominantly second-generation Irish and German to first urban-generation African American—southern migrant and Caribbean. By 1915, when the block was predominantly black, households showed a remarkable diversity.

Households selected consist of odd- and even-numbered houses (1–78 on 131st Street as well as the corner houses on Lenox and Fifth Avenues). For purposes of this study, the residential block rather than the typical census block was chosen for two reasons. First, New York State census takers were inconsistent in the selection of house numbers in 1905, 1915, and 1925 and sometimes but not always included 132nd Street in their enumeration of the block. I wanted to study residents of the same houses and only on 131st Street. Second, I wanted to examine a neighborhood block, houses on each side of a street, the way neighbors were likely to describe a city block. This block was chosen primarily because of its location in central Harlem; the ratio of foreign-born to native black residents, which most closely reflected their representation in the total population; the variety of housing available—from the one-family brownstone to elevator apartments to tenement-like walk-ups; the manageable size of the block—over 1,000 but under 2,000 residents; and the several well-known residents, including the Paytons, Petionis, Randolphs, and others whose identities provide narrative context. The data from this block form the basis for a comparison of black native-born and immigrant households in chapter 3 ("On to Harlem").

The first set of tables (I) examine the ethnic composition of the block, beginning with 1905 but focusing primarily on the number of foreign-born and native-born black heads of household in 1915 and 1925. These households and all other data were counted by hand and categorized on the basis of gender and nativity. Enumerators generally identified the European foreign-born by country of origin, but unfortunately they did not usually specify the birthplace of most Caribbean immigrants. Those from the various British colonies were designated as "B.W.I." (British West Indian). To simplify my analysis in the tables, I identify black residents as either native or foreign born.

Tables in the next category (II) focus on occupations of heads of household by gender and nativity for 1905 and 1925. A table showing a detailed occupational distribution of all working-age residents is included for 1915, on the basis of nativity. This socio-economic ranking of occupations and job descriptions on the block in 1915 is adapted from the scheme used by Herbert Gutman in his much larger sample of black Harlem in 1925. (See Gutman, *The Black Family in Slavery and Freedom* 1750–1925 [New York:

Pantheon, 1976], Appendix A. Table 42. p. 512.) For all occupation tables, distributions are broken down into five basic categories: unskilled laborers and service workers, skilled workers, white collar, professional, and entrepreneurial.

A third set of tables (III) describe age distribution, a fourth (IV) lodgers, and a fifth (V) cross-cultural marriages in Payton block households in 1915 and 1925.

I. Heads of Household 1905, 1915, and 1925

Table I-1	by Nativity 1905	
	Foreign-born	Native-born
Male	87	255
Female	17	57
Totals	104	312

Table I-2	by Nativity 1915	
	Foreign-born	Native-born
Male	76	201
Female	13	73
Totals	89	274

Table I-3	by Nativity 1925	
	Foreign-born	Native-born
Male	53	211
Female	12	82
Totals	65	293

II. Occupational Distribution 1905 and 1925

Table II-1	Female Heads of Household 1905	
	Foreign-born	Native-born
Unskilled	0	2
Skilled	0	4
White collar	0	2
Professional	1	2
Entrepreneurial	1	3
No occupation	15	44

Table II-2	Male Heads of Household 1905	
	Foreign-born	Native-born
Unskilled	13	22
Skilled	34	32
White collar	14	127
Professional	2	13
Entrepreneurial	14	41
Miscellaneous	0	8
No occupation	10	12

Table II-3	Female Heads of Household 1925	
	Foreign-born	Native-born
Unskilled	12	72
Skilled	0	7
White collar	0	0
Professional	0	1
Entrepreneurial	0	2
No occupation	0	0

Table II-4	Male Heads of Household 1925	
	Foreign-born	Native-born
Unskilled	21	148
Skilled	19	29
White collar	3	20
Professional	4	3
Entrepreneurial	6	11
No occupation	0	0

Table II-5 Occupations of Native Blacks and Caribbean Immigrants
Payton Block 1915

| Occupation | 1. Unskilled Laborers and Service Workers | |
	Native-born	Foreign-born
bellman	5	4
bldg. engineer/fireman	5	2
butler	5	5
caretaker	2	0
caterer	2	0
chauffeur	15	4
cook	15	9
domestic worker	274	82
drygoods	1	0
elevator operator	19	34
housekeeper	2	0
houseworker	28	7
janitor	10	5
laborer	63	5
laundress	2	2
longshoreman	1	0
maid	2	2
manicurist	1	0
messenger	4	0
porter	65	28
presser	1	1
railroad porter	6	0
seaman	2	2
stevedore	1	0
steward	4	1
superintendent	8	1
unemployed	2	1
valet	4	0
waiter	30	26
waitress	2	4
Totals	581	225

Table II-5 Occupations of Native Blacks and Caribbean Immigrants (*cont.*)

| | 2. Skilled Workers | |
	Native-born	Foreign-born
actor	11	0
actress	1	0
artist (photo)	2	0
barber	0	3
bookbinder	1	0
carpenter	2	1
cigar maker	2	4
corker	1	0
dressmaker	23	10
electrician	3	2
hairdresser	4	1
machinist	2	1
mechanic	0	1
musician	27	2
painter	0	2
photographer	0	2
piano maker	0	1
printer	2	2
salesman	1	2
seamstress	4	0
shoemaker	1	1
silversmith	0	1
singer	1	0
stagehand	1	0
tailor	4	5
Totals	93	41

Table II-5 Occupations of Native Blacks and Caribbean Immigrants (*cont.*)

	3. White Collar	
	Native-born	Foreign-born
advertising agent	1	0
bookkeeper	3	2
broker	0	1
cashier	1	0
city employee	0	0
clerk	34	2
custom house worker	1	0
editor	3	0
insurance agent	1	0
railroad inspector	1	0
real estate agent	1	0
stenographer	1	0
telephone operator	3	2
U.S. customs worker	1	0
Totals	51	7

	4. Professional	
	Native-born	Foreign-born
law clerk	1	1
lawyer	1	0
minister	1	1
music teacher	1	0
physician	3	0
teacher	3	1
teacher (Boy Scouts)	1	0
Totals	11	3

	5. Entrepreneurial	
	Native-born	Foreign-born
contractor	2	1
jeweler	1	1
merchant	3	1
Totals	6	3

III. Age Distribution

Table III-1	Age of Residents 1925
Under 15	108
15–24	168
25–34	354
35–44	335
45–54	219
Over 55	53

IV. Lodgers Living in Payton Block 1905, 1925

Table IV-1	Lodgers 1905, 1925	
1905	Foreign-born	Native-born
Male	18	40
Female	6	5
Totals	24	45
1925	Foreign-born	Native-born
Male	96	258
Female	60	144
Totals	156	402

V. Cross-Cultural Marriages 1915, 1925

Table V-1	Marriages 1915
Foreign-born Males to Native-born Females	17
Foreign-born Females to Native-born Males	4

Table V-2	Marriages 1925
Foreign-born Males to Native-born Females	7
Foreign-born Females to Native-born Males	6

Notes

1. Introduction

1. Wallace Thurman and William Jourdan Rapp, "Harlem as Others See It," *Negro World*, April 13, 1929; Doming Romero, typescript in Edward Bruce Papers, Box 3 Manuscripts Archives and Rare Books Division, Schomburg Center for Research in Black Culture, the New York Public Library, Astor, Lenox and Tilden Foundations (hereafter SCRBC); William Whyte, ed., *The WPA Guide to New York City* (1939; reprint, New York: Random House, 1982), p. 257.

2. Only a few studies focus on the social history of African Americans in Manhattan. See Seth Scheiner, *The Negro Mecca* (New York: New York University, 1965); Roi Ottley, *The Negro in New York: An Informal Social History* (Dobbs Ferry, New York: Oceana, 1967); Gilbert Osofsky, *Harlem: The Making of a Ghetto, 1890–1930* (New York: Harper and Row, 1963). The most important of the latter is Osofsky's 1963 volume, a judiciously researched community study focusing on the period between 1890 and 1930. Only a few pages are devoted to Harlem's heterogeneity, and for him the central theme in intraracial ethnic relations is conflict which "served to weaken a Negro community in great need of unity." See p. 135. Relatively recent cultural studies include James De Jongh, *Vicious Modernism: Black Harlem and the Literary Imagination* (New York and Cambridge: Cambridge University Press, 1990); Jervis Anderson, *This Was Harlem* (New York: Farrar Straus Giroux, 1982); David Levering Lewis, *When Harlem Was in Vogue* (New York: Oxford University Press, 1979). Both Lewis and Anderson devote sections of their books to the presence of Caribbean immigrants in Harlem. Harold Cruse's pioneering *Crisis of the Negro Intellectual* (Boston: Little, Brown, 1967) raised important questions about race and ethnicity in Harlem's intellectual community.

3. Social science scholarship has focused upon the themes of race, ethnicity, and identity in late twentieth-century black communities. Most of this work, which also examines migration patterns and adjustment, deals with the post-1965 Caribbean immigrant communities in New York City and elsewhere. See Philip Kasinitz, *Caribbean New York: Black Immigrants and the Politics of Race* (Ithaca: Cornell University Press, 1992); Nancy Foner, ed., *New Immigrants in New York* (New York: Columbia University Press, 1987); Constance Sutton and Elsa Chaney, eds., *Caribbean Life in New York City* (New York: Center for Migration Studies, 1987); Roy Simon Bryce-Laporte, *Sourcebook on the New Immigration: Implications for the United States and the International Community* (New Brunswick: Transaction Books for the Smithsonian Institution, 1980); Virginia Dominguez, *From Neighbor to Stranger: The Dilemma of Caribbean Peoples in the United States* (New Haven: Yale University Press, 1975); Helen Safa and Brian Du Toit, eds., *Migration and Development* (The Hague: Mouton, 1975). One important recent historical study is Marilyn Halter's *Between Race and Ethnicity: Cape Verdean American Immigrants 1860–1965* (Urbana: University of Illinois Press, 1993).

4. Barbadian lecturer and Harlem activist Richard B. Moore and others have pointed out that the word *Caribbean*, derived from *Carib*, the original inhabitants of the islands, is a more appropriate designation for the people of the region than the term *West Indian*, derived from the errors of Western explorers. Here *Caribbean* is the preferred term and is interchanged with *black immigrant*

and similar designations for stylistic purposes. See Richard B. Moore, *Caribs, "Cannibals," and Human Relations* (New York: Pathway Publishers, 1972), p. 8.

5. *New York Times*, August 16, 1900; *New York Tribune*, July 27, 1905. By 1920 African American Harlem extended from 130th to 145th Streets, bounded on the east by Madison Avenue and on the west by Seventh Avenue. Later these boundaries would expand to the south, touching 110th Street and north to the 150s.

6. See Calvin B. Holder, "The Causes and Composition of West Indian Immigration to New York City, 1900–1952," *Afro-Americans in New York Life and History* (January 1987); "The Rise of the West Indian Politician in New York City, 1900–1952," *Afro-Americans in New York Life and History* (January 1980); John C. Walker and Jill Louise Ansheles, "The Role of the Caribbean Migrant in the Harlem Renaissance," *Afro-Americans in New York Life and History* (January 1977).

7. Lionel M. Yard, *Biography of Amy Ashwood Garvey 1897–1969* (Washington, D.C.: The Associated Publishers, 1990), p. 37; Claude McKay, *A Long Way from Home* (New York: Lee Furman, 1937), p. 48. James Weldon Johnson wrote of Harlem in 1930 that "it is not a slum, nor is it a quarter consisting of dilapidated tenements. . . . It is a section of new-law apartment houses and handsome dwellings, with streets as well paved, as well lighted, and as well kept as in any other part of the city." James Weldon Johnson, *Black Manhattan* (1930; reprint, New York: Atheneum, 1972), p. 146. But to be sure, by 1930 Harlem had its "Valley," a slum area extending from 130th to 140th Street, east of Seventh Avenue. There was also the "Market," a stretch from 110th to 115th Street on Seventh Avenue, which was frequented by streetwalkers. At the other extreme and more closely fitting Johnson's description was "Golden Eagle," the part of the neighborhood facing Central Park, which housed many of the professional class. And "Sugar Hill," the section of Harlem's upper class, was located along Edgecombe, Convent, and St. Nicholas Avenues. Another haven of the upper class was "Strivers Row," located on 138th and 139th Streets. Susan Edmiston and Linda D. Cirno, *Literary New York* (1976; reprint, New York: Peregrine Smith Books, 1991), p. 272.

8. This quotation actually referred to the Garvey movement and was written right after the first UNIA international convention, attended by 25,000 mostly native African Americans in Madison Square Garden in August 1920. Du Bois would soon characterize Garvey's followers as "ignorant Negroes." W. E. B. Du Bois, "The Rise of the West Indian," *Crisis* 20 (September 1920), p. 214.

9. See Stephen Steinberg, *The Ethnic Myth* (Boston: Beacon, 1990), for a discussion of what he terms ethnic heroes and ethnic villains; Henry Louis Gates, Jr., "The Trope of the New Negro and the Reconstruction of the Image of the Black," *Representations* 24 (Fall 1988), p. 137. See also Paul Lawrence Dunbar, "Representative American Negroes," in Booker T. Washington et al., *The Negro Problem* (1903; reprint, New York: AMS, 1970).

10. In their 1945 classic, *Black Metropolis,* St. Clair Drake and Horace R. Cayton wrote that on Chicago's southside "to open a successful business in Bronzeville makes any man something of a hero." Drake and Cayton, *Black Metropolis,* vol. 2 (New York: Harcourt, Brace & World, 1962), p. 488.

11. Ira De Augustine Reid, *The Negro Immigrant* (New York: Columbia University Press, 1939), pp. 33, 244; Roy Garis, *Immigration Restriction* (New York: The Macmillan Company, 1927), p. 172; Malcolm J. Proudfoot, *Population Movements in the Caribbean* (1950; reprint, New York: Negro Universities Press, 1970), p. 88. Only independent nations of the Western Hemisphere qualified in its nonquota category. The exception made for Western Hemispheric nations was probably in the interest of positive relations with border countries such as Mexico and Canada. The demand for migrant labor was also a consideration in the case of Mexico. There were 20,336 foreign-born blacks in the United States in 1900; 73,803 in 1920; and 98,620 in 1930. Only 8,500 entered the country between 1925 and 1930, reflecting the effect of the 1924 law. Many of the latter individuals were the immediate family members of naturalized citizens. However, these totals do not include migrants from the U.S. Virgin Islands or the estimated 43,452 native-born black persons of foreign-born parentage. By 1930 the number of black persons residing in the United States who were foreign-born

or the children of foreign-born was 150,000. Approximately 50 percent of these individuals lived in New York City. United States Bureau of the Census, *Negroes in the United States, 1920–1932, Population* Vol. II (Washington, D.C.: U.S. Government Printing Office, 1934), pp. 67–73.

12. *Negroes in the United States*, pp. 17–21

13. W. A. Domingo, "Gift of the Black Tropics," in Alain Locke, ed., *The New Negro* (New York: Albert and Charles Boni, 1925), p. 342.

14. Ira De A. Reid's 1939 sociological study is the most comprehensive on black immigrants of this period and is highly useful.

15. Booker T. Washington, *Up from Slavery,* in John Hope Franklin, *Three Negro Classics* (1900; reprint, New York: Avon, 1965), p. 83.

16. McKay, *A Long Way from Home,* pp. 8–9.

17. James Weldon Johnson, *Along This Way* (New York: Viking Press, 1969), p. 65.

18. Ira De A. Reid, *The Negro Immigrant,* p. 204; *The Negro World,* July 2, 1927; July 17, 1926.

19. Peter Gottlieb, "Rethinking the Great Migration: A Perspective from Pittsburgh," in Joe William Trotter, Jr., *The Great Migration in Historical Perspective* (Bloomington: Indiana University Press, 1991), p. 72; Dowridge-Challenor Family Letters 1905–1917, Manuscript Division, SCRBC. Letters between Aletha Dowridge and her family and friends in Barbados illustrate the importance of emotional as well as financial support.

20. See Herbert Gutman, *The Black Family in Slavery and Freedom, 1750–1925* (New York: Pantheon, 1976). Family letters and the records of community organizations provide a fuller but still incomplete portrait of family networks.

21. Philip Payton later became president of the Afro-American Realty Company. Referred to as the "pioneer [N]egro real estate agent in New York," Payton became one of the first black managers of white-owned buildings in Harlem. When vacancies became available he rented to blacks. See *New York Times,* June 16, 1991; New York State Manuscript Census (hereafter NYSMC) 1905: ED41 AD31 Block A; 1915: ED15 AD21 Block 1; 1925: ED35 AD119 Block 1, New York Public Library. State of New York, *Report of the Secretary of State of the Enumeration of Inhabitants, 1915* (New York: J.B. Lyon Company, 1916). All published reports are located in the Municipal Archives Library of the City of New York.

22. Darlene Clark Hine, "Black Migration to the Urban Midwest: The Gender Dimension 1915–1945," in Trotter, ed., *The Great Migration in Historical Perspective,* pp. 128–29. Walter Laidlaw, ed., *Population of the City of New York 1890–1930* (New York City Census Committee, 1932), p. 8. Laidlaw's tables, based on census reports, tend to support contemporaries' observation that New York City attracted more migrating southern women than men.

23. W. E. B. Du Bois, "The Black North in 1901—New York," reprinted in Dan Green and Edwin Driver, *W. E. B. Du Bois, On Sociology and the Black Community* (Chicago: University of Chicago Press, 1978), p. 141, from *The Black North in 1901—A Social Study* (1901; reprint New York: Arno Press, 1969).

24. See *Manifest of Alien Passengers for the United States between 1890 and 1930,* Department of National Archives of the United States, (hereafter, DNA), New York City. The researcher is impressed by the number of Caribbean women arriving classified as "nonimmigrant aliens" and therefore not counted in the permanent immigration statistics for the period.

25. Mary White Ovington, *Half a Man: The Status of the Negro in New York* (New York: Longman, Green and Company, 1911), p. 177.

26. Today, any leader, including African heads of state, can be seen speaking on the corner of 125th Street and Adam Clayton Powell Boulevard in Harlem.

27. McKay, *A Long Way from Home,* p. 49.

28. Osofsky, *Harlem: The Making of a Ghetto,* p. 134.

29. John Higham, *Strangers in the Land: Patterns of American Nativism, 1860–1925* (New Brunswick: Rutgers University Press, 1955), preface to 2nd edition.

2. Panama Silver Meets Jim Crow

1. J. F. Dowridge to Aletha Dowridge, September [4?], 1904; Mrs. H. Dowridge to Aletha Dowridge, June 10, 1905. In Dowridge-Challenor Family Letters, Manuscript Division, SCRBC; Interview with Dorothy Challenor Burnham, November 12, 1993.

2. See Eric Williams, *From Columbus to Castro: The History of the Caribbean, 1492–1969* (New York: Harper and Row, 1970); Dawn Marshall's overview is particularly relevant here. She points out that "the history of the Caribbean can be seen as a succession of waves of migration. The population of the countries of the Caribbean are almost wholly the result of migration: from initial settlement after discovery, forced immigration during slavery and indentured immigration during the nineteenth century, to the present outward movement to the metropolitan core countries. Nevertheless observers tend to see the present outward movements as a recent phenomenon and are not generally aware that, certainly from the Commonwealth Caribbean, people have been moving out of their islands for 150 years." See Dawn Marshall, "A History of West Indian Migration: Overseas Opportunities and 'Safety-Valve' Policies," in Levine, ed., *The Caribbean Exodus* (New York: Praeger, 1987), p. 15.

3. E. Ethelred Brown, "Labor Conditions in Jamaica Prior to 1917," *Journal of Negro History* 4 (October 1919), p. 358.

4. Jamaica Census of 1921, Abstract G, *Occupations*.

5. Frank W. Knight, *The Caribbean: The Genesis of a Fragmented Nationalism* (New York: Oxford University Press, 1978), p. 144; Eric Williams, *From Columbus to Castro*, p. 447.

6. George Roberts, "Emigration from Barbados," *Social and Economic Studies* 4 (September 1955), p. 281.

7. Knight, pp. 143–44.

8. Such a migratory history may account for the presence of the Suey family, who resided on the Payton block in 1925. Also Anna Petioni, who had emigrated from Trinidad in 1918 to join her husband, Charles, was of Chinese extraction. New York State Manuscript Census 1925, ED35, AD19, p. 19, New York City Municipal Archives.

9. Michael M. Horowitz, ed., *Peoples and Cultures of the Caribbean* (Garden City, New York: Natural History Press, 1971), p. 32.

10. David Lowenthal, *West Indian Societies* (New York: Oxford University Press, 1972), p. 91.

11. Interview, Tyrell Wilson, March 7, 1978; Gordon Heights, Long Island, New York. Tyrell Wilson mentioned color stratification as a factor retarding the ambitions of the young, dark-skinned middle class.

12. David McCullough, *The Path between the Seas: The Creation of the Panama Canal, 1870–1914* (New York: Touchstone, 1977), p. 575.

13. The building of the Canal was a gigantic enterprise, and many young men felt not only a need but an urge to go to Panama.

Albert Peters of the Bahamas recalled that in 1906, " . . . while reading the daily papers I saw where they were digging a canal from ocean to ocean on the Isthmus of Panama and needed thousands of men. I and two of my pals read it over and we suggested to take a trip over. We were all eager for some adventure and experience." And E. W. Martineau of Grenada, who left home for Panama in 1912, wrote, "I came to the Republic of Panama . . . not in search of work, but to find a better field of endeavor." Martineau brought with him the equipment to start a carbonated-drinks factory and soon after his arrival set up a business in Gatun. "Most of us came from homelands in search of work and improvements," he added. "We turned out to be pioneers in a foreign land." Isthmian Historical Society. "Competition for the Best True Stories of Life and Work on the Isthmus during Construction Days by Non-United States Citizens Who Worked on the Isthmus Prior to 1915," [hereafter "Life and Work"], (Canal Zone Library, 1963), p. 1, 186.

14. McCullough, p. 472.

15. George Westerman, *The West Indian Worker on the Canal Zone* (National Civil League, 1951), p. 10. Jamaican laborer Daniel T. Lawson, who had come to the Isthmus in 1906, reported that "between the years of 1906 and 1908 from what I had seen daily, I manifest my doubt as to whether the death toll on the Canal Zone had, and could be, correctly estimated. As for me personally I escaped death three times by train, hand car and by drowning in the Chagres river." "Life and Work," p. 153.

16. Quoted in Reid, p. 63, from Carleton Beals, *America South* (Philadelphia: Lippincott, 1937), p. 158.

17. McCullough, p. 561.

18. Eric Walrond, *Tropic Death* (1926; reprint, New York: Collier, 1972), p. 181.

19. Walrond, p. 187.

20. Melville J. Herskovits, *Trinidad Village* (New York: Octagon, 1964), p. 76; Margaret Katzin, "'Partners': An Informal Savings Institution in Jamaica," *Social and Economic Studies* 8 (December 1959), pp. 436–40; Clifford Gertz, "The Rotating Credit Association: A Middle Rung in Development," *Economic Development and Cultural Change* 10 (April 1962), pp. 241–63.

21. Roberts, p. 275.

22. Edwin Slossen and Gardner Richardson, "The Story of a Martinique Girl," *Independent* 60 (April 19, 1906), pp. 924–25.

23. Annual Report of the Isthmian Canal Commission [hereafter ARICC], 1906, p. 116.

24. Frederic J. Haskins, *The Panama Canal* (New York: Doubleday, Page, 1913), p. 161.

25. McCullough, p. 577.

26. S. A. Gilbert Cox, "Editorial," *Our Own* 1 (July 1, 1910), p. 4.

27. *New York Age,* June 28, 1917. For other reactions to Jim Crow in Panama, see Harvey Patterson and Thomas C. Saint, "American Democracy in the Panama Canal Zone," *Crisis,* June 1920, p. 84; "The West Indian in Panama," *Crisis,* April 1927, p. 57. A *Crisis* article explained the existence of prostitution in the context of the impoverished conditions of families: "The families that are able to rent two rooms are very few in number. A small room which would ill-accommodate the most unpretentious bachelor generally houses a family of four to eight, some of them full-grown young women. The absence of privacy in the home and the deep wounds inflicted by the fangs of abject poverty drive these young women—most of them not quite past the age of sixteen—to prostitute their bodies in order to appease the gnawing pangs of hunger. . . ." G. Victor Cools, "Semi-Peonage in Panama," *Crisis,* April 1922, p. 276.

28. ARICC, 1914, p. 27.

29. Z. H. McKenzie, "Life and Work," p. 181.

30. Interview Charles Zampty, February 26, 1977. Detroit, Michigan; Robert Hill, ed. *The Marcus Garvey and Universal Negro Improvement Association Papers* [hereinafter *MGP*] I, p. 37.

31. McCullough fails to explore the contribution of skilled black workers on the Canal project. G. Victor Cools noted that "when the first group of American engineers landed in Panama in 1904, they found there a nucleus of efficient black men—artisans and laborers—who were originally identified with the French Canal Company. A number of these men occupied positions of trust in the office personnel of the company, while in the field of construction they held positions ranging from superintendent of construction to skilled mechanics and shopmen. The usefulness of these men was immediately recognized by these American pioneers and they were allowed to serve in their various capacities." When southern whites came, according to Cools, black men were "surreptitiously removed. Those whose places could not be conveniently filled were retained. The artisans and shopmen were given another designation. From skilled mechanics they came to be known as helpers," Cools, *Crisis,* April 1922, p. 272.

32. Hill, *MGP* II, p. 74, n. 2.

33. Richard Kluger, *Simple Justice* (New York: Vintage, 1977), p. 316.

34. A community of English- and French-speaking immigrants grew during the World War I years (1913–1918) as revenues from sugar sales gave Cuba "the highest per capita tax income of

any Latin American country. . . ." The total population was 1,500,000 in 1900. John Edwin Fagg, *Latin America: A General History* (New York: MacMillan, 1963), p. 748. Official estimates are lower than the actual emigration, but a recorded 22,000 persons, mostly men but some women, left Jamaica permanently for Cuba between 1911 and 1921 and there joined compatriots and relatives who had emigrated earlier. Roberts, *Economic Development of Jamaica*, p. 139. Permanent Haitian immigration between 1912 and 1920 rose above 33,000. By the end of the decade the Cuban government, alarmed that its black population was growing larger than its white, moved to restrict this migratory flow. Reid, p. 65.

35. Cools, "Semi-Peonage in Panama," *Crisis*, April 1922, p. 276.

36. Amy Ashwood to Marcus Garvey, March 6, 1917, in Hill, ed., *MGP* I, p. 205.

37. For a discussion of lynching, see Arthur F. Raper, *The Tragedy of Lynching* (Chapel Hill: University of North Carolina Press, 1933); Walter White, *Rope and Faggot: A Biography of Judge Lynch* (1929; reprint New York: Arno and New York Times, 1969); NAACP, *Thirty Years of Lynching in the United States, 1889–1918* (New York, 1919).

38. Claude McKay, *My Green Hills of Jamaica*. ed. Mervyn Morris. (Kingston: 1979) p. 86–87.

39. *Pittsburgh Courier*, July 9, 1918.

40. Paule Marshall, "Black Immigrant Women in *Brown Girl, Brownstones*," in Roy Bryce-Laporte, ed., *Female Immigrants to the United States: Caribbean, Latin American and African Experiences* (Washington D.C.: Research Institute on Immigration and Ethnic Studies, Smithsonian Institution, 1981), p. 5.

41. Ibid.

42. Mrs. H. Dowridge to Aletha Dowridge, September 29 circa 1908.

43. Ibid.

44. J. F. Dowridge to Aletha Dowridge, ibid.; Harriet Dowridge to Aletha Dowridge, March 26, circa 1910; Interview, Dorothy Burnham, November 12, 1993.

45. H. Dowridge to Aletha Dowridge, June 4, n.d. circa 1907.

46. H. Dowridge to "Dearest lea," n.d., circa 1907.

47. Dowridge-Challenor Family Letters, Willie to Lee, September 14, 1907.

48. H. Dowridge to Aletha Dowridge, n.d., circa spring 1908.

49. Quoted in *Negro World*, November 10, 1923, from the Barbados *Weekly Herald*, n.d., circa October or November 1923.

50. Interview, Violet Murrell, September 2–3, 1994, St. Michael, Barbados. Violet Murrell died in 1995.

51. *Daily Gleaner*, December 14, 1920.

52. Quoted in *Daily Gleaner*, July 30, 1920.

53. Tony Martin, *Race First* (Wesport, Connecticut: Greenwood Press, 1976), p. 95; see *Negro World, passim* 1920–1930.

54. *Negro World*, March 19, 1921.

55. Amy Ashwood to Marcus Garvey, June 10, 1917, in Hill, *MGP* I, p. 207.

56. *Jamaica Gazette*, October 10, 1918. See also September 6, September 12, and October 4, 1918. John Bruce, "Bruce Grits Column," clipping in John Bruce papers, n.d., circa 1920. SCRBC.

57. *Jamaica Gazette*, October 10, 1918.

58. *New York Age*, December 10, 1932.

59. Department of National Archives, Manifest of Alien Passengers to the United States, SS *Korona*, April 6, 1911; *Negro World* (n.d., circa 1920) in Bruce Papers, SCRBC.

60. Ross Hazeltine to Secretary of State, August 8, 1916. National Archives. Record Group 59, Box 8896, State Decimal File 1910–1929.

61. *Baltimore Afro-American*, April 28, May 5, 1922. *New York Amsterdam News* [hereafter *NYAN*], June 8, 1927.

62. See Michael Cohn and Michael K.H. Platzer, *Black Men of the Sea* (New York: Dodd, Mead, 1978).

63. *NYAN,* June 8, 1927.

64. *Chicago Defender,* January 14, 1922. See also Charles L. Latham to Secretary of State, March 18, 1922. This report was sent to the State Department by the Postmaster in the town of Douglass: "It appears that Mrs. Paul and one of the girls had a disagreement over household work and the girl became enraged and threw various cooking utensils at Mrs. Paul who became frightened and called the Police Department who came and took the girl to the city jail where she was placed in the women's ward with plenty of bedding and good food. No charges were filed against the girl by any of the Paul family and she was held on a charge of disturbing the peace, preferred by the policeman who made the arrest. No hearing was held on this charge, however, and after being held two days, she was released at the intercession of J. R. Rector, a colored minister of this city, who obtained lodging for her at a lodging house for colored people. Her conduct while at this place was such that she was not permitted to remain only for a few days." The fate of this woman or her companions is not known. C. A. Overluck, Postmaster, to Inspector-in Charge, Washington, D.C., April 20, 1922, National Archives, Record Group 59, Box 8896, State Decimal File.

65. Interview, Hope R. Stevens, March 9, 1978.

66. Paule Marshall, "Black Immigrant Women in *Brown Girl, Brownstones,*" p. 5.

67. G. W. Roberts, "Emigration from the Island of Barbados," *Social and Economic Studies* 4 (September 1955), p. 275.

68. Joyce Moore Turner and W. Burghardt Turner, *Richard B. Moore, Caribbean Militant in Harlem* (Bloomington: Indiana University Press, 1988), p. 23.

69. Hill, "W. A. Domingo," in Appendix I, *MGP* I, p. 528.

70. Kluger, *Simple Justice,* p. 316.

71. Turner and Turner, *Richard B. Moore,* p. 58.

72. Grace Campbell to Claude McKay, Dec. 10, 1921, in Claude McKay Papers of the James Weldon Johnson Collection, in the Yale Collection of American Literature Beinecke Rare Book and Manuscript Library, Yale University.

73. Grace P. Campbell was one of the best-known Harlem radicals.

74. Immigration and Naturalization Service. Reports of the Commissioner General of Immigration, 1920–1924.

75. Mary White Ovington, *Half a Man,* p. 147.

76. Hudsy Smith, "Partial History of White Rose Mission and Industrial Association," Manuscript Division, SCRBC.

77. Lasalle Best, "White Rose Mission" (WPA Research Paper, SCRBC); William Fielding Ogburn, "The Richmond Negro in New York City" (M.A. thesis, Columbia University, 1918), p. 26. The White Rose Home was located at 217 East 86th Street before being moved to Harlem in 1918. While providing protection to young women against the immorality of the city, the home also sought to imbue the new arrival with middle-class values as well as proper training in the domestic arts. In 1911 the mission maintained a Penny Provident Fund to encourage the "habit of saving." The cooking class was of practical "value to girls in their home-life and will fit them for greater usefulness in whatever sphere they may work." The mission also maintained a lodging department, but women were required to move after a stay of a few weeks. The mission described its purpose: "to establish and maintain a Christian, non-sectarian Home for Colored Working Girls and Women, where they may be trained in the principles of practical self-help and right living." *Annual Report White Rose Industrial Association,* 1911, pp. 1–10, SCRBC.

78. *Negro World,* March 3, 1923, April 7, 1923; *NYAN,* March 7, 1923.

79. David John Hellwig, "The Afro-American and the Immigrant, 1880–1930: A Study of Black Social Thought" (Ph.D. diss., Syracuse University, 1973), p. 216. *Congressional Record,* December 31, 1914, p. 805; *Crisis,* February 15, 1915, p. 190.

80. *Chicago Defender,* January 16, 1915.

81. *New York Age,* January 7, 1915.

82. *Kingston Daily Chronicle,* January 19, 1915. Clippings, West India Research Library, Institute of Jamaica, Kingston.

83. Ibid., January 20, 1915. Quoted from the *Boston Post.*

84. Alfred H. Kelly and Winfred A. Harbison, *The American Constitution, Its Origins and Development* (New York: W. W. Norton, 1976), p. 666.

85. Robert F. Foerster, *The Racial Problems Involved in Immigration from Latin America and the West Indies to the United States* (Washington, D.C.: Government Printing Office, 1925), p. 57.

86. *New York Age,* July 19, 1924. As editor of the *Age,* a competitor of Garvey's *Negro World,* and a politician targeted by Caribbean stepladder speakers, Moore was harsh in his denunciation of what he described as "disloyalty" and criticism of the "flag under which they now live." "If they were consistent in their attitude, it would be expected that they would embark on the first vessel sailing for their former home, but not so. They criticize America and Americans, but cling to the opportunities they have found here."

87. W. E. B. Du Bois, "West Indian Immigration," *Crisis,* December 1924, p. 57.

88. *Baltimore Afro-American,* December 2, 1921.

89. Harry Robinson, "West Indian Immigrants in New York City" (WPA Research Paper), (SCRBC); Reid, *The Negro Immigrant,* p. 26; rhyme is from "West Indies Blues," by Edgar Dowell, Spencer Williams, and Clarence Williams. (New York: Clarence Williams Music Publishing Co., 1924). Interview, Viola Scott Thomas, New York City, July 24, 1980.

90. Oral History interview with Maida Springer Kemp by Betty Balaniff, Chicago, January 4, 1977, in *Black Women's Oral History Project,* Schlesinger Library, Radcliffe College, p. 2.

3. "On to Harlem"

1. Gerald Moore, "The Sugar Hill Pioneers," *Afro-Americans in New York Life and History* (July 1988), p. 35.

2. San Juan Hill was so called because of the steep incline peaking at West 62nd Street where many battles between black and Irish residents occurred.

3. Adam Clayton Powell, Sr., *Against the Tide: An Autobiography* (New York: R. R. Smith, 1938), p. 70.

4. Gary Ward Moore, "A Study of a West Indian Group" (M.A. thesis, Columbia University, 1913); Harry Robinson, "West Indian Immigrants in New York City."

5. Gerald Moore, "The Sugar Hill Pioneers," p. 35. Gary Ward Moore, "Study of a West Indian Group," p. 9.

6. In a speech before the YMCA clubs in 1906, the Rev. Dr. Morris gave this description of the dives and taverns of the Tenderloin:

> These dens of infamy are little less than a corner of Hell. Thousands of our young men and women who might have otherwise been a help to society and the race have been drawn into these cesspools of vice, and their lives and character blasted forever. Fathers and mothers away down south or far off in the West Indies, little know of the shame and degradation that have overtaken many of their sons and daughters who have come to this city to improve their condition and perhaps aid their parents, but have been lost to them and the world.
> *New York Age,* March 29, 1906.

7. *New York Age,* March 30, 1911; Adam Clayton Powell, Sr., *Against the Tide,* p. 70.

8. Minutes of the Bermudian Benevolent Society, June 12, 1912. Minute Book 2, p. 1, Box 5, SCRBC.

9. Osofsky, *Harlem,* p. 79.

10. Richard B. Moore, "African Conscious Harlem," in Turner and Turner, *Richard B. Moore,* p. 161.

11. Jeffrey S. Gurock, *When Harlem was Jewish, 1870–1930* (New York: Columbia University Press, 1979), p. 17.

12. On neighboring streets similar elegance was evident. On 130th Street a group of 28 three-story homes, known as Astor row, had been constructed in the 1890s. Known as one of the most attractive residential areas of Manhattan, the tree-lined block "presented a picture of domestic tranquillity and comfort . . . which few other blocks in the city possess." *New York Times,* November 21, 1920; Osofsky, *Harlem,* p. 79.

13. *New York Age,* December 5, 1912.

14. Wilbur Young, "Sketch of James C. Thomas" (WPA Research Paper, SCRBC).

15. George Edmund Haynes, *The Negro at Work in New York City* (New York: Columbia University Press, 1912), pp. 132, 136; Roi Ottley and William J. Weatherby, eds., *The Negro in New York*, p. 236; Wilfred Bain, "Negro Real Estate Brokers" (WPA Research Paper, SCRBC n.d. circa 1939). *New York Age,* April 9, 1921.

16. Osofsky, *Harlem,* p. 120; Bain, "Negro Real Estate Brokers"; *New York Age*, February 19, 1921.

17. Theodore Poston, "Negro Millionaire Solomon Riley" (WPA Biography).

18. T. J. Woofter, Jr., *Negro Problems in Cities* (New York: Doubleday, 1928), p. 141. Woofter's data show that the percentage of homeowners in northern cities contrasts sharply with ownership in large southern cities, such as Memphis, where in several wards black ownership was over 50 percent.

19. Interview, Hope Stevens, New York City, March 9, 1978.

20. Ivan Light, *Ethnic Business Enterprises in America* (Berkeley: University of California Press, 1972), p. 34. See also Bonnett, A. W., "An Examination of Rotating Credit Associations among Black West Indian Immigrants in Brooklyn," in *Sourcebook on the New Immigration*, pp. 271–83.

21. Fred Challenor to Aletha Dowridge Challenor, May 4, 1910, in CDFL in SCRBC. Mrs. Payne appears to have been operating the association among a group of Barbadian immigrants in Brooklyn. In April Fred had written Aletha, "Mrs. Payne's turn will be starting next week, I believe, and I am going to draw in it and as soon as she gives you will have it." Fred Challenor to Aletha Dowridge Challenor, April 10, 1910.

22. The head of the household, Charlie Suey, a shoemaker, was identified as black, but his birthplace was identified as China. His wife, Julia, and their three children were also identified as black and had all been born in the United States. Some Caribbean people were born in the British-held colony of Hong Kong.

23. Recorded as the head of household, she lived at No. 13 with a niece and nephew and a lodging couple. The Paytons' fortune had declined after the collapse of the Afro-American Realty Company, and although she did not work in 1905, it is conceivable that Payton, like most black women, would have worked as a domestic to help support the family. In any case, Philip Payton died in the Allentown house in 1917, and Maggie sold No. 13 in 1919.

24. Marshall, "Black Immigrant Women," p. 7.

25. Interview, Muriel Petioni, New York City, November 18, 1991.

26. Interview, Dorothy Burnham, November 12, 1993; Fred Challenor to Aletha Dowridge, April 10, 1910.

27. Addie to Aletha Dowridge Challenor, September 10, 1910.

28. NYSMC 1915 AD21 ED15, p. 3. For fuller discussion of Spence, see chapter 10.

29. James Weldon Johnson, "The Making of Harlem," *Survey Graphic* (1925), p. 635.

30. Bruce Kellner, ed., *The Harlem Renaissance, A Historical Dictionary for the Era* (New York: Methuen, 1984), p. 117. Europe was killed by one of his bandmembers during a concert in Boston in 1919.

31. Bernardo Vega, *The Memoirs of Bernardo Vega* (1977; New York: Monthly Review Press, 1984), p. 22.

32. High rents and the lack of space promoted what was known as the "hot bed system," the double renting of a lodging room by the head of a household. The room, or "bed," would be rented to both a day worker and a night worker; one slept in the daytime and the other at night. "Very often the rooms of children in the family are let out to the night workers." New York Urban League, "Twenty-Four Hundred Negro Families in Harlem: An Interpretation of Living Conditions of Small Wage Earners," (1927), p. 11. Typescript SCRBC.

33. L. Hollingsworth Wood, "The New York Colored Mission—Good Samaritan Inn," *Opportunity,* March 1927, p. 82; Interview, Muriel Petioni, Dec. 23, 1993.

34. According to Mary White Ovington, residents considered the "railroad-train tenements" a better alternative to the "double-decker tenements," where there were four apartments to each floor and residents shared two "water closets" in the hallway. In the railroad tenement rent was "twenty to twenty-four dollars a month." "Only two flats are on a floor and each apartment is likely to have a private bath." Mary White Ovington, "The Negro and the New York Tenement," *Voice of the Negro,* June 1907, p. 104.

35. Interview, Muriel Petioni, November 21, 1991.

36. Ibid.

37. Spero and Harris, *The Black Worker,* p. 178.

38. Muriel Petioni, ibid. After the beginning of nursing desegregation in the 1940s, this profession became a beachhead attracting new Caribbean immigrant women. Mable Staupers, who immigrated to New York from Barbados in 1903 and trained as a registered nurse, became a pioneer in the fight to desegregate the profession in her role as president of the National Association of Colored Graduate Nurses. See Darlene Clark Hine, "Mable K. Staupers and the Integration of Black Nurses into the Armed Forces," in John Hope Franklin and August Meier, eds., *Black Leaders of the Twentieth Century* (Urbana: University of Illinois Press, 1982).

39. Ira de Reid, *The Negro Immigrant,* p. 207.

40. Marshall, "Black Immigrant Women in *Brown Girl, Brownstones,*" p. 7.

41. Paule Marshall, *Brown Girl, Brownstones* (1959; reprint, New York: Feminist Press, 1981), pp. 287–88.

42. Marshall, "Black Immigrant Women in *Brown Girl, Brownstones,*" p. 9.

43. Gerald L. Moore, p. 35; NYSMC 1915 AD 21 ED 15, p. 26.

44. Interview, Charles Zampty, Detroit, Michigan, February 26, 1977.

45. Interview with Alma John, July 31, 1980.

46. Interview, Alma John; interview with Tyrell Wilson, Gordon Heights, Long Island, New York, March 7, 1978.

47. Hugh Mulzac, *A Star to Steer By* (New York: International Publishers, 1963), pp. 78–79. There was perhaps never a more classic case of racial discrimination in employment than that confronting Hugh Mulzac, a native of Union Island (near St. Vincent). In 1918 after becoming licensed he began a twenty-four-year effort to become master of an ocean vessel. After long periods of unemployment and family deprivation, the War Shipping Department in 1942 granted Mulzac a commission as a captain of the *Booker T. Washington.* Still, Mulzac was not allowed to operate a ship on which crew or passengers were predominantly white.

4. Churches, Benevolent Associations, and Ethnicity

1. James Weldon Johnson, *Black Manhattan,* p. 157.

2. *New York Evening Graphic,* December 21, 1921 (Clipping, Alexander Gumby Collection, Columbia University).

3. The Caribbean home societies included organizations such as the American Virgin Islands Association, American West Indian Ladies Aid Society, Anguilla Benevolent Society, Antillian League, Bermuda Benevolent Association, British Jamaicans Benevolent Association, British Virgin

Islands Society, Dominica Benevolent Society, Grenada Mutual Association, Montserrat Progressive Society, St. Vincent Benevolent Association, Sons and Daughters of Barbados, Sons and Daughters of Nevis, Sons and Daughters of St. Christopher Society, and Victoria Benevolent Association. Similar organizations from southern states included the Sons and Daughters of South Carolina, Sons and Daughters of Georgia, Sons and Daughters of Florida, etc. Roi Ottley and William J. Weatherby, eds., *The Negro in New York: An Informal Social History* (New York: Oceana, 1967), p. 194.

4. Odette Harper, "Organizations Formed by Migrant Southerners in New York," (WPA Research Paper, 1939). Caribbean immigrants organized numerous social clubs: Isthmica (comprised of Panamanian immigrants), Club Aristocrat, L'Arc en Ciel, Emanon, Altaire, Zodiac, Concordia, Golden Glen, Clair du Lune, Karma, La Vivia, Lilac, Ajax, Solidarité, Astor Social and Literary Club, Dutch Guiana League, Trinidad Athletic League, Cosmopolitan Tennis Club, etc. Harry Robinson, "The Negro Immigrant in New York" (WPA Research Paper, SCRBC).

5. Eulalie Spence, "The Starter," in *Opportunity* (1927), p. 211.

6. The Dorcas societies, good-works groups usually affiliated with the urban black church of the nineteenth century, were run by black women. The name *Dorcas* refers to the New Testament biblical character in Acts 9:36–43.

7. James Weldon Johnson, *Black Manhattan,* p. 163.

8. The extent to which Caribbean immigrants were drawn into storefront denominations during this period cannot be determined from the available evidence. We do know that storefront denominations, including the Pentecostal movement, attracted large numbers of southern migrants. The Harlem figure Steamboat Bill, a street corner preacher, is said to have started the storefront church movement in this period. During the 1930s Father Divine attracted large numbers of Caribbean immigrants. Robert Weisbort, *Father Divine and the Struggle for Racial Equality* (Urbana: University of Illinois Press, 1983), p. 61. Today storefront churches are very widespread among Caribbean immigrants.

9. Report of the New York Federation of Churches, 1929, p. 25.

10. Interview, Dorothy Burnham, NYC, November 12, 1993; Interview, Violet Murrell, September 2, 1994. Dorothy Burnham, one of Fred and Aletha Challenor's three daughters, recalled Rector George Frazier Miller's black immigrant church members felt he showed ethnic bias. See also *New York Age*, September 10, 1927; *NYAN,* April 16, 1930.

11. Osofsky, *Harlem,* p. 13; Woofter, *Negro Problems in Cities* (New York: McGraw Hill, 1928).

12. St. Philips Episcopal, which largely attracted and perhaps even catered to a native-born elite, was identified by some contemporaries as perpetuating differences in the black community based on color. Certain pews, these observers claimed, were reserved for the lightest-complexioned and upper-class members. St. Philips was the only black church in Manhattan which used the pew system—the assigning of pews to certain individuals and families based upon their contributions. "The older families of well-to-do free negroes who count on an unspotted family life for two centuries gather at St. Philips . . . ," noted Du Bois in 1901. W. E. B. Du Bois "The Black North in 1901: New York," in Dan S. Green and Edwin Driver, *W. E. B. Du Bois, On Sociology and the Black Community* (Chicago: University of Chicago Press, 1978), pp. 151–52. "The Negro in New York," ibid.

13. Dunbar, "Factors in the Cultural Background of American and West Indian Negroes," p. 24.

14. In 1958 St. Cyprian was torn down to make way for the Lincoln Center Development for the cultural arts. Woofter, *Negro Problems*, pp. 253–55.

15. Woofter, *Negro Problems*, pp. 253–55. H. C. Banks, Vicar, St. Cyprian Church to "Dear Friend," October 8, 1943, in James Watson Papers, SCRBC.

16. Dunbar, "Factors in the Cultural Background of American and West Indian Negroes," pp. 22–23; *New York Post*, May 9, 1958; Gary Hunter, "'Don't Buy from Where You Can't Work': Black Urban Boycott Movements during the Depression" (Ph.D. diss., University of Michigan, 1977), pp. 183–85; John H. Johnson, "Don't Buy Where You Can't Work," in *Harlem, the War and Other Addresses* (New York: Malliet, 1942), pp. 60–68. See St. Martin's Episcopal Church (Vertical

File, Schomburg Collection); John H. Johnson, *A Place of Adventure, Essays and Sermons* (Greenwich, Connecticut, 1955).

17. Interview, G. James Fleming, October 14, 1977.

18. *NYAN,* January 26, 1928.

19. *New York Age*, March 30, 1911.

20. Hill, ed., *MGP,* V, p. 688, n. 4.

21. William Welty, "Black Sheperds: A Study of the Leading Negro Clergymen in New York City" (Ph.D. diss., New York University, 1969), p. 139; *New York Age,* May 7, 1908; November 19, 1921.

22. The Jamaican Baptist Church was formed in the eighteenth century by the American-born black preacher George Liele, who had established the first black Baptist Church in Savannah, Georgia, in 1777. Liele had been freed by his master before the Revolutionary War, but after his former master's death he was "obliged to come to Jamaica as an indented servant" in payment of a debt he owed a Georgia Tory who fled to the island after the war. Liele spent the rest of his life in Kingston, where he set up a thriving Baptist community among slaves and freed persons. See "Letters Showing the Rise and Progress of the Early Negro Churches of Georgia and the West Indies," *Journal of Negro History* I (1916), pp. 69–92. Mechal Sobel, *Trabelin' On: The Slave Journey to an Afro-Baptist Faith* (Princeton: Princeton University Press, 1988), p. 106.

23. Robinson, "West Indians in New York" (WPA Research Paper, SCRBC); see also Arthur Huff Fauset, *Black Gods of the Metropolis* (1944; reprint, University of Pennsylvania, 1971); Joseph R. Washington, Jr., *Black Sects and Cults* (New York: Anchor, 1973); E. Franklin Frazier, *The Negro Church in America* (New York, 1964; original publication 1964).

24. Interview, Tyrell Wilson, March 7, 1978. See also Edward Maynard, "Endogamy among Barbadian Immigrants to New York City" (Ph.D. diss., New York University, 1972).

25. Harold Cook Phillips, "The Social Significance of Negro Churches in Harlem" (M.A. thesis, Columbia University, 1922), p. 25.

26. Hill, ed., *MGP,* p. 239, n. 1. Quoted by Morrison-Reed in *Black Pioneers in a White Denomination*, p. 81, from Brown, "A Statement Presented to the Special Committee Appointed by the American Unitarian Association to Inquire into the Circumstances Leading to the Removal of My Name from the Official List of Unitarian Ministers," December 14, 1931, in Brown Papers, Unitarian Universalist Association, Boston.

27. Paul E. West to American West Indian Ladies Aid Society, September 4, 1933, in West Indian Ladies Aid Society Papers, SCRBC.

28. John H. Johnson, *A Place of Adventure*, p. 27.

29. Phillips, "The Social Significance of Negro Churches in Harlem," p. 25.

30. Schomburg to Horace Mann Bond, February 13, 1936. Schomburg Papers, SCRBC.

31. *NYAN,* January 6, 1926. In explaining his determination to continue the church's mission in 1935, Brown wrote: "Harlem needs a liberal church—needs it first as a neutralizing influence staying the poisonous spread of superstition, ignorance and fanaticism—and needs it also as a means of getting together those who have intellectually and ethnically outgrown the fundamental doctrines of the older churches, to make of them the living apostles of a rational and practical religion." "Religious Liberalism in Harlem," in Notebooks, dated June 30, 1929. Brown Papers, Box 4, Folder I, Manuscript Division, SCRBC.

32. "The Failure of the Negro Church," *Messenger*, October 1919, p. 6.

33. Kelly Miller, *Out of the House of Bondage* (New York: Neale Publishing Company, 1914), p. 208.

34. See Elizabeth-Clark Lewis, "'This Work Had an End': African American Household Workers in Washington, D.C., 1910–1940," in Carol Groneman and Mary Beth Norton, eds. *To Toil the Live Long Day* (Ithaca: Cornell University Press, 1987), pp. 196–212. Emma Carroll recalled that while working as a live-in household worker she appropriated the time to attend church ser-

vices at her own church, although her employers were not willing to spare her even on Sundays at first. She prepared the meal for the day, and after her employers, who were Catholic, returned from early morning Mass, she simply dressed and left for her own church. Interview, Emma Carroll, August 19, 1991, Yonkers, New York.

35. Mark D. Morrison-Reed, *Black Pioneers in a White Denomination* (Boston: Beacon, 1980), p. 98.

36. Ibid.; see also Ethelred Brown, "Religious Liberalism in Harlem," dated June 30, 1929. Notebooks, Box 4, Folder 1, Brown Papers, SCRBC. The families of at least two Harlem radicals, Moore and Domingo, joined the church. Turner and Turner, *Richard B. Moore*, p. 45. In Brown the Caribbean journalist Hodge Kirnon and Jamaican poet Ben Burrell are listed among the lasting supporters of the Church.

37. Morrison-Reed, *Black Pioneers*, p. 82.

38. Ibid.; Brown, "Religious Liberalism in Harlem," in Brown Papers, Box 4, Folder 1; Welty, *Black Shepherds*, p. 139.

39. Brown, "If Jesus Came to Harlem Whom Would He Denounce?" December 1934 (Sermons and Notebooks), p. 1, Brown Papers, Box 4, Folder 2. Brown became a member of the Harlem Socialist party and ran unsuccessfully for Congress in 1928, City Council in 1929, and the State Assembly in 1930.

40. Ethelred Brown, "Fifteen Years of Unitarianism," in E. Ethelred Brown Papers, SCRBC Manuscript Division, pp. 66–67.

41. *New York Times*, August 6, 1924. The *Negro World* declared that the Good Shepherd Church had "50 communicants" shortly after it organized. Most of these early members appear to have been Caribbean immigrants. But McGuire himself was known widely among African Americans as a brilliant orator, and he gained support for his ideas with black Episcopalians, whom he had served while a missionary priest in the American South. McGuire was mentioned as a successor to Garvey should the UNIA leader remain incarcerated on charges of mail fraud. *Negro World*, October 8, 1921. Tony Martin, *Race First* (Westport, Connecticut: Greenwood Press, 1976), p. 70.

42. *Negro World*, October 8, 1921.

43. James D. Browning, "The Beginnings of Insurance Enterprise among Negroes," *Journal of Negro History* 22 (1937), p. 423.

44. Ottley and Weatherby, eds., *The Negro in New York*, pp. 134–35.

45. Many of the members in both societies proudly bore Dutch surnames (Ten Eyck, Van Horne, etc). And many were recruited from the "Negro 400," the tiny black upper class known for having acquired "a measure of wealth." Willard B. Gatewood, *Aristocrats of Color* (Bloomington: Indiana University Press, 1990), p. 222.

46. *New York Age*, August 30, 1929. In San Juan Hill the Caribbean community was actively involved in benevolent societies and lodges. Gary Ward Moore listed the following: Guiding Star of Moses, Mt. Tabor Union House, Household of Ruth, Temple House of Moses, Love and Charity, Cricket Club, St. Cyprian Athletic Club, Mothers Club of Lincoln Day Nursery, West End Civic League, etc. Moore, "A Group of West Indian Negroes," p. 37.

47. Constitution and By-Laws of the Sons and Daughters of Florida (Revised 1931) in AWILAS Papers, SCRBC.

48. Myrtle Evangeline Pollard, "Harlem as Is" (M.A. thesis, City University of New York, 1937), pp. 346–47.

49. Harper, "Organizations Formed by Migrant Southerners," p. 1.

50. Ibid., p. 3.

51. Ibid.

52. *Constitution and By-Laws of the Bermuda Benevolent Association, Containing a Brief Sketch of the History of the Association* (New York: 1927), pp. 5–8, in Bermuda Benevolent Association Papers, SCRBC.

53. Ibid., pp. 20–36.

54. *Constitution and By-Laws of the Bermuda Benevolent Association* (New York: 1911), p. 17.

55. Robert Hill, "General Introduction," *Marcus Garvey Papers*, vol. I, p. lxii.

56. Mrs. Helena Benta, "Address to a Group of Benevolent Associations," April 1933, quoted by Pollard, pp. 346–47.

57. Cornelia Jackson, April 10, n.d., 70 West 142 Street, to American West Indian Ladies Aid Society; another note read: "From this you will learn that I am in receipt of the aid you sent me[,] the sum of $3.00. Please accept a heart brimful of gratitude for your kindness." E. Carey to AWILAS, n.d., in AWILAS Papers, Manuscript Division, SCRBC.

58. Pollard, "Harlem as Is," p. 80.

59. Interviews, Dorothy Burnham and Violet Murrell.

60. White insurance companies charged blacks much higher rates than whites for health and death insurance, and local hospitals, too, frequently denied them and black physicians access to medical facilities.

61. Hodge Kirnon, *Montserrat and Montserratans* (New York: Kirnon, 1925), p. 42.

62. Pollard, "Harlem as Is," p. 343. Pollard quotes from Helena Benta's speech made before a group of Caribbean benevolents in April 1933; Benta recognized that Caribbean women needed to participate more in public affairs and that their achievements needed more recognition. An aim of the Federation read: "To stimulate the interest of West Indian women in all problems and matters concerning national development and accord to their efforts and achievements every encouragement and recognition."

63. Ashley Totten to Society, p. 2 of letter, n.d. (circa 1925), in AWILAS Papers, SCRBC.

64. Emily Thomas and Redalia Matthews to Ashley Totten, September 28, 1933, AWILAS Papers, SCRBC. The officers turned down another of Totten's requests "on account of economic conditions." See *The Declaration of Independence and the U.S. Constitution* (Washington D.C.: U.S. Government Printing Office, 1979), p. 36.

65. Richard B. Moore, "Afro-Americans and Radical Politics," in Turner and Turner, *Richard B. Moore*, p. 217; Joyce Moore Turner, "Radical Politics," p. 55. Moore mentions that Hendrickson was active as a street speaker as well as an activist of the Harlem Tenants League. Her occupation is not clear, but in 1928 Hendrickson advertised as the proprietor of a dress shop at 58 West 140th Street. See "Souvenir Programme," July 12, 1928, in AWILAS.

66. See Pollard, "Harlem as Is," p. 344. Partial support for her claim might have been found in an observation of some of the British Caribbean benevolents' activities, especially when they reminded themselves and other Harlemites of their ties to the Crown. In 1910, " . . . each of several Benevolent Societies offered suitable resolutions of condolence on the occasion of the death of King Edward VII. The [Bermuda Benevolent] Association had its resolution engrossed, and copies suitable for framing may be secured for a nominal sum." In 1937 immigrants from the British-held Caribbean conducted a re-enactment of the George VI Coronation at the St. Ambrose Episcopal Church. By the 1930s some prominent Caribbean Harlemites received honors from the British Crown, though such ceremonies increasingly rankled growing anticolonial feelings in the community. When the Rev. Jedidiah Edmead, pastor emeritus of the Church of the Crucifixion, received the insignia of the Order of the British Empire, a newspaper account announced that Edmead was "commended for his assistance to the British Consul in aiding natives of the British West Indies in New York City." Even colonial officials recognized the importance of a stabilized Caribbean community in New York.

67. "Sketch" in *Constitution and By-Laws of the Bermuda Benevolent Association* (1911), p. 12.

68. William A. Muraskin, *Middle-Class Blacks in a White Society, Prince Hall Freemasonry in America* (Berkeley: University of California Press, 1975), p. 26.

69. Lasalle Best, "History of the Lebanon Foresters" (WPA Research Paper, SCRBC, 1939), n.p.

70. "Biography of Distinguished Men," *West Indian American*, November 3, 1927.

71. Baxter Leach, "Fraternal Orders in Harlem" (WPA Research Paper, SCRBC 1939), p. 1.

72. Hill, ed., *MGP* I, p. lxi.

73. See Arthur Schomburg Papers. Schomburg's correspondence with the Masons throughout the United States reflects his involvement with the organization. See also fraternal news in various major black papers, such as the Chicago *Defender* and the Baltimore *Afro-American*.

74. *NYAN*, August 28, September 4, 1929.

75. *Fraternal Review*, February, August, 1929; Henry, "Culture of Afro-West Indies," p. 451.

5. Politics and the Struggle for Autonomy

1. McKay, *Harlem, Negro Metropolis*, p. 125.

2. As president of the "Colored Republican Club," Anderson worked hard for Theodore Roosevelt's campaign and enlisted the talent of James Weldon Johnson as chairman of the house committee. According to Johnson, Anderson, a friend for a number of years, approached him with the request that he serve as house committee chairman. The Club was located across the street from the Marshall, Manhattan's most famous black hotel, popular with musicians and athletes. The Republican Club was to be furnished in good style, billiard and pool room in the basement, assembly room on the main floor, lounge and card room on the second floor, and committee rooms on the top. All expenses were paid by the white Republican party in the city. Anderson's political influence was based on his own track record in the Republican party, a record of favors and loyalties, which gave him direct access to powerful Republicans in and outside the city. He was promoted from gauger to private secretary to the Collector of Internal Revenue, to Chief Clerk in the State Treasury, to Supervisor of Accounts for the New York Racing Commission, and finally to Collector of Internal Revenue. Anderson punished his political enemies but took good care of his friends. According to Johnson's autobiographical account, after Roosevelt's election, Anderson approached James Weldon Johnson with the idea of becoming a member of the diplomatic service and secured his appointment through Elihu Root, Roosevelt's Secretary of State, as ambassador to Venezuela. James Weldon Johnson, *Along This Way* (New York: Viking, 1968), p. 219.

3. Johnson, *Along This Way*, p. 219.

4. Herbert Aptheker, ed., *The Correspondence of W. E. B. Du Bois* (Amherst: University of Massachusetts Press, 1973), vol. 1, p. 201. Du Bois described Morton as a "close and enduring friend."

5. Osofsky, *Harlem*, p. 160.

6. *Crisis*, July 1925, p. 116.

7. One institution established to help migrating women adjust to the city, the White Rose Industrial Home, founded by Victoria Earle Matthews in 1897, gained the approval of Booker T. Washington and no doubt sought the local support of Charles W. Anderson. See *Annual Report White Rose Home*, 1911 and 1912. SCRBC.

8. Calvin Holder, "The Rise of the West Indian Politician in New York City, 1900–1952," *Afro-American in New York Life and History* (January 1980); Waring Cuney, "The United Colored Democracy" (WPA Research Paper, 1939), pp. 2–3.

9. *NYAN*, December 15, 1926.

10. Ibid.; Cuney, "United Colored Democracy," p. 3.

11. Edgar H. Grey, "The West Indian in Harlem Politics," *NYAN*, December 29, 1927. Henderson, p. 55.

12. *New York Age*, April 13, 17; October 4, 1930.

13. As a result of the primary elections in 1929, Harlem elected two members to the Republican State Committee, Charles W. Fillmore from the Nineteenth Assembly district and Charles W. B. Mitchell, co-leader of the twenty-first, (elected a member with a half vote). The rules governing the composition of the State Committee stipulated that it be comprised of two members from each dis-

trict, one of whom shall be a woman. It is important to note that as blacks began entering the party councils, black women, though they were a substantial block of Harlem voters, were not nominated for important political positions. Mitchell's nomination and election to the Committee meant that two male members, one white and one black, were members of the committee with one vote divided between them. *Age*, October 4, 1930.

14. *NYAN*, December 15, 1926.
15. Holder, "Rise of the West Indian Politician," p. 48.
16. *NYAN*, January 4, 1936.
17. Holder, "Rise of the West Indian Politician," p. 50.
18. *New York Age*, November 22, 1924.
19. *New York Age*, November 22, 1917.
20. Samuel Duncan to James Watson, July 30, 1918, foreign-born protective society flier, in James Watson papers, Box 7, Civic and Community Activities folder, SCRBC; Hill, *Marcus Garvey: Life and Lessons* (Berkeley: University of California Press, 1987), pp. 381, 402. In cooperation with a number of native-black Americans, including lawyer and one-time Democratic candidate for State Assembly, Louis Lavelle, Duncan was a founding member of Garvey's UNIA. According to Garvey, Duncan and Lavelle attempted to turn the UNIA into a political club primarily to promote their own ambitions. Both men split with Garvey, and Duncan returned to the West Indian Protective Society, giving it various UNIA-sounding names. Lavelle became an outspoken critic of Garvey and an open competitor with Caribbean-born politicians. Duncan later wrote British colonial officials warning them about Garvey's agitation among workers in the Caribbean.
21. *Pittsburgh Courier*, February 4, 1928.
22. Grey, "The West Indian in Harlem Politics," *NYAN*, December 29, 1927.
23. *New York Age*, August 28, 1920.
24. *Pittsburgh Courier*, February 4, 1928.
25. Jamaica Progressive League Bylaws, SCRBC. See also Harry Robinson, "West Indians in New York" (WPA Research Paper), p. 19. In an effort to mobilize home people toward independence, a group of Jamaicans in Harlem organized the Jamaica Progressive League and published a pamphlet, *Onward Jamaica* (New York: Jamaica Progressive League, 1937).
26. *NYAN*, December 29, 1927; *New York Age*, April 21, 1928; see also January 21, March 24, 1928.
27. Ibid., April 28, 1928.
28. Ibid., March 15, 1917.
29. *NYAN*, October 3, 1923; see also May 30, October 10, 1923. For quite different reasons, Caribbean immigrant editor of the radical *Crusader Magazine*, Cyril Briggs felt all eligible Harlemites should become voters to "strengthen the radical movement." He made this appeal to his readers in his 1921 election-month issue:

> Those who have votes must help the disenfranchised ones to get their votes. Those who were not born in the United States and are not naturalized *must naturalize* not because it's better to be an American citizen than a British subject (or vice versa), but because it's better to be a *Negro than to be either of the others*, and because the Negro's Strength in America *must be developed* before it can exert political, moral or financial influence upon the liberation struggle. (*Crusader*, November 1921, pp. 15–16)

30. *NYAN*, December 29, 1927.
31. Ira Reid, *Negro Immigrant*, p. 163. Although figures are not available for New York City, in 1930 25.6 percent of black foreign-born individuals twenty-one years old and over living in the United States were naturalized and 10.5 percent had taken first papers. In contrast 60.4 percent of the white foreign-born were naturalized and 9.6 percent had first papers. *Fifteenth Census of the United States, 1930*. Population, vol. II, p. 405. Although moves to naturalize were slower among

Caribbean immigrants, other immigrants were determined to remain in New York as "citizens" when legal channels of naturalization presented too many obstacles. In 1932 the *New York Age* attributed the following quotation to Police Commissioner Mulrooney, formerly police captain at the 135th Street precinct in Harlem:

> There are West Indian, low class Mexican, low class Argentineans, low class Peruvians. They also come from East Indies and India. All of them, however, when arrested, invariably are "Porto Rican" [*sic*]. In fact the incoming of these people is responsible for a new racket in that section [Spanish Harlem] of the city—the Porto Rican birth certificate. We have come across groups lately in Harlem who are selling fake Porto Rican birth certificates for $30 each.

New York Age, March 9, 1932. In the late twenties thousands of Puerto Ricans began immigrating to the mainland. "Harlem seems to be the most popular objective," noted the *Age*. Their numbers, about 40,000, compared favorably to the large number of African Caribbean people in Central Harlem. In East Harlem they added a more complex texture to the community and authorities found it more difficult to prove, for instance, that an individual born in the Dominican Republic was not in fact born in Puerto Rico.

32. Interview, Dorothy Challenor Burnham, November 12, 1993; interview, G. James Fleming, Baltimore Maryland, October 14, 1977; McKay, *Harlem: Negro Metropolis*, p. 135.

33. Grey, *NYAN*, December 29, 1927.

34. *Pittsburgh Courier*, July 9, 1927. Malliet, a Harlem journalist, wrote a series of articles called "Why I Cannot Become Americanized" for the *Pittsburgh Courier* in July and August of 1927 and again in 1930.

35. *Negro World*, June 17, 1922.

36. Vertical File, "West Indians in New York," clipping, n.d., SCRBC.

37. Correspondence of C. D. B. King and INS officers in UNIA Records of the Central Division, 1918–1959, SCRBC.

38. Watson was elected as one of Harlem's first two municipal judges from the newly created 10th Municipal District in 1930. Watson's campaign flier in American West Indian Ladies Aid Society Papers, SCRBC.

39. Holder, "The Rise of the West Indian Politician," p. 51.

40. Joseph McGoldrick, "The New Tammany," *The American Mercury* (September 1928), p. 9.

41. McKay, *Harlem: Negro Metropolis*, p. 132.

42. Interview, Hope Stevens, March 8, 1978.

43. Claude McKay, *Harlem: Negro Metropolis*, p. 132.

44. Henderson, "Harlem Confronts the Machine," *NYAN*, p. 56. November 16, 1927. McGoldrick, "The New Tammany," p. 8.

45. Thomas Henderson, "Harlem Confronts the Machine: The Struggle for Local Autonomy and Black District Leadership," *Afro-Americans in New York Life and History* (July 1979), p. 55.

46. Henderson, ibid.

47. *New York Age*, December 20, 1930; *NYAN*, July 20, 1927.

48. *NYAN*, March 9, 1933; Will Haywood, *King of the Cats: The Life and Times of Adam Clayton Powell, Jr.* (New York: Houghton Mifflin, 1993), pp. 35–37.

49. James S. Watson campaign brochure in AWILAS Papers, SCRBC.

50. Hill, *MGP* I, p. 255.

51. Henderson, "Harlem Confronts the Machine," p. 60.

52. Henderson, ibid., p. 61; *NYAN*, June 28, 1933.

53. Fliers and form letter correspondence of the Council in the James Watson Papers.

54. Quoted in "Foreign-Born Citizens League" flier n.d. (circa January 1934), Watson Papers, SCRBC.

55. Quoted in "Foreign-Born Citizens League" flier.

56. "Foreign-Born Citizens League" flier in Watson Papers, SCRBC.

6. Stepladder to Community

1. Jervis Anderson, *A. Philip Randolph: A Biographical Portrait* (New York: Harvest, 1972), p. 77.

2. *New York News*, 1926. Clipping, Gumby Collection, Columbia University, n.d.

3. Richard B. Moore, "Afro-Americans and Radicals Politics," in Turner and Turner, *Richard B. Moore*, p. 217.

4. McKay, *Negro Metropolis*, p. 192.

5. Audley Moore, interview conducted by the Black Women's Oral History Project, Schlesinger Library, Radcliffe College, p. 23.

6. Harry Robinson, "West Indians in New York," (WPA Research Paper, SCRBC).

7. A list of Harlem's female radicals remains incomplete, as does biographical information about women whose names recur in the literature. More information about the following women's activities may help us understand distinctions between female and male activism in this period: Helen Holman, Layle Lane, Hermie Huiswood, Williana Burroughs, Anna Brown, Claudia Jones, Elizabeth Hendrickson, Grace Campbell, Maude White, Marie Houston, Bonita Williams, Louise Thompson, Audley Moore, and others. See Mark Naison, *Communists in Harlem during the Depression*; Philip S. Foner, *American Socialism and Black Americans*; Angela Davis, *Women, Race and Class* (New York: Random House, 1981).

8. "In Chicago the street university centered around Washington Park and State Street. Here Noble Drew Ali recruited many of the ten-thousand member Peace Movement of Ethiopia followers. Scores of Garveyites, Communists, Socialists, and black labor organizers could be found haranguing crowds along Southside Chicago Streets." Gary Hunter, "Don't Buy from Where You Can't Work: The Jobs for Negroes Campaign of the 1930s" (Ph.D. diss., University of Michigan, 1977), p. 35.

9. *New York News*, August 28, 1926.

10. A. Philip Randolph, quoted in Jervis Anderson, *A. Philip Randolph* (New York: Harcourt Brace Jovanovich, 1972), p. 77.

11. *New York News*, August 28, 1926.

12. Frank Crosswaith, "The Newer Negro," *Vanguard Press*, July 1928, Clipping in Vertical File, Schomburg Collection; "New Negro" was a term the World War I generation applied to themselves, a generation attempting to make a clean and permanent break with past censorship of free expression and the councils of accommodation. See Alain Locke, *The New Negro*, pp. 7–8.

13. *Harlem Magazine*, December 1916, quoted in Anderson, p. 77.

14. McKay, *A Long Way from Home*, p. 41; *New York News*, August 28, 1926.

15. Charles W. Anderson to Booker T. Washington, September 10, 1911, in Booker T. Washington Papers, Box 52, Library of Congress.

16. Charles W. Anderson to Washington, October 30, 1911, in ibid.

17. Eric Foner, *American Socialism and Black Americans* (Westport, Connecticut: Greenwood Press, 1977), p. 206. Foner quotes from Samuel M. Romansky to Julius Gerber, New York, October 12, 1911, in Local New York Socialist Party Papers, Tamiment Institute, Bobst Library, New York University.

18. Anderson to Booker T. Washington, in Washington Papers.

19. Quoted by Wilfred Samuels, "Hubert Harrison and the 'New Negro Manhood Movement,'" *Afro-Americans in New York Life and History* (January 1981), p. 34. According to J. A. Rogers, Harrison used to come to blows with Irish Catholics when he lectured on New York street corners on birth control. J. A. Rogers, "Hubert Harrison" (WPA Biography, 1939, SCRBC).

20. Wilfred Samuels, "Hubert Harrison," p. 32.

21. Elinor Des Verney Sinnette, *Arthur Alfonso Schomburg, Black Bibliophile and Collector* (Detroit: New York Public Library and Wayne State University Press, 1989), pp. 36, 126.

22. Richard B. Moore, "Africa Conscious Harlem," in John Henrik Clarke, *Harlem USA* (New York: Collier, 1964), pp. 37–38; Elinor Des Verney Sinnette, p. 86.

23. Hubert Harrison, "A Tender Point," in *When Africa Awakes* (New York: Porro Press, 1920), p. 86.

24. J. A. Rogers, "Hubert Harrison"; *NYAN*, February 3, 1923.

25. According to the *Pittsburgh Courier*, December 31, 1927, Harrison was hired by Columbia as a lecturer on contemporary civilization in that year; Rogers, "Hubert Harrison"; McKay, *A Long Way from Home*, p. 113.

26. Harrison to Pickens, n.d., in Pickens Papers, SCRBC.

27. *Boston Chronicle*, December 31, 1927.

28. *Negro World*, December 31, 1927.

29. *Pittsburgh Courier*, December 31, 1927.

30. Jervis Anderson, *A. Philip Randolph: A Biographical Portrait* (New York: Harcourt Brace Jovanovich, 1973), p. 58.

31. Ibid., p. 61.

32. Ibid., p. 80. In 1917 Randolph and Owen became editors of the *Hotel Messenger* at the request of the Headwaiters and Sidewaiters Society, but were fired eight months later for exposing unfair practices within the Society. Two months later they launched their own monthly magazine, *The Messenger*, Anderson points out, with the financial backing of Lucille Randolph. Without her help, Anderson quotes Randolph as saying, "we could not have started the *Messenger*." The *Messenger* became, even by the admission of its critics, one of the best-edited monthlies of the period.

33. Anderson quotes a survivor of the prewar (WWI) soapbox era, p. 78.

34. Quoted by Anderson, p. 78. Anderson also quotes a former associate of Randolph's in the Independent Political Council who "never knew him to do any work for a salary, but I never saw him without a starched collar, a carefully knotted tie, a white handkerchief in his breast pocket, and a blue serge suit that looked like he had just bought it from Brooks Brothers. It was his wife, of course. She had a good hairdressing business, and she was a sweet and motherly woman. He was lucky to have had a wife like that. Only she could have put up with all those people he used to bring home from political meetings two, three times a week to talk till one, two, three o'clock in the mornings."

35. Anderson, ibid. A major problem faced by Harlem radicals was the ability to finance their undertakings. Here their personal and public affiliations are important to understanding the social context in which they operated. After the loss of his post office job, Harrison apparently had personal financial problems in supporting his large family. Raising money to support his independent operations (after he cut all ties with the Socialists) was also a problem in his public undertakings. It was perhaps the Liberty League's inability to raise funds that led to its demise and, as some historians have suggested, its takeover by the UNIA's more capable financial networks. Randolph's debt to Lucille Randolph's successful hairdressing business was acknowledged by him on several occasions. Richard B. Moore's occupation as an elevator operator and later book dealer was apparently not sufficient to support a family *and* his far-ranging community activities. (See Turner and Turner, *Richard B. Moore*, p. 58.) At times Ethelred Brown's earnings from his Socialist street meetings were his only income, desperately needed to support a family and an invalid wife.

36. Moore, "Afro-Americans and Radical Politics," p. 217 in ibid. For an analysis of black Socialists' activities, see Philip Foner, *American Socialism and Black Americans.*

37. Joyce Moore Turner, "From Barbados to Harlem," in Turner and Turner, *Richard B. Moore*, p. 30.

38. Ibid.

39. Ibid.

40. Ibid., p. 29.

41. Harrison, *When Africa Awakes*, pp. 9–10.

42. Harrison, *When Africa Awakes*, p. 63.

43. *New York Times*, May 31, 1917.

44. Ibid., May 27, 1917.

45. Ibid., June 7, 1917.

46. Ibid., July 5, 1917.

47. Ibid.

48. Harrison, *When Africa Awakes*, pp. 16–17.

49. Edwin C. Walker to Editor, *Crusader* 1, no. 4 (December 1918), p. 31. Miller was actually the first black person ever nominated for Congress in New York. See Hill, *MGP* I, p. 345.

50. Frank Crosswaith, "The Newer Negro," *Vanguard Press* (July 1928). Clipping in Vertical File, SCRBC. Based on an interview with Richard B. Moore, Joyce Moore Turner has stated that Owen actually appealed for order when members of the crowd harangued and booed Roosevelt. His intent was to have Roosevelt finish his statement so that the Socialists could answer him. Turner and Turner, *Richard B. Moore*, p. 31.

51. Anderson, *A. Philip Randolph*, p. 95. *Messenger*, November 1920; Richard B. Moore, "Africa Conscious Harlem," *Freedomways* (Summer 1963), III, pp. 319–20.

52. *New York Age*, September 6, 1924; Richard B. Moore, "Afro-Americans and Radical Politics," in Turner and Turner, p. 217.

53. Hill, *MGP* IV, p. 688.

54. Hill, ibid.

55. A friend of Briggs, Harry Haywood, a fellow Communist, noticed that he stuttered less when he was angry. On one occasion during a dispute with Garvey, who resisted Briggs's attempts to draw the UNIA into a more class-conscious political stance, the UNIA leader publicly denounced the fair-complexioned Briggs as "a white man trying to pass himself off as a Negro." Haywood recounts the following anecdote: "Friends told me that this account sent Briggs into such a rage that he mounted a soapbox at Harlem's 135th Street and Lenox Avenue and assailed Garvey for two hours without a stutter." Harry Haywood, *Black Bolshevik* (Chicago: Liberator Press, 1978), p. 127.

56. Theodore Vincent, *Black Power and the Garvey Movement* (San Francisco: Ramparts Press, 1971), p. 75. According to Vincent one ABB recruit, a Mr. White, read the *Crusader* and was so impressed that he walked all the way to New York City from South Carolina to join the movement.

57. *New York Times*, June 20, 1921.

58. Hill, *MGP* II, p. 40.

59. Hill, *MGP* I, "Account by W. A. Domingo of Marcus Garvey's St. Mark's Church Hall Lecture," pp. 191–92.

60. Anderson, *A. Philip Randolph*, p. 122.

61. Johnson, *Black Manhattan*, p. 253.

62. Clipping from "Bruce Grit" column in John E. Bruce papers, SCRBC.

63. *New York Age*, August 28, 1920. Morris and Powell escaped injury, but years later Ethelred Brown was not so lucky. In 1928 Brown, actually one of Garvey's milder critics, held a meeting at his church to give an "impartial assessment of the Garvey legacy" following the UNIA leader's deportation. At the session's opening, Brown began by presenting what he considered some of Garvey's weaknesses, whereupon a disappointed listener rose, approached the pulpit, clubbed the Reverend over the head with a blackjack, and quickly departed, leaving a black derby initialed P. H. as the only clue to his identity. *New York Age*, January 21, 1928.

64. Haywood, *Black Bolshevik*, pp. 126–31.

65. *MGP* VI, p. 311; *NYAN*, June 26, 1929.

66. The *Harlem Liberator*, December 7, 14, and 21, 1929.

67. Haywood, *Black Bolshevik*, p. 145.

68. *NYAN*, March 2, 1935.

69. Negro Labor Committee Papers, Biographical Sketch of Frank Crosswaith, SCRBC; *NYAN*, March 2, 1935. In 1930 Crosswaith was also in demand by progressive church groups. The Students Literary and Debating League invited him to Brooklyn's Trinity Baptist Church. "So insistent have been the entreaties for Mr. Crosswaith to speak since last he spoke under the auspices of the League . . . that it has actually taken on the form of a demand; therefore in order not to disappoint the public the meeting was arranged by the officers of the club." *NYAN*, October 22, 1930.

70. *NYAN*, March 2, 1935.

71. *Boston Chronicle*, August 4, 1928.

72. Anderson, *A. Philip Randolph*, p. 154; see the *Civic* (August 1955), organ of the American Virgin Islands Civic Association, for more information on Totten.

73. Crosswaith, "The Newer Negro," *Vanguard*, July 1928.

74. *NYAN*, September 19, 1926.

75. *NYAN*, September 29, 1926.

76. A. Philip Randolph, "Free Speech in Harlem," *Messenger*, November 1926.

77. Williana J. Burroughs to Dear Friend, October 4, 1926, in Gumby Clipping Collection, Columbia University; Mark Naison, *Communists in Harlem during the Depression* (Urbana: University of Illinois Press, 1983), p. 53.

78. Claude McKay, *Long Way from Home*, p. 224. A concern with pragmatic solutions and methods appears to have been at the core of other women's activism as well. Caribbean immigrant and radical Bonita Williams and southern migrant Audley Moore were "effective street speakers who could argue for Communist policies in the cadence of the Garvey movement and the church," notes historian Mark Naison. During the jobs campaign Bonita Williams led a "flying squad of black housewives . . . through the streets of Harlem demanding that butchers lower their prices by 25 percent." According to a *Daily Worker* account: "So great was the sense of power of the workers that when butchers agreed to cut prices, housewives jumped on tables in front of stores and tore down old price signs and put up new ones. . . . No store held out for more than five minutes after the pickets arrived." From *Daily Worker*, June 3, 1935, pp. 136, 149.

79. Audley Moore, interview, BWOHP (Schlesinger Library), p. 33.

80. Audley Moore, ibid., p. 24. Powell had been involved in community activism previously, but Moore's account is interesting for its revelations about the strategy used by some women activists in selecting well-known ministers to "head" community-initiated movements.

81. Audley Moore, ibid.

82. Wallace Thurman, "Odd Jobs in Harlem," typescript, Thurman Papers, James Weldon Johnson Collection, Yale University.

83. *NYAN*, August 8, 1928, p. 192. The writer Ivan Taylor was probably referring to men such as St. William Grant, a Garveyite who was involved in a number of violent clashes.

84. See Frank R. Crosswaith, "The Newer Negro," clipping dated July 1928, in Vertical File, SCRBC.

85. Pollard, "Harlem as Is," p. 132.

86. *NYAN*, November 3, 1937.

87. Sadie Hall, "Stepladder Speakers" (WPA Research Paper) SCRBC.

88. Tyrell Wilson, interview, March 7, 1978, Gordon Heights, Long Island, New York. Program of "Testimonial Dinner in Honor of Tyrell S. Wilson, Sr.," May 1, 1971.

89. *New York News*, 1926. Clipping Gumby Collection.

7. Marcus Garvey

1. J. Edgar Hoover to Ridgely, October 11, 1919. DNA RG 60 #198940.

2. Hill, "Introduction," *MGP* III, p. xxxiii.

3. Tony Martin, *Race First: The Ideological and Organizational Struggles of Marcus Garvey and the Universal Negro Improvement Association* (Westport, Connecticut: Greenwood Press, 1976), p. 8.

4. Marcus Garvey, "West Indies in the Mirror of Truth," *The Champion* (January 1, 1917), p. 26.

5. Ibid.

6. Hoover to Ridgely, October 11, 1919, ibid.

7. *NYAN,* July 6, 1940.

8. Walker agent Marjorie Hill Joyner performed a recitation at Garvey's birthday celebration in Edelweiss park in Jamaica in 1929, and the Walker convention was held in Jamaica at the same time as the UNIA annual convention. By 1938 Joyner had become president of the Walker company and a speaker for the New York Garvey Club. Hill, ed., *Marcus Garvey: Life and Lessons,* pp. 437–38; *Negro World,* July 24, 1926; *NYAN,* July 16, 1940.

9. Ida Wells Barnett, *Crusade for Justice,* p. 180. Wells and Randolph did not attend since the U.S. government denied passports to most African Americans who wanted to attend. A Haitian envoy attended instead. The lack of understanding about the political roles diaspora blacks should take in Africa continued to plague the repatriation movement as it had in the nineteenth century. Neither diaspora black radicals nor moderates seriously considered self-rule as a viable alternative for Africans in the former German-held territories.

10. Marcus Garvey, "Autobiography: Articles from the Pittsburgh Courier," in Hill, *Marcus Garvey: Life and Lessons,* p. 36.

11. For a discussion of the UNIA's ties to the African American Church, see Randall K. Burkett, *Black Redemption: Churchmen Speak for the Garvey Movement* (Philadelphia: Temple University Press, 1978).

12. Burkett, *Black Redemption,* pp. 3–4; Hill, "Introduction," *MGP* I, p. lxii.

13. William Seraille, "Henrietta Vinton Davis and the Garvey Movement," *Afro-Americans in New York Life and History* (July 1983), pp. 13–15. Another woman organizer, Maymie Leona Turpeau De Mena (1891–1953), of African Nicaraguan descent, became a "lauded speaker in the Garvey movement and 'electrified'" audiences in Chicago, Detroit, Cleveland, Washington, D.C., Norfolk, and other American cities. See Hill, *MGP,* VI, p. 117.

14. Burkett, *Black Redemption,* p. 46.

15. *NYAN,* July 16, 1940. Martin, *Race First,* p. 11, 25; Hill, "Introduction," *MGP* III, p. xxxiii; *Negro World,* February 12, 1921. The *Negro World* was not only read widely by new arrivals in Harlem, but it was redistributed among relatives and friends back home. During the height of its circulation the paper was dispersed in black communities all over the United States and in the Caribbean, South and Central America, and many African colonies. One Caribbean immigrant, Charles Zampty, a UNIA official, recalled first receiving the paper in Panama through Japanese seamen who had sailed from New York. Charles Zampty, interview, February 26, 1977, Detroit, Michigan.

16. *Chicago Defender,* September 6, 1919.

17. W. E. B. Du Bois, "The Rise of the West Indian," *Crisis,* September 1920, p. 214. In his autobiography Du Bois recalled: "My first effort was to explain away the Garvey movement and ignore it; but it was a mass movement that could not be ignored. I noted this movement from time to time in the *Crisis.* . . ." *Dusk of Dawn* (New York: Harcourt, Brace, 1940) p. 278.

18. "Report by the American Protective League to the Bureau of Investigation," NYC, June 3, 1918, in Hill, *MGP,* p. 244.

19. Anonymous to Justice Department from New York City, August 11, 1919. DNA RG 60 Amy Jacques Class Subfile 198940 (Micro #55).

20. Louis Post, Asst. Secretary of Labor to Attorney General A. Mitchell Palmer, August 16, 1919. DNA RG 60 File 198940. Informants from other cities also wrote government officials.

George Thomas of Key West wrote Attorney General Harry Daughterly about "an alien organization . . . know[n] as the UNIA and has for its leader an alien by the name of Marcus Garvey." This writer urged the Attorney General to "send to this city at once some Government investigators in order that they may run down these West Indie [*sic*] Aliens that are connected with this organization as they are formenting [*sic*] a lot of unrest amongst ignorant negroes in this city against our government." George Washington, 615 Thomas Street, Key West, Florida, to Harry Daughterly, April 28, 1921, in DNA RG 60 A. J. Class File 198940. See also Hill, *MGP* III, pp. 375–76.

21. Asst. Attorney General R. P. Steward to Secretary of Labor, October 14, 1919, DNA RG 60 Class File 198940.

22. The network of correspondence between consuls in the Caribbean and from these locations to the State Department supports this view, but it is also interesting for the kind of information the letters contain. For example, correspondents report what they believed to be the sums of money collected at meetings as well as the details of the topics covered. The consul at Jamaica, Charles L. Latham, reported in his September 1920 account that the question of an alliance with Indian nationalists and with Japan and China as well as with Bolshevik Russia were issues discussed. He also reported on Garvey's support of a recent police strike and other labor agitation in Kingston. Latham to Secretary of State, September 12, 1920. DNA RG 59.

23. "Evidence to this end might be obtained from Adrian Richardson of 14 West 107th, New York." Charles Latham to Secretary of State, August 24, 1921, ibid.

24. Telegram from Walter Smith to Secretary of State Charles Evans Hughes, July 1, 1921. DNA RG 59 State Decimal File, 1910–1929, Box 7371.

25. William Jennings Price to Secretary of State, May 18, 1921; DNA RG 59 (811. 108) G191/16; Wilbur J. Carr to Charles L. Latham, March 25, 1921, DNA RG 60, Box 7371.

26. Richard W. Flournoy, Jr., to J. Preston Doughten, June 21, 1921. Hill, *MGP* III, p. 482.

27. Martin, *Race First*, p. 186.

28. Hill, *MGP* IV, p. 6

29. Earlier, when he was detained in New Orleans, Garvey sent a telegram to Secretary of State Charles Evans Hughes placing the blame on "many enemies, members of my race and others" who had made "false representations" and because of "jealousy" were attempting to prevent his returning to the United States. Garvey to Charles Evans Hughes, July 13, 1921, DNA RG 59 811. 108 G 191/32.

30. Years later in an unsuccessful bid to obtain a visa to travel in the U.S. in 1935, Garvey wrote the State Department: "Through my being an alien, although I had signified my intention of becoming an American Citizen by taking out my first papers, a great amount of jealousy among the members of my race sprung up over my apparent success in leading the organizations with which I was identified." Marcus Garvey to Secretary of State from St. Andrew, Jamaica, January 7, 1935. DNA RG 60 Amy Jacques Garvey Class File 198940. One Harlem contemporary agreed with Garvey's position. Writer Wallace Thurman, in an unpublished essay, noted contentiousness of editors like Moore, Randolph, and Du Bois. "Their zeal in fighting him does not all times seem to have been purely for the benefit of the race. How dare [Garvey] come along and get more followers in one year than they had been able to garner in a decade? They appreciated the more ridiculous aspects of the dream and righteously denounced them. But they did not and would not appreciate its more cogent elements, which they might well have incorporated into their own programs." James Weldon Johnson Papers, Small Collections, Thurman Papers, Beinecke Library, Yale University.

31. Hill, "General Introduction," *MGP* I, p. lxxx.

32. Ibid., p. lxxiv.

33. W. E. B. Du Bois, "Back to Africa," *Century Magazine* 105 (February 1923), pp. 542, 546.

34. John Bruce believed this to be the case with the white press in New York. In a 1922 letter to the editors of the *World*, he stated, "I venture the statement that there isn't a White man in the City of New York who possesses first hand information of the real aims and objects of what is

called the Garvey Movement, and that there is not a Negro now opposing it who knows anything worth remembering, concerning the Movement." John Bruce to Editor of the *World*, January 17, 1922, in John Bruce Papers, SCRBC.

35. Charles S. Johnson to James Weldon Johnson, March 1, 1922; James Weldon Johnson to Charles S. Johnson, March 3, 1922. Library of Congress, NAACP Administrative File, Box C-385.

36. James Weldon Johnson to Rev. Franklin Jones, October 11, 1921, NAACP Administrative File.

37. To the dismay of Du Bois and Senegalese delegate Blaise Diagne, some UNIA sympathizers were among the Congresses' delegates, including one UNIA member from Haiti who passed out the *Negro World* at the 1919 Congress. Du Bois admitted in his report to the NAACP Board of Directors that differences in opinion between himself and some of the black delegates residing in Paris nearly disrupted the Congress. Following the 1921 Brussels Congress a new, permanent Pan-African Congress secretary, who sympathized with the UNIA program of industrial cooperation, wanted to extend the Pan-African idea to include industrial and commercial cooperation with Africa, Africans in the Caribbean, and the United States. W. E. B. Du Bois, "The Pan-African Movement," in George Padmore, ed., *History of the Pan-African Congress* (London: Hammersmith, 1945), p. 22; Du Bois, "Opinion," *Crisis,* December 1925, p. 57; Martin, *Race First,* pp. 122, 288.

38. "American Delegates Sail for Pan-African Congress" (News Release) in LC NAACP Administrative File, Box C-385.

39. Clipping, LC NAACP Administrative File, Box C-385.

40. *Negro World,* September 11, October 1, October 29, November 26, and December 3, 1921. Bruce stated that he was sorry he could not afford the "$350-$750" expense package for the trip. "I wish it the success it deserves and I sincerely hope that enough Negro millionaires will be found on this side of the salt pond to make up a respectable delegation of American Negroes." *Negro World,* March 19, 1921.

41. *Negro World,* September 30, 1927; W. E. Du Bois, *The World and Africa* (1946; reprint edition New York: International Publishers, 1965), pp. 242–43. It is important to note African American women's less public roles in the promotion of the Pan-African idea. In 1919 two prominent African American women, Madame C. J. Walker and Dr. Verina Morton Jones, were among those who contributed to a fund for Du Bois's travel to the first Pan-African Congress. See "Expense Report," Pan-African Congress Folder 1918–1919, Library of Congress, NAACP Administrative File Box C-385. Walker apparently saw no conflict in her financial backing of Garvey's programs during the same period. In 1926 Addie Hunton of the Circle for Peace and Foreign Relations sent the following letter to the NAACP Board of Directors:

> In pursuance with one of the purposes of the organization, which is the promotion of understanding and unity among the darker races, the Circle believes it a duty to promote the fourth Pan-African Conference rather than see the splendid results of the previous Conferences go for naught. Therefore, it has voted to raise an amount sufficient to hold the fourth Conference in New York City next summer and has asked Dr. Du Bois to direct it in the same manner as previously.

Addie W. Hunton to Mary White Ovington, November 4, 1926, NAACP Administrative File C-385, Pan-African Congress Folder.

42. *New York World,* June 20, 1923, clipping in Alexander Gumby Collection, Scrapbook no. 32.

43. *Messenger* (July 1922), p. 477.

44. W. A. Domingo, "Open Forum: The Policy of the Messenger on West Indian and American Negroes," *Messenger* (March 1923), p. 640.

45. Chandler Owen, "Open Forum," ibid., p. 641.

46. Roscoe Conkling Bruce was the son of a black Mississippi reconstruction senator, Blanch K. Bruce.

47. *Messenger* (April 1922), p. 387.

48. Walter White to A. Philip Randolph, August 7, 1922, and Randolph to Walter White, August 25, 1922, in LC NAACP Papers Administrative File, Box 304-C.

49. Clippings in Pickens Papers, SCRBC, *Public Journal,* August 1922; *Baltimore Afro-American,* August 11, 1922.

50. *Baltimore Afro-American,* September 29, 1922.

51. *Negro World,* September 23, 1922. One reason Pickens proved so reprehensible to the UNIA and the Garvey camp was that at one point he had been considered an ally and a possible writer for the *Negro World.* As recently as May 1922, Garvey had invited him to attend the UNIA convention in August as a delegate and to serve as a high-ranking officer in the UNIA. "We have lined up some of the ablest men of the country for our new administration, and I am counting on you as one of those to be in our new cabinet . . . ," Garvey confided. "I write you in a friendly way." He added, "because I know that your heart beats right, and I feel the same toward you." Garvey to Pickens, May 15, 1922. Pickens Papers, SCRBC. Pickens had previously written mildly favorable reviews of the Garvey movement in various journals and publications, but he had been under considerable pressure from the NAACP to discontinue such reviews. See *Nation,* December 28, 1921; *Negro World,* December 17, 1921.

52. New York *News* reprinted in *The World,* July 16, 1922; UNIA supporters at Liberty Hall headquarters applauded Garvey's bravery. According to a *Negro World* account, when the telegram announcing the KKK meeting was read, "The applause which greeted the reading . . . shook the rafters of the building and it was some time before it subsided." *Negro World,* July 22, 1922. Charles Zampty, a Garvey lieutenant who was present at the meeting, recalled that when Garvey held a widely publicized mass meeting in Atlanta, the Grand Wizard invited him to come for an interview. "We were not afraid of anything" and wanted to make it clear they were just as "proud to be black as the klansman were to be white." Interview, Charles Zampty; Maurice Warren, "Moses and the Messenger: The Crisis of Black Radicalism 1921–1922," Senior Honors Essay, Harvard College, 1973, p. 93.

53. Hill, "General Introduction," *MGP* I, p. lxxxiii.

54. Hill, "General Introduction," *MGP* IV, p. xxxiv.

55. *New York Age,* February 11, 1925; *Richmond Planet,* August 16, 1923; *Pittsburgh Courier,* August 12, 1923.

56. E. Franklin Frazier, "Garvey: A Mass Leader," *The Nation* 123 (August 18, 1926), pp. 147–48; *NYAN,* August 5, 1925.

57. *New York Herald Tribune,* August 16, 1926.

58. Quoted in *Negro World,* September 3, 1927.

59. *NYAN,* August 3, 1927.

60. John Sargent to Coolidge, November 12, 1927. DNA, RG 204, 42–473.

61. Du Bois, "Marcus Garvey and the NAACP," *Crisis,* February 1928.

8. Ethnic and Race Enterprise

1. W.E.B.DuBois,ed., *The Negro in Business* (Atlanta: Atlanta University Publications, 1899), p. 5; Booker T. Washington, *The Negro in Business* (Boston: Hertel, Jenkins, and Company, 1907).

2. *New York Age,* March 23, 1924.

3. *Negro World,* September 3, 1925.

4. *Crusader passim.* In its July 1919 issue, Briggs highlighted the Art Publishing Company at 208 West 64th Street as "A Great Race Enterprise." Again in August the magazine recommended the Sarco Realty Company as a race investment opportunity and described the Intercolonial Supply Company as an "Up to Date Grocery."

5. St. Clair Drake and Horace Cayton, *Black Metropolis, The Story of Negro Life in a Northern City,* vol. 2 (New York: Harcourt Brace Jovanovich, 1945), p. 432.

6. Quoted in *Negro World*, August 14, 1926.

7. Ida B. Wells, *Crusade for Justice* (Chicago: University of Chicago Press, 1970), pp. 47–55.

8. George Edmund Haynes, *The Negro at Work in New York* (New York: Columbia University, 1912), pp. 100–102, 108.

9. This statement by a Barbadian immigrant informant in W. E. B. Du Bois's 1899 study illustrates a pattern among Caribbean entrepreneurs. Apprenticed to a watchmaker in his hometown of Bridgetown until he had a "fair knowledge of the trade," the informant also received a "good grammar course" before trying his luck in America. "After about four months after my arrival in this country, I applied for work at some of the leading jewelry stores [of Kansas City] and found out for the first time that the roads to success in this country for the black man were not so free and open as those of his brother in white. So I worked as [a] porter for two years, and then encouraged by the success of pleasing my friends with private work done for them during my leisure hours . . . I bought a small frame building, opened a watch repairing shop and became Kansas City's first Negro jeweler." Du Bois, *The Negro in Business*, p. 41.

10. *NYAN*, May 13, 1925.

11. George Edmund Haynes, *The Negro at Work*, p. 126.

12. Ibid., p. 114.

13. *New York Age*, December 21, 1929.

14. Interview, George Schuyler, May 24, 1960. Oral History Research Office, Columbia University.

15. See *New York Age* survey of black business, July 1920, April 1921.

16. Herbert Gutman, *The Black Family in Slavery and Freedom* (New York: Pantheon, 1976).

17. Gutman, *The Black Family*, p. 514. A popular and scholarly notion maintains that in business a "significant distinction" existed between Caribbean immigrants and native blacks. While this may have been the case in the types of businesses engaged in, census evidence tends to show less contrast than previously believed, at least in terms of the numbers engaged. Claude McKay provides valuable insight about the historical roots of Caribbean immigrants' participation in business:

> West Indians are foremost in . . . little businesses of push carts, fruit and vegetable stands, candy stores and grocery stores. . . . Because of their energy and tenacity in this line, their American cousins call the West Indians the black Jews of Harlem. They even credit them with superior business acumen. But the truth is that the English-speaking West Indians, like the Spanish-speaking, show aptitude in this sphere because of their background. In the English-speaking islands the Negroes are over 90 percent of the population. The small white aristocracy are all high officials, heads and subheads of departments and large landed proprietors. The upper layer of the wealthy mulatto group are politicians, big merchants and civil servants. Enterprising Negroes therefore enter the field of petty commerce which is wide open to them and in which their competitors are immigrant Chinese and East Indians whose standard of existence is on a lower level than the Negroes'. When these Negroes migrate to America they see in the black belts a special field in which their native background is helpful.

McKay, *Harlem: Negro Metropolis*, p. 93.

18. Anonymous, "Negro Printers and Print Shops" (WPA Research Paper).

19. Pollard, "Harlem as Is," p. 152.

20. The *New York Age* urged southern blacks as well as Caribbean immigrants to use home connections to promote black retail business in Harlem. *New York Age*, August 21, 1920.

21. Pollard, "Harlem as Is," p. 152. Interview, Joyce and Burghardt Turner, September 30, 1978.

22. *New York Age*, April 30, 1916.

23. Ibid., March 19, 1921.

24. Edgar M. Grey, "The New Negro Slavery in Harlem," *NYAN*, May 13, 1925.

25. *New York Age*, March 8, 1924. Gurock, *When Harlem Was Jewish*, 1870–1930, p. 147.

26. *NYAN,* November 5, 1930. T. R. Woofter, *The Negro at Work,* pp. 280–81.

27. *New York Age,* March 12, 1921.

28. In general Afro-Americans applied the same attitude to Chinese, who, if merchants, were categorized with white ethnic businesses. However, those Asians who emigrated from the Caribbean and settled in Harlem were "race people." South Asian Indian Hucheshwar G. Mudgal, for instance, a native of Trinidad, succeeded T. Thomas Fortune as editor of the *Negro World.* See Roi Ottley, *New World A' Coming,"* for discussion of Chinese business people.

29. Spero and Harris, *The Black Worker,* pp. 48–54.

30. *New York Age,* February 26, 1921; W. A. Domingo, "The Gift of the Black Tropics," in Alain Locke, *The New Negro,* p. 345; *New York Age,* February 26, 1921.

31. Ibid., September 27, 1924; *NYAN,* December 24, 1930.

32. *New York Age,* August 7, 1920; *NYAN,* December 20, 1922.

33. *New York Age,* February 19, 1922. At least two of the stores in the Renaissance Building were leased to black immigrants. Hart and cigar store owners L. Casanova and P. Perez manufactured a new brand of cigar which they named "The Dunbar," for black poet Paul Laurence Dunbar.

34. *Negro World,* July 27, 1929.

35. *NYAN,* March 8, 1933.

36. *New York Age,* October 18, 1930; *NYAN,* March 8, 1933.

37. *NYAN,* June 29, 1929. According to the *Age,* white firms charged blacks from 25 to 30 percent interest for business loans, March 19, 1921.

38. Arthur Gray, "The Negro in Business" (WPA Research Paper).

39. *NYAN,* September 19, 1928.

40. *New York Age,* September 22, 1928; *NYAN,* September 3, 1930; October 8, 1930.

41. *New York Times,* November 6, 1933; Pollard, vol. 2, p. 205. When the depression hit soon after the Dunbar Apartments' opening, even the carefully screened middle-class tenants could not pay the rent. Rockefeller sold the building to a real estate agent in 1937.

42. Ivan Light, *Ethnic Enterprise in America* (Berkeley: University of California Press, 1972), p. 34. Light quotes from personal correspondence from Amy Jacques Garvey, dated February 12, 1968.

43. Interview, Dorothy Burnham, November 12, 1993.

44. Roi Ottley, *The Negro in New York,* p. 231. An important business community leader, Francis was born in Jamaica in 1882 and worked in Costa Rica as a retail store manager before immigrating to the United States in 1916. He worked as a hotel clerk, law clerk, and manager of a New York bakery and restaurant before setting up his own business in 1924, when he also became a naturalized citizen. The Urban League industrial secretary, Samuel Allen, nominated Francis for the Harmon Award for business leadership in 1930. Library of Congress, Harmon Foundation Papers, Box 37.

45. *New York Age,* October 1927.

9. The Underground Entrepreneur

1. *New York Age,* May 24, 1924.

2. Ottley, *New World A' Coming,* p. 151.

3. McKay, *Harlem: Negro Metropolis,* p. 110.

4. *New York Sun,* November 20, 1935.

5. *New York Age,* July 5, 1924.

6. Numbers banker Martin Harris was an usher in the Abyssinian Baptist Church.

7. Osofsky, in *Harlem,* treats numbers briefly but gives no consideration to its social or economic significance. See St. Clair Drake and Horace Cayton, *Black Metropolis,* vol. 2, and Richard

W. Thomas, *Life for Us Is What We Make It: Building Black Community in Detroit, 1915–1945* (Bloomington: Indiana University Press, 1992).

8. Edgar M. Grey, "Is the Numbers an Evil in Harlem?" *New York News,* December 17, 1927.

9. McKay, *Harlem: Negro Metropolis,* p. 110.

10. Drake and Cayton, *Black Metropolis,* p. 482. A major complaint of political insurgents against Ferdinand Q. Morton was that he turned his head to vice and racketeering in the community.

11. *NYAN,* August 27, 1928.

12. Drake and Cayton, *Black Metropolis,* II. p. 481.

13. Grey, *New York News,* December 17, 1927.

14. Ottley, *New World A' Coming,* p. 216.

15. *New York Times,* November 11, 1925.

16. *New York Age,* December 6, 1924; May 3, 1924.

17. *Evening Graphic,* December 21, 1926.

18. *NYAN,* August 27, 1938.

19. Ibid., September 3, 1938.

20. Ibid.

21. Ibid., August 27, 1937.

22. Ibid.

23. William Brashler, *Josh Gibson: A Life in the Negro Leagues* (New York: Harper and Row, 1978) p. 59. Colored leagues sometimes used white stadiums when white teams were not playing.

24. *NYAN,* August 27, 1938.

25. *New York Times,* June 24, 1931.

26. Ibid.

27. *NYAN,* September 4, 1929.

28. Ibid.

29. Ibid.

30. Ibid., October 9, 1929.

31. Ibid., December 18, 1930.

32. Ibid., September 9, 1929; October 30, 1929.

33. Ottley, *The Negro in New York,* pp. 273–74.

34. *New York Post,* March 4, 1960.

35. *NYAN,* August 27, 1938.

36. Ibid.

37. *Post,* February 29, 1960. See McKay, *Harlem: Negro Metropolis,* p. 111.

38. Sadie Hall, "Casper Holstein" (WPA Biography, 1939).

39. Charles W. Turnbull and Christian J. Lewis, *Casper Holstein, Unusual Humanitarian* (St. Thomas: Virgin Islands Department of Education, 1974), p. 9.

40. *New York Age,* January 3, 1927.

41. *Pittsburgh Courier,* January 29, 1927, clipping in Hubert Harrison Vertical File, SCRBC. When Harrison died in December 1927, Holstein, assisted by Edgar Grey, was in "entire charge of the funeral arrangements." *NYAN,* December 28, 1927. There is no account of Harrison ever having criticized his fellow Virgin Islander from the stepladder.

42. *Opportunity,* October 1926, p. 319.

43. Langston Hughes, *The Big Sea,* p. 214.

44. *New York News,* December 17, 1927; *New York Age,* February 11, 1928. Turnbull and Lewis, *Casper Holstein,* p. 9.

45. *Chicago Defender,* March 5, 1927.

46. Turnbull and Lewis, *Casper Holstein,* p. 7.

47. Ibid.

48. *NYAN,* August 3, 1927; August 10, 1927; September 26, 1928.

49. *NYAN*, September 26, 1928.

50. *New York Age*, August 20, 1927.

51. Ibid., December 24, 1927.

52. Ibid., February 11, 1928.

53. *New York Times*, September 24, 1928; *New York Age*, September 29, 1928.

54. *NYAN*, October 3, 1928.

55. Interview, G. James Fleming, Baltimore, Maryland, October 14, 1977.

56. Turnbull and Lewis, *Casper Holstein*, p. 14.

57. Sadie Hall, "Casper Holstein" (WPA Biography).

58. Drake and Cayton, *Black Metropolis* II, p. 486.

59. *NYAN*, August 27, 1938.

60. *New York Age*, May 24, 1924.

61. Ibid.

62. Ibid., September 27; December 6, 1924.

63. Ibid.

64. *New York Age*, July 12, 1924.

65. *New York Age*, June 7, 1924; see also July 19, 1924; September 27, 1924.

66. Grey, *New York News*, December 17, 1927. In 1926 the Urban League's *Opportunity* editors, Charles S. Johnson and Eric Walrond, nominated Holstein for the Harmon Foundation Award in the category of race relations. Holstein's references included Forest Bailey, Director of the ACLU; Judge L. J. Malmin of Chicago; and Charles W. Anderson, Collector of Internal Revenue, New York City. The Harmon Foundation and the Julius Rosenwald Fund were considered two of the most influential philanthropic organizations supporting African American achievement. Harmon Foundation Papers, Box 57, Library of Congress.

67. Thurman, *Negro Life in New York's Harlem* (Girard, Kansas: Haldeman Julius, 1928), p. 12.

10. Harlem Writers and Intraracial Ethnicity

1. Philip Kasinitz, *Caribbean New York: Black Immigrants and the Politics of Race* (Ithaca: Cornell University Press, 1990), p. 52. The Caribbean media in New York includes the weekly newspapers the *Carib News* and the *Observateur; Everybody's* and *Haiti Observateur Magazine* are both monthly magazines. Kasinitz, p. 71.

2. James Weldon Johnson, *Black Manhattan*, p. 251.

3. McKay, *Home to Harlem* (New York: Harper, 1928), p. 81.

4. W. A. Domingo, "Gift of the Black Tropics," in Locke, *The New Negro* (New York: Boni, 1925) p. 343.

5. Claude McKay, *Home to Harlem*, p. 82.

6. Eric Walrond, "Englishman, What Now?" in *The Daily Gleaner* June 1, 1935.

7. Ibid.

8. McKay, *Home to Harlem*, p. 130.

9. McKay, *A Long Way from Home*, p. 49. McKay's biographer points out the following: "New York, with its great concentration of population and teeming impersonality, tolerated the existence of a large though officially repressed homosexual community whose members found regular, if illicit, outlets for their sexual and social taste. McKay enjoyed this almost clandestine aspect of New York life, and after the dissolution of his marriage he pursued a love life that included partners of both sexes." Wayne Cooper, *Claude McKay: Rebel Sojourner of the Harlem Renaissance* (New York: Schocken, 1987), p. 75.

10. *Negro World*, May 6, 1922.

11. Rudolph Fisher, "City of Refuge," in Alain Locke, *The New Negro* (1925; reprint, New York: Atheneum, 1969), p. 64.

12. Ira De Augustine Reid, *The Negro Immigrant,* p. 193.

13. Wallace Thurman, *The Blacker the Berry* (1929; reprint, New York: MacMillan, 1970), pp. 111–12.

14. Marshall, "Black Immigrant Women in *Brown Girl, Brownstones,*" pp. 7–8.

15. Elizabeth Brown-Guillory, *Their Place on the Stage* (New York: Praeger, 1990), pp. 4, 19.

16. Elizabeth Brown-Guillory, ed., *Wines in the Wilderness: Plays by African American Women from the Harlem Renaissance to the Present* (New York: Praeger, 1990), pp. 39–40. Noah D. Thompson of *Opportunity* nominated Spence for the Harmon Foundation Award in literature for 1927. Harmon Foundation Papers, Library of Congress, Box 51. For contemporary reviews of Spence's plays, see *Herald Tribune* May 7, 1927 and *Billboard* May 14, 1927.

17. Lionel Yard, *Biography of Amy Ashwood Garvey, 1897–1969, Co-founder of the Universal Negro Improvement Association* (Washington, D.C.: Associated Publishers, n.d.), p. 105; *New York Age,* August 20, 1927.

18. Yard, p. 109.

19. Wayne Cooper, *Claude McKay,* p. 139.

20. Harrison, in *Negro World,* March 12, 1921.

21. Eric Walrond, "On Being Black," *New Republic* (November 1, 1922), p. 246. Bruce Kellner, *The Harlem Renaissance: An Historical Dictionary for the Era* (New York: Methuen, 1984), p. 375; Hill *MGP* II, p. 182.

22. *Negro World,* April 1, 1922.

23. Ibid., May 6, 1922; July 22, 1922.

24. Walrond is known to have continued his affiliation with the organization in England for some twenty years after he left the United States in 1928. See *MGP* II. p. 182.

25. Claude McKay to Schomburg, September 9, 1925, Schomburg Papers. Langston Hughes, p. 218.

26. See *Opportunity* November 1926; Bruce Kellner, *The Harlem Renaissance,* p. 235.

27. *Opportunity* announced its third contest for the "Holstein awards in literature and musical compositions" in its November 1926 issue, p. 343.

28. *Pittsburgh Courier,* March 5, 1927; *Messenger,* January 1927, pp. 27–28.

29. *New York Herald Tribune,* December 5, 1926.

30. See Walrond, *Tropic Death.* See also McKay's *Banana Bottom* (New York: Harper and Row, 1933).

31. Langston Hughes, "Third American Writers Congress Address," Carnegie Hall, June 2, 1939, quoted in Ottley, *The Negro in New York,* p. 261.

32. Robert Kerlin, ed., *Voice of the Negro* (New York: E.P. Dutton and Company, 1920), p. ix; Associated Negro Press, in Kerlin, p. 1.

33. In 1930, one of Harlem's major newspapers, the *Amsterdam News,* was owned by prominent immigrant businessman Dr. P. M. H. Savory and native-born physician C. B. Powell, Jr. Marcus Garvey's *Negro World* was the only paper self-consciously recognizing its multiethnic audience for a brief period in its Spanish, French, and English sections. The content of the articles, however, was primarily racial.

34. *MGP* V, p. 4, n. 1.

35. Robert Hill, "Introduction: Racial and Radical: Cyril Briggs, *The Crusader Magazine,* and the African Blood Brotherhood, 1918–1922," in facsimile edition of the *Crusader* vol 1 (New York: Garland, 1987), p. v. Harrison was an experienced journalist, though not a businessman by the time he launched his *Voice* in 1917. As early as 1906 his articles appeared in New York white dailies—the *New York Times* and later the *Sun* and *Call.* His articles in the *Masses* gained him exposure to a wide range of leftist thinkers. But he was never happy with the position of the left on race or black labor. In a series for the *Call,* Harrison tried to instruct Socialists about the special needs and conditions of black labor. To gain black supporters he began organizing in 1911 an African American Socialist

club at 60 West 134th Street in Harlem, where he gave lectures on African and African American history and "Socialism and the Negro Problem." See *New York Call*, December 4, 16, and 26, 1911. It is not clear what Harrison's ties were with other native-born African American Socialists, but he was aware of the work of black California Socialist Rev. George Washington Woodbey. The nature of Harrison's early relationship with Du Bois is also unclear. According to correspondence between local Socialist party officials, Harrison was a "close friend" of Du Bois, who regarded him as a man of "intelligence and ability" and recommended Harrison as a Socialist party speaker during the *Crisis* editor's brief sojourn with the party in 1911. Philip Foner, *American Socialism and Black Americans from the Age of Jackson to World War II* (Westport, Connecticut: Greenwood Press), p. 206. Foner quotes Samuel Romansky to Julius Gerber, October 12, 1911, in Socialist Party Papers, Tamiment Institute, Bobst Library, New York University.

36. Harrison claimed he initially wrote the "Descent of Du Bois" article as a report solicited by Major Walter H. Loving, one of a half dozen African American U.S. Military Intelligence agents reporting on the activities of radicals in Harlem. Harrison's actions, he claimed, were prompted by Du Bois's famous article, which appeared in the June 1918 issue of the *Crisis*. Here the editor called on African Americans to "close ranks" with white Americans in support of the allied nations. The "Close Ranks" article, which appeared at the height of lynchings, Jim Crow, mob law, and violence against the African American people, sent shock waves through the black press, which roundly condemned the article's premise. Harrison wanted to assure Loving that Du Bois no longer represented thinking African Americans. Harrison believed and boldly reported in *Africa Awakes* that his summary of the situation, incorporated in Loving's report to the government, convinced officials not to offer Du Bois a captaincy in Military Intelligence for which he was being considered. Du Bois would have been captain of a unit set up to encourage and monitor African American participation in the war. It now seems clear that the *Crisis* editor wrote "Close Ranks" in exchange for the expected captaincy. Du Bois biographer David Levering Lewis reports that Loving's "indefatigable" intelligence work probably helped officials make their final decision. Still, Harrison's collaboration with a known government agent is curious. But his admitted involvement with Loving demonstrates he was not merely a stepladder lecturer aloof from political maneuvering, whether inside or outside the native black establishment. *When Africa Awakes* (New York: Porro Press, 1920), p. 56; W. E. B. Du Bois, *Crisis*, July 1918; David Levering Lewis, *W. E. B. Du Bois, Biography of a Race* (New York: Henry Holt), p. 559–60.

37. At least one African American leader, the very fair-complexioned Walter White, wrote about the subject in an article for Alain Locke's *New Negro* (1925). Acknowledging that the "color line within the color line" shaped community dynamics in Harlem, White pointed out that "even among intelligent Negroes there [is] the belief that black Negroes are less able to achieve success." But White attributed the heightened consciousness about this subject to the "presence of some 40,000 Negroes from the West Indies" and to Marcus Garvey. In his opinion, immigrants from the Caribbean defined social relations in Harlem on the basis of tripartite divisions between whites, mulattos, and black-skinned people in their former homes. Walter White, "The Paradox of Color," in Alain Locke, *The New Negro*, pp. 366–67. White was not correct to blame long-standing tensions about color prejudice on the presence of dark-skinned Caribbean immigrants. However, the presence of talented dark-skinned immigrants was not irrelevant to a rise in color tensions in Harlem. A predominantly light-skinned African American elite held on to leadership positions and denied the color issue validity in political discourse.

38. *New York News,* August 11, 1928.

39. *MGP* Vol. I, pp. 211–12.

40. *NYAN*, July 6, 1927; August 3, 1927.

41. *New York Age,* January 28, 1928; *MGP* I, p. 211.

42. Robert Hill, "Racial and Radical," p. xxii. According to Hill's account, Briggs had not been fired. The publishers did not really disagree with his editorials. The *Crusader,* in fact, received

direct support from *NYAN* staff through its field agents. The final separation was effected when publisher Edward A. Warren was summoned at the height of the Red Scare in June 1918 to Washington, D.C., with other African American editors. They were asked to "assist the government in winning the war." Warren and other black editors were pressured into issuing statements calling upon the black community to support the war effort and the League of Nations. With this new policy in effect, Briggs believed he had no further role on the paper and therefore resigned.

43. Robert Miller, "The Ku Klux Klan," in Irwin Unger, *The American Past* (New York, 1971), p. 229.

44. The *Harlem Liberator*, December 14, 1929.

45. See Burghardt Turner, "Joel Augustus Rogers: An Afro-American Historian," *Negro History Bulletin* (February 1972), pp. 35–36.

46. *Negro World*, January 7, 1922; Roi Ottley, *New World A Coming*, p. 102; Sydney French, "J. A. Rogers" (WPA Biography, 1940), p. 3.

47. *Negro World*, January 7, 1922.

48. Hughes, *The Big Sea*, p. 234; Theodore Vincent, *Voices of a Black Nation*, p. 32.

49. Arthur Schomburg, "The Negro Digs Up His Past," in Alain Locke, *The New Negro*, p. 236. In a barb aimed at someone, probably a certain caliber of stepladder speaker, Schomburg continued:

> The blatant Caucasian racialist with his theories and assumptions of race superiority and dominance has in turn bred his Ethiopian counterpart—the rash and rabid amateur who has glibly tried to prove half of the world's geniuses to have been Negroes and to trace the pedigree of nineteenth-century Americans from the Queen of Sheba.

50. *Negro World*, August 14, 1926.

51. Amy Jacques Garvey, "Acquit Yourselves like Men," *Negro World*, April 30, 1927.

52. Mark D. Matthews, "Our Women and What They Think: Amy Jacques Garvey and the *Negro World*," *The Black Scholar* (May–June 1979), p. 6; also, *Negro World* February 5, 1927, November 27, 1926, April 9, 1927.

53. *Negro World*, August 21, 1926.

54. *Negro World*, February 2, 1924. Matthews, "Our Women," p. 5; Paula Giddings, *When and Where I Enter: The Impact of Black Women on Race and Sex in America* (New York: Bantam, 1984), p. 194. See also Anna Julia Cooper, *A Voice from the South* (Xenia, Ohio, Aldine Publishing House, 1892).

55. *Negro World*, January 9, 1926.

11. Conclusion

1. Hubert Harrison in *Pittsburgh Courier*, Jan 21, 1927.

2. *Pittsburgh Courier*, January 29, 1927.

3. Addie ("your true friend") to Aletha Challenor Dowridge, September 6, 1910.

4. Many Spanish-speaking immigrants also settled in Central Harlem, though most settled among the Puerto Rican and other Hispanic groups between 100th and 116th Streets, and Lexington and Morningside Avenues in East Harlem.

5. *Clustering* is the word Reid appropriately uses to describe patterns of black immigrant settlement in Harlem. For instance, as many as thirty families of Martiniquians and Guadeloupeans lived on the southern end of Harlem at 111th Street between Eighth and Madison Avenues. Reid, *The Negro Immigrant*, p. 95.

6. Herbert Gutman's sample of the entire community in 1925 confirms that there were very few occupational distinctions between most of Caribbean immigrants and native African Americans. See Appendix of this book and Herbert Gutman, *The Black Family in Slavery and Freedom, 1750–1925*, Appendix. pp. 507–19.

7. Suzanne Model, "Work and Family: Blacks and Immigrants from the South and Eastern Europe," in Virginia Yans-McLaughlin, *Immigration Reconsidered: History, Sociology and Politics* (London: Oxford University Press, 1990), p. 139–40.

8. Although the Payton block occupational data does not convey this point, one specialized area which initially distinguished some Caribbean from native-born women was their employment as workers in New York's garment industry. Known for its employment of immigrant women, particularly Jews and Italians, the needle trades systematically excluded black women. Although more research is needed on this topic, contemporaries such as W. A. Domingo noted that Caribbean women served as "pioneers and shock troops," opening this field for African Americans. But for years most black women were excluded from advancement to the higher and more skilled tasks. See W. A. Domingo, "Gift of the Black Tropics," in Locke, *The New Negro*, p. 345.

9. Interview, Tyrell Wilson, March 7, 1978.

10. See Reid, *The Negro Immigrant*, pp. 167–69.

11. Charles Tilly, "Transplanted Networks," in *Immigration Reconsidered*, pp. 93–94.

12. W. A. Domingo, "Gift of the Black Tropics," p. 346.

13. Wayne Cooper, *Claude McKay: Rebel Sojourner in the Harlem Renaissance*, p. 351. Harlem's literary establishment was proudest of McKay's poetry. His *Home to Harlem* received the most negative reviews from old-line custodians of the Harlem Renaissance movement because of its perceived departure from respectability. See *Crisis*, June 1928, p. 202. McKay's noncitizenship status did, however, prevent him from obtaining WPA work during the depression. He finally became naturalized on April 13, 1940.

14. See Floyd J. Calvin, "West Indian-American Relations: A Symposium," *The Boston Chronicle*, September 8, 1928.

15. See Stanley Lieberson, *A Piece of the Pie* (Berkeley: University of California Press, 1980); Lawrence H. Fuch, "The Reactions of Black Americans to Immigration," in Yans McLaughlin, pp. 293–314.

16. Claude McKay, *Harlem: Negro Metropolis*, p. 132.

17. Hubert Harrison, *Pittsburgh Courier*, January 29, 1927.

18. Domingo, "Gift of the Black Tropics," p. 348.

Selected Bibliography

Manuscript and Archival Collections

Schomburg Center for Research in Black Culture (SCRBC)

American West Indian Ladies Aid Society Records
Bermuda Benevolent Association Records
Ethelred Brown Papers
John Edward Bruce Papers
Challenor-Dowridge Family Letters—Eddos and Yams
Frank Crosswaith Papers
Richard B. Moore Collection of Documents
Negro Labor Committee Papers
William Pickens Papers
Schomburg Papers
UNIA Records of the Central Division 1918–1959
James A. Watson Papers

Library of Congress

Harmon Foundation Papers
NAACP Papers
National Urban League Papers
Booker T. Washington Papers

Yale University-Beinecke Rare Book and Manuscript Library

James Weldon Johnson Collection:
    James Weldon Johnson Papers
    Claude McKay Papers
    Wallace Thurman Papers

National Archives of the United States

Manifest of Alien Passengers for the United States at Port of Arrival: SS *Korona* and
    SS *Stephen*
General Records of the Department of State
General Records of the Department of Justice

New York University-Tamiment Institute, Elmer Holmes Bobst Library

Local New York Socialist Party Papers
Socialist Labor Party Papers

Municipal Archives of the City of New York

New York State Manuscript Census, 1905, 1915, 1925

Jamaica Archives, Spanish Town, Jamaica

Census of Jamaica
Register of Dispatches 1914–1917

Published Manuscript Collections

Herbert Aptheker, ed., *The Correspondence of W. E. B. Du Bois* (Amherst: The University of Massachusetts Press, 1973).
Robert Hill, ed., *The Marcus Garvey and Universal Negro Improvement Association Papers* vols. I–VII (Berkeley: University of California Press, 1983–1987).

Newspapers, Magazines, and Journals

Baltimore Afro-American
Boston Chronicle
Chicago Defender
Civic
Colored American Magazine
Crisis
Crusader
Daily Worker
Evening Graphic
Harlem Liberator
Kingston Daily Gleaner
Messenger
Negro World
New York Age
New York Amsterdam News
New York Call (Leader)
New York Herald Tribune
New York News
New York Post
New York Sun
New York Times
Opportunity
Pittsburgh Courier
West Indian American

Newspaper Clipping Files

Alexander Gumby Collection, Columbia University Library, Special Collections.
Vertical Files, Schomburg Center for Research in Black Culture.
West India Research Library, Institute of Jamaica, Kingston.

Interviews

Burnham, Dorothy Challenor. New York City, November 12, 1993.
Carrol, Emma. Yonkers, New York, August 19, 1991.
Fleming, G. James. Baltimore, Maryland, October 14, 1977.
Griffith, Eva. Christ Church, Barbados, September 3, 1994.
John, Alma V. New York City, July 31, 1980.
Murrell, Violet. Flint Hall, St. Michael, Barbados, September 2, 3, 1994.
Petioni, Muriel. New York City, November 18, 1992; December 23, 1993.
Thomas, Viola Scott. New York City, July 24, 1980.
Turner, Joyce and Burghardt. Patchogue, Long Island, New York, September 30, 1978.
Stevens, Hope R. New York City, March 7, 1978.
Wilson, Tyrell. Gordon Heights, Long Island, New York, March 7, 1978.
Zampty, Charles. Detroit, Michigan, February 26, 1977.

Published Interview Collections

Interviews of the Columbia University Oral History Project (George Schuyler)
Interviews of the Black Women's Oral History Project, Radcliffe College Schlesinger Library
    (Maida Springer Kemp and Audley Moore)

Testimonials, Reports, and Official Documents

Isthmian Historical Society. *Competition for the Best True Stories of Life and Work on the Isthmus during Construction Days by non-United States Citizens Who Worked on the Isthmus Prior to 1915.* Canal Zone Library, 1963.
National League on Urban Conditions among Negroes. *Housing Conditions Among Negroes in Harlem, New York City,* 1915.
New York Urban League. "Twenty-Four Hundred Negro Families in Harlem: An Interpretation of Living Conditions of Small Wage Earners." Typescript, Schomburg Collection, 1927.
Report of the Joint Legislative Committee Investigating Seditious Activities, Filed April 24, 1920, New York State Senate, Albany, New York: J. B. Lyon, 1920.
Temporary Commission on the Condition of the Urban Colored Population. *Report to the Legislature of the State of New York,* 1938.
United States Bureau of the Census. *Negroes in the United States, 1920–1932.* Washington, D.C., United States Government Printing Office, 1935.
United States Bureau of the Census. *Negro Population in the United States, 1790–1915.* 1918. Reprint. New York: *New York Times* and the Arno Press, 1968.
White Rose Industrial Association. *Annual Reports.* 1911, 1912.

Dissertations, Theses, and Unpublished Studies

Connolly, Harold X. "Blacks in Brooklyn from 1900 to 1960." Ph.D. dissertation, New York University, 1972.
Dunbar, Barrington. "Factors in the Cultural Background of the American Southern Negro and the British West Indian Negro That Condition Their Adjustment in Harlem." Master's thesis, Columbia University, 1935.

Gunner, Frances. "A Study of Employment Problems of Negro Women in Brooklyn." Master's thesis, Columbia University, 1930.

Haynes, Elizabeth Ross. "Negroes in Domestic Service in the United States." Master's thesis, Columbia University, 1923.

Hellwig, David John. "The Afro-American and the Immigrant, 1880–1930: A Study of Black Social Thought." Ph.D. dissertation, Syracuse University, 1973.

Henry, Keith Stanley Augustine. "The Place of the Culture of Migrant Commonwealth Afro–West Indians in the Political Life of Black New York in the Period Circa 1918 to Circa 1966." Ph.D. dissertation, University of Toronto, 1973.

Hopper, Ernest J. "A Northern Group of Negroes." Master's thesis, Columbia University, 1912.

Hunter, Gary. "'Don't Buy from Where You Can't Work': Black Urban Boycott Movements during the Depression." Ph.D. dissertation, University of Michigan, 1977.

Johnstone, Robert Zachariah. "The Negro in New York—His Social Attainments and Prospects." Master's thesis, Columbia University, 1911.

Lewis, Rupert. "A Political Study of Garveyism in Jamaica and London: 1914–1940." Master's thesis, University of the West Indies, Kingston, Jamaica, 1971.

Locke, Benjamin H. "The Community of Life of a Harlem Group of Negroes." Master's thesis, Columbia University, 1913.

Marshall, Dawn I. "The Caribbean Diaspora: A Caribbean Position." Typescript in Research Institute for the Study of Man, New York City.

Moore, Gary Ward. "A Study of a Group of West Indian Negroes in New York City." Master's thesis, Columbia University, 1913.

Mosell, John Albert. "The Political Behavior of Negroes in New York City." Ph.D. dissertation, Columbia University, 1951.

Newton, Velma. "British West Indian Emigration to the Isthmus of Panama, 1850–1914." Master's thesis, University of the West Indies, Kingston, Jamaica, 1968.

Paul, Seymour. "A Group of Virginia Negroes in New York City." Master's thesis, Columbia University, 1912.

Phillips, Harold Cook. "The Social Significance of Negro Churches in Harlem." Master's thesis, Columbia University, 1922.

Pollard, Myrtle Evangeline. "Harlem as Is: The Negro Business and Economic Community." Master's thesis, City College of New York, 1937.

Sanford, Delacy Wendell, Jr. "Congressional Investigation of Black Communism, 1919–1967." Ph.D. dissertation, State University at Stony Brook, 1973.

Spurling, John Jasper. "Social Relationships between American Negroes and West Indian Negroes in a Long Island Community: An Exploratory Examination of Intergroup Relationship in the Addisleigh Park Neighborhood of St. Albans, Long Island, New York." Ph.D. dissertation, New York University, 1962.

Warren, Maurice Ira. "Moses and the Messenger: The Crisis of Black Radicalism 1921–1922." Senior Honors Essay, Harvard College, 1973.

Welty, William M. "Black Shepherds: A Study of the Leading Negro Clergymen in New York City 1900–1940." Ph.D. dissertation, New York University, 1969.

Westerman, George. "The Problems of West Indian Offspring in Panama." Unpublished manuscript, New York Public Library, 1944.

White, Noel A. "The Contribution of West Indian Immigrants to the Negro Community in the United States." Master's thesis, Columbia University Teachers College, 1968.

Writers Program, New York City. "Negroes of New York." Research Studies of the Works Projects Administration in New York City, 1936–1941.

Articles

Ardener, Shirley. "The Comparative Study of Rotating Credit Associations." *Journal of the Royal Anthropological Institute* 94 (1904), 201–29.

Bascom, William R. "The Esusu: A Credit Institution of the Yoruba." *Journal of the Royal Anthropological Institute* 82 (1952), 63–69.

Batterham, E. Rose. "Negro Girls and the Y.W.C.A." *Southern Workman* (1919), 437–41.

Brown, Elsa Barkley. "Womanist Consciousness: Maggie Lena Walker and the Independent Order of St. Luke." In M. Malson, E. Mudimbe-Boyi, J. F. O'Barr, and Mary Wyer, *Black Women in America, Social Science Perspectives* (University of Chicago Press, 1990), 173–196.

Brown, E. Ethelred. "Labor Conditions in Jamaica Prior to 1917." *Journal of Negro History* 4 (October 1919), 358.

Browning, James B. "The Beginning of Insurance Enterprise among Negroes." *Journal of Negro History* 22 (October 1937), 117–32.

Bryce-Laport, Roy Simon. "Black Immigrants." *Journal of Black Studies* 2 (September 1972), 31.

Colored American Magazine. "Woman Suffrage." XV, I (January 1909), 202.

Coombs, Orde. "West Indians in New York: Moving beyond the Limbo Pole." *New York Magazine*, July 13, 1970, pp. 28–32.

Crowder, Ralph L. "John Edward Bruce: Pioneer Black Nationalist." *Afro Americans in New York Life and History* II, 2 (July 1978), 47–66.

Derrick, W. B. "Bishop W. B. Derrick to the Young People of the Race." *Colored American Magazine* XV, I (January 1909), 655–58.

Dickson, Lynda F. "Toward a Broader Angle of Vision in Uncovering Women's History: Black Women's Clubs Revisited." In Hine, ed., *Black Women in United States History* vol 9 (New York: Carlson Publishers, 1990). 103–119.

Domingo, W. A. and Owen Chandler. "The Policy of the *Messenger* on West Indian and American Negroes." *Messenger* (March 1923), 639–45.

Domingo, W. A. "Gift of the Black Tropics." In Alain Locke, *The New Negro* (New York: Albert and Charles Boni, Inc., 1925). Reprint Atheneum, 1969, 341–49.

———. "Garvey." *Public Opinion* (October 9, 1964).

———. "Socialism, The Negroes' Hope." *Messenger* (July 1919), 22.

Du Bois, W. E. B. "Back to Africa." *Century Magazine* (February 1923), 539–48.

———. "A Lunatic or a Traitor." *Crisis* (May 1924), 8–9.

———. "Marcus Garvey." *Crisis* (December 1920), 58–60.

———. "Marcus Garvey." *Crisis* (January 1921), 112–15.

———. "Inter-Racial Implications of the Ethiopian Crisis." *Foreign Affairs* (October 1935), 82–92.

———. "The Rise of the West Indian." *Crisis* (September 1920), 214.

E. U. Essien-Udom. "The Nationalist Movements of Harlem." *Freedomways* (Summer 1963), 337.

Frazier, E. Franklin. "The Garvey Movement." *Opportunity* (November 1926), 346–47.

Gottlieb, Peter. "Migration and Jobs: The New Black Workers in Pittsburgh, 1916–1930." *The Western Pennsylvania Historical Magazine* 61, I (January 1978).

Henderson, J. M. "Negroes of Beautiful Bermuda." *The Colored American* XVI, 6 (June 1909), 367–72.

Henderson, Thomas M. "Harlem Confronts the Machine: The Struggle for Local Autonomy and Black District Leadership." *Afro-Americans in New York Life and History* (July 1979), 51–68.

Henry, Keith. "Caribbean Migrants in New York: The Passage from Political Quiescence to Radicalism." *Afro-Americans in New York Life and History* II, 2 (July 1978), 29–41.

Hine, Darlene Clark. "Mabel K. Staupers and the Integration of Black Nurses into the Armed Forces." In *Black Women in American History* (New York: Carlson Publishing Co, 1990), 241–57.

———. "Lifting the Veil, Shattering the Silence, Black Women's History in Slavery and Freedom." In Hine, ed., *The State of Afro-American History: Past, Present, Future* (Baton Rouge: Louisiana State University Press, 1986).

Holder, Calvin B. "The Causes and Composition of West Indian Immigration to New York City, 1900–1952." *Afro-Americans in New York Life and History* (January 1987), 7–26.

———. "The Rise of the West Indian Politician in New York City, 1900–1952." *Afro-Americans in New York Life and History* (January 1980), 45–59.

Garvey, Marcus. "West Indies in the Mirror of Truth." *Champion* (January 1917).

———. "Why the Black Star Line Failed." In John Henrik Clark, *Marcus Garvey and the Vision of Africa.* (New York: Vintage Books, 1973).

Gates, Henry Louis, Jr. "The Trope of a New Negro and the Reconstruction of the Image of the Black." *Representations* 24 (Fall 1988), 129–53.

Gertz, Clifford. "The Rotating Credit Association: A Middle Rung in Development." *Economic Development and Social Change* 10 (April 1962), 241–63.

Johnson, Charles S. "Black Workers and the City." *Survey Graphic* (March 1925), 641–43.

Johnson, James Weldon. "The Making of Harlem." *Survey Graphic* (March 1925), 635–39.

Katzin, Margaret. "Partners: An Informal Savings Institution in Jamaica." *Social and Economic Studies* 8 (December 1959), 436–40.

Kusmer, Kenneth. "The Black Urban Experience in American History." In Hine, ed., *The State of Afro-American History* (Baton Rouge: Louisiana State University Press, 1986).

Malcioln, Jose V. "Panama." *Freedomways* (Summer 1964), 383–91.

Malliet, A. M. Wendell. "On West Indian Colonization in British Guiana." *Education, A Journal of Reputation* I, (July–August 1935), 3.

———. "Prominent West Indians." *Opportunity* (November 1926), 351.

Marshall, Dawn I. "Mobility, Identity and Policy in the Eastern Caribbean." *Pacific Viewpoint* 26, no. 1 (April 1985).

McDougald, Elise Johnson. "The Double Task." *Survey Graphic* (March 1925), 689–91.

McDowell, Deborah E. "The Neglected Dimension of Jessie Redmon Fauset." *Afro-Americans in New York Life and History* (July 1981), 33–49.

McKay, Claude. "Garvey as a Negro Moses." *Liberator* (April 1922), 8–9.

Miller, Kelly. "The Harvest of Race Prejudice." *Survey Graphic* (March 1925), 683.

Moore, Gerald L. "The Sugar Hill Pioneers." *Afro Americans in New York Life and History* (July 1988), 35–38.

Moore, Richard B. "Africa Conscious Harlem." *Freedomways* (Summer 1963).

———. "Caribbean Unity." *Freedomways* (Summer 1964), 295–311.

Morgan, Charlotte T. "Finding a Way Out: Adult Education in Harlem during the Great Depression." *Afro-Americans in New York Life and History* (January 1984), 17–29.

Ramsey, Priscilla. "Freeze the Day: A Feminist Reading of Nella Larsen's *Quicksand* and *Passing.*" *Afro-Americans in New York Life and History* (January 1985), 27–40.

Raphael, Lennox. "West Indians and Afro-Americans." *Freedomways* (Summer 1964), 438–45.

Reid, Ira. "Negro Immigration to the United States." *Social Forces* (March 16, 1938), 411–17.

———. "Let Us Prey." *Opportunity* (September 1926), 274–78.

Rogers, J. A. "The West Indies." *Messenger* (November 1922), 528.

Samuels, Wilfred. "Hubert H. Harrison and 'The New Negro Manhood Movement.'" *Afro-Americans in New York Life and History* (January 1981), 29–43.

Schomburg, Arthur. "The Negro Digs Up His Past." *Survey Graphic* (March 1925), 670–73.

Seraille, William. "Henrietta Vinton Davis and the Garvey Movement." *Afro-Americans in New York Life and History* (July 1983), 8–24.

Smith, Albert Edgar. "West Indians on the Campus." *Opportunity* (August 1933), 239–41.

Sutherland, Louis G. "Panama Gold." *Opportunity* (November 1934), 336–39.

Thom, William T. "The True Reformers." *U.S. Department of Labor Bulletin* 41 (July 1902), 807–814.

Thomas, Bert J. "Historical Functions of Caribbean-American Benevolent/Progressive Associations." *Afro-Americans in New York Life and History* (July 1988), 45–58.

Walker, John C. "Frank Crosswaith and the Negro Labor Committee in Harlem, 1925–1939." *Afro-Americans in New York Life and History* (July 1979), 35–49.

———. "Frank R. Crosswaith and Labor Organization in Harlem, 1939–1945." *Afro-Americans in New York Life and History* (July 1983), 47–58.

Walker, John C. and Jill Louise Ansheles. "The Role of the Caribbean Immigrant in the Harlem Renaissance." *Afro-Americans in New York Life and History* (January 1977), 49–64.

Walrond, Eric D. "The Black City." *Messenger* (January 1924), 13–14.

———. "On Being Black." *New Republic* (November 1, 1922), 244–46.

———. "Imperator Africanus." *The Independent* (January 3, 1923).

Westerman, George W. "Gold Men and Silver Men." *Crisis* (December 1947), 365–67.

Woodson, Carter G. "Insurance Business among Negroes." *Journal of Negro History* XIV (April 1929), 202–26.

———. "The Negro Washerwoman: A Vanishing Figure." *Journal of Negro History* XV (July 1930).

———. "Racial Purity: An Advantage in Race Consciousness." Baltimore *Afro-American*, November 7, 1931.

Books

Anderson, Jervis. *A. Philip Randolph: A Biographical Portrait.* New York: Harcourt, Brace, Jovanovich, 1973.

———. *This Was Harlem: A Cultural Portrait 1900–1950.* New York: Farrar, Straus, Giroux, 1982.

Best, Ethel L. *Economic Problems of the Women of the Virgin Islands of the United States.* United States Department of Labor, Women's Bureau, No. 142, 1936.

Borchert, James. *Alley Life in Washington: Family Community, Religion, and Folklife in the City, 1850–1970.* Chicago: University of Illinois Press, 1980.

Brown-Guillory. *Wines in the Wilderness: Plays by African American Women from the Harlem Renaissance to the Present.* New York: Praeger, 1990.

Brownstone, David J.; Brownstone, Douglass L.; and Franck, Irene M. *Island of Hope, Island of Tears, Migration through Ellis Island.* New York: Rawson, Wade Publishers, Inc., 1979.

Bryce-Laporte, Roy S. and Mortimer, Delores M. *Female Immigrants to the United States: Caribbean, Latin American* and *African Experiences.* Washington, D.C.: Research Institute on Immigration and Ethnic Studies, Smithsonian Institution, 1981.

Burkett, Randall. *Black Redemption*. Philadelphia: Temple University Press, 1978.

Carpenter, Niles. *Immigrants and Their Children*. Washington, D.C.: United States Government Printing Office, 1927.

Clark, John Henrik, ed. *Marcus Garvey and the Vision of Africa*. New York: Vintage Books, 1974.

Cohn, Michael, and Platzer, Michael K. H. *Black Men of the Sea*. New York: Dodd, Mead and Company, 1978.

De Jongh, James. *Vicious Modernism: Black Harlem and the Literary Imagination*. Cambridge: Cambridge University Press, 1990.

Du Bois, W. E. B. *Dark Princess*. New York: Harcourt, Brace, Jovanovich, 1928.

——. *Dusk of Dawn*. 1940. Reprint. New York: Schocken Books, 1968.

Fisher, Rudolph. *The Walls of Jericho*. New York: Alfred A. Knopf, 1928.

Foerster, Robert F. *The Racial Problem Involved in Immigration from Latin America and the West Indies to the United States*. Washington, D.C.: Government Printing Office, 1925.

Foner, Philip. *American Socialism and Black Americans from the Age of Jackson to World War II*. Westport, Connecticut: Greenwood Press, 1977.

Garvey, Amy Jacques. *Garvey and Garveyism*. 1963. Reprint. New York: Atheneum, 1970.

——. *Philosophy and Opinions of Marcus Garvey*. 1923, 1925. Reprint. New York: Atheneum, 1969.

Grey, Brenda Clegg. *Black Female Domestics during the Depression in New York City*. New York: Garland Publishing, Inc. 1993.

Gurock, Jeffrey S. *When Harlem Was Jewish, 1870–1930*. New York: Columbia University Press, 1979.

Gutman, Herbert. *The Black Family in Slavery and Freedom*. New York: Pantheon Books, 1976.

Hamilton, Charles V. *Adam Clayton Powell, Jr.: The Political Biography of an American Dilemma*. New York: Atheneum, 1991.

Harrison, Hubert. *The Negro and the Nation*. New York: Cosmo Advocate Publishing Company, 1917.

——. *When Africa Awakes*. New York: Porro Press, 1920.

Haywood, Harry. *Black Bolshevik: Autobiography of an Afro-American Communist*. Chicago: Liberator Press, 1978.

——. *Negro Liberation*. New York: International Publishers, 1948.

Henri, Florette. *Black Migration: Movement North, 1900–1920*. New York: Anchor Books, 1976.

Hine, Darlene Clark. *Black Women in White: Racial Conflict and Cooperation in the Nursing Profession*. Bloomington: Indiana University Press, 1989.

——, ed. *The State of Afro-American History: Past, Present, and Future*. Baton Rouge: Louisiana State University Press, 1986.

Huggins, Nathan. *Harlem Renaissance*. London: Oxford University Press, 1971.

Hughes, Langston. *The Big Sea, An Autobiography*. New York: Hill and Wang, 1940.

——. *The Weary Blues*. New York: Alfred Knopf, 1926.

——. *Fine Clothes to the Jew*. New York: Alfred Knopf, 1927.

Hull, Gloria. *Color, Sex and Poetry: Three Women Writers of the Harlem Renaissance*. Bloomington: Indiana University Press, 1987.

Johnson, James Weldon. *Along This Way: The Autobiography of James Weldon Johnson*. 1933. Reprint. New York: Viking Press, 1968.

——. *Autobiography of an Ex-Colored Man*, New York: Sherman French, 1912.

————, ed. *The Book of Negro Verse*. New York: Harcourt, Brace, Jovanovich, 1922.

————. *Black Manhattan*. 1930. Reprint. New York: Atheneum, 1972.

Jones, Jacqueline. *Labor of Love, Labor of Sorrow: Black Women, Work, and the Family, from Slavery to the Present*. New York: Vantage Books, 1986.

Kasinitz, Philip. *Caribbean New York: Black Immigrants and the Politics of Race*. Ithaca: Cornell University Press, 1990.

Katznelson, Ira. *Black Men, White Cities*. New York: Oxford University Press, 1973.

Kirnon, Hodge. *Montserrat and Montserratans*. New York: Kirnon, 1924.

Knight, Frank. *The Caribbean: The Genesis of a Fragmented Nationalism*. New York: Oxford University Press, 1978.

Kusmer, Kenneth L. *A Ghetto Takes Shape: Black Cleveland, 1870–1930*. Chicago: University of Illinois Press, 1976.

Laidlow, Walter, ed. *Statistical Sources for Demographic Studies of New York*. New York: World Council of Churches, 1913.

Lewis, David. *When Harlem Was in Vogue*. New York: Alfred Knopf, 1981.

Lieberson, Stanley. *A Piece of the Pie: Blacks and White Immigrants Since 1880*. Berkeley: University of California Press, 1980.

Light, Ivan A. *Ethnic Enterprise in America: Business and Welfare among Chinese, Japanese and Blacks*. Berkeley: The University of California Press, 1972.

Little, Kenneth. *Negroes in Britain: A Study of Race Relations in English Society*. Boston: Routledge and Kegan Paul, 1948.

————. *West African Urbanization: A Study of Voluntary Association in Social Change*. New York: Cambridge University Press, 1965.

Locke, Alain. *The New Negro*. 1925. Reprint. New York: Atheneum, 1969.

Lowenthal, David. *West Indian Societies*. New York: Oxford University Press, 1972.

Malson, Michelle R.; Mudimbe-Boyi, Elisabeth; O'Barr, Jean F.; and Wyer, Mary, eds. *Black Women in America: Social Science Perspectives*. Chicago: University of Chicago Press, 1988.

Marks, Carole. *Farewell—We're Good and Gone: The Great Black Migration*. Bloomington: Indiana University Press, 1989.

Martin, Tony. *Race First: The Ideological and Organizational Struggles of Marcus Garvey and the Universal Negro Improvement Association*. Westport, Connecticut: Greenwood Press, 1976.

McCullough, David. *The Path between the Seas: The Creation of the Panama Canal, 1870–1914*. New York: Simon and Schuster, 1977.

McKay, Claude. *A Long Way from Home*. New York: Lee Furman, 1937.

————. *Harlem: Negro Metropolis*. New York: E. P. Dutton & Company, Inc., 1940.

Morrison-Reed, Mark D. *Black Pioneers in a White Denomination*. Boston: Beacon Press, 1980.

Mossell, N. E. *The Work of the Afro-American Woman*. Philadelphia: George Ferguson Co, 1908. Reprint, New York: Oxford University Press, 1988.

Mulzac, Hugh. *A Star to Steer By*. New York: International Publishers, 1963.

Naison, Mark. *Communists in Harlem during the Depression*. Urbana: University of Illinois Press, 1983.

Orsi, Robert Anthony. *The Madonna of 115th Street: Faith and Community in Italian Harlem, 1880–1950*. New Haven: Yale University Press, 1985.

Ottley, Roi. *New World A' Coming*. Boston: Houghton Mifflin Company, 1943.

————. ed. *The Negro In New York: A Social History, 1626–1940*. New York: Praeger, 1969.

Ovington, Mary White. *Half a Man: The Status of the Negro in New York*. 1911. Reprint. New York: Shocken Books, 1969.

———. *The Walls Came Tumbling Down*. New York: Harcourt, Brace and Company, 1947.

Ranson, Reverdy C. *The Pilgrimage of Harriet Ranson's Son*. Nashville: Sunday School Union of the A.M.E. Church.

Reid, Ira De Augustine. *The Negro Immigrant, His Background, Characteristics, and Social Adjustment, 1899–1937*. New York: Columbia University Press, 1939.

Richardson, Bonham C. *Caribbean Migrants, Environment and Human Survival on St Kitts and Nevis*. Knoxville: The University of Tennessee Press, 1983.

Sinnette, Elinor Des Verney. *Arthur Alfonso Schomburg: Black Bibliophile and Collector*. Detroit: Wayne State University Press and the New York Public Library, 1989.

Spero, Sterling D., and Harris, Abram H. *The Black Worker*. New York: Atheneum, 1969.

Thurman, Wallace. *The Blacker the Berry*. New York: Macaulay Company, 1929.

Toomer, Jean. *Cane*. New York: Boni and Liveright, 1923.

Trotter, Joe. *The Great Migration in Historical Perspective: New Dimensions in Race, Class, and Gender*. Bloomington: Indiana University Press, 1992.

Turner, Joyce Moore and Burghardt. *Richard B. Moore: Caribbean Militant in Harlem*. Bloomington: Indiana University Press, 1988.

Vega, Bernardo. *Memoirs of Bernardo Vega*. New York: Monthly Review Press, 1984.

Vincent, Theodore. *Black Power and the Garvey Movement*. San Francisco: Ramparts Press, 1971.

———. *Voices of a Black Nation: Political Journalism in the Harlem Renaissance*. San Francisco: Ramparts Press, 1973.

Walrond, Eric. *Tropic Death*. New York: Boni and Liveright, 1926.

Wells, Ida B. *Crusade for Justice*. Chicago: University of Chicago Press, 1970.

Westerman, George. *The West Indian Workers on the Canal Zone*. New York: National Civic League, 1951.

Index

Abbott, Robert, 27, 116
Abyssinian Baptist Church, 57, 88, 105
Adams, Jane, 80
African Americans: ambivalence of native-born
    toward black ethnicity, 28–29; nativism and,
    80–81, 113, 171–72; political influence of in
    Chicago, 87; roles of clergymen in larger
    community of, 58–59, 62. *See also*
    Caribbean, immigrants from; Nativism;
    Violence against
African American Socialist Club, 214–15n.35
African Blood Brotherhood (ABB), 103–104,
    110, 159, 204n.56
African Caribbeans. *See* Caribbean, immigrants
    from
African Methodist Episcopal (A.M.E.) Church,
    57, 59, 115, 168
African Orthodox Church, 57, 63–64
Afro-American Realty Company, 42, 187n.21,
    193n.23
Ali, Noble Drew, 202n.8
Americanization, Caribbean immigrants and, 84
American West Indian Association, 44
American West Indian Ladies Aid Society, 26, 56,
    61, 68, 70, 71, 108, 168–69, 198n.57
American and West Indian News (newspaper), 160
Amsterdam News (newspaper), 160, 214n.33
Ancient Order of Shepherds, 72
Anderson, Charles H., 133
Anderson, Charles W., 42, 75–76, 78, 90, 95, 96,
    199n.2, 203nn.34,35
Anderson, Jervis, 41, 98–99, 185n.2
Andrews, William T., 89–90
Anglican Church, 57
Anticolonialism. *See* Colonialism
Antillean Holding Company, 43, 128, 135
Art Publishing Company, 209n.4
Ashwood, Amy, 2, 17, 18, 22, 37, 117, 155
Ashwood, Michael, 17
Asian Caribbeans, as immigrants to Harlem, 12,
    188n.8, 193n.22, 211n.28

Associated Negro Press, 124, 158
Associated Press, 120
Association of Colored Women's Clubs, 109
Augustine, Bernard, 131
Austin, A. A., 43, 128, 135
Austin, William H., 85

Bagnall, Robert, 122–23
Bahamas, emigration from, 13
Banking industry, business, 133–34, 174
Baptist Church, 57, 61, 196n.22
Barbados, emigration from, 11, 12, 20–21;
    St. Michael, 19, 21
Barnett, Ida Wells, 113, 114, 206n.9
Barrow, Rev. Reginald Grant, 57
Baseball, "Negro Leagues," 140, 212n.23
Beavers Democratic Club, 91
Benevolent associations, ethnicity and evolution
    of black community in Harlem, 56–74.
    See also Voluntary organizations
Benta, Helena, 68, 70, 74, 168, 198n.62
Bermudian Benevolent Association, 40, 44, 67–68
Bermudian Home Club, 40
Bethel A.M.E. Church, 40, 100
Blacker the Berry (Thurman), 153
Black Manhattan (Johnson), 149
Black Metropolis (Drake and Cayton), 146
Black Star Steamship Line, 23, 105, 114, 115
Black Yankees, 140
Bolshevik Revolution, 93, 163
Book dealers, in Harlem, 96
Book of Negro Poetry (Johnson), 156
Boulin, H. S., 90
Briggs, Cyril, 25, 103, 126, 160–61, 200n.29,
    204n.55, 209n.4, 215–16n.42
Briggs, Valentine, 158
British Guiana, emigration from, 12, 20
Brooklyn Heights Holy Trinity Episcopalian
    Church, 57
Brooklyn and Long Island Informer, The
    (weekly), 156

229

Irma Watkins-Owens is Associate Professor of African American and African Studies at Fordham University-Lincoln Center Campus.